"A SMALL MIRACLE . . .

It goes on that small shelf of books that are both
a pleasure to read and worth consulting."

—Christopher Lehmann-Haupt,
The New York Times

M O N E Y
Whence It Came, Where It Went

by JOHN KENNETH GALBRAITH

A Book-of-the-Month Club Featured Alternate
A selection of the *Fortune* Book Club, McGraw-
Hill Book Clubs and Macmillan Book Clubs

*A fascinating book
about the world's second
most interesting subject.*

MONEY

"The most prestigious intellectual figure in modern economic history . . . manages to bring life and clarity to a subject long known in university circles for inducing dull, glazed expressions."

—*New Republic*

———————

"Demystifying literacy and razor-edged wit . . . A fascinating book."

—*Newsweek*

———————

"A landmark . . . a book that an intelligent but nonprofessional citizen can use to cut through the pompous esoterica of the politicians and experts to find out how much greed and how little sense often underlies their decisions."

—*Chicago Tribune Book World*

JOHN KENNETH GALBRAITH

MONEY

Whence It Came,
Where It Went

*This low-priced Bantam Book
has been completely reset in a type face
designed for easy reading, and was printed
from new plates. It contains the complete
text of the original hard-cover edition.*
NOT ONE WORD HAS BEEN OMITTED.

MONEY: WHENCE IT CAME, WHERE IT WENT

*A Bantam Book / published by arrangement with
Houghton Mifflin Company*

PRINTING HISTORY

Houghton Mifflin edition published July 1975
2nd printing...................July 1975
3rd printing...............August 1975
4th printing.........September 1975
5th printing.........November 1975

Book-of-the-Month Club edition published April 1975

McGraw Hill Book Club edition published May 1975

Macmillan Book Club edition published June 1975

Portions of this book have appeared in HARPER'S,
HORIZON, BANKER'S MAGAZINE, BOOK DIGEST, BUSINESS
& SOCIETY REVIEW, East/West Network *and* Metropolitan
Sunday Newspapers.

Bantam edition / September 1976
2nd printing

Cover Photograph by Nancy Crampton

ISBN 0–553–02688–7

Published simultaneously in the United States and Canada.

In memory of Jim Warburg

and with love
for Joan

Acknowledgments

THIS BOOK was, in an innocent way, its own progenitor. Initially it was to have been a long essay on the problems of economic management and monetary stabilization, and their origins. It was a timely undertaking. I could draw on a lifetime of reading, casual or otherwise, for these are matters of which an economist is expected to have knowledge—and I had always found the history of money, early and late, exceedingly engaging. So interesting was the task that the essay became a book, and the book became a long one. As may conceivably be evident, it was, as these things go, a joyful task.

No small part of the pleasure was from my partners in the enterprise. One of these was David Thomas, a highly faithful, intelligent and charming assistant, now, alas, lost to me in the practice of law. He had a remarkable ability to find both the things I needed and those on which I needed correction. Any malefactor so fortunate as to fall in his hands will be saved by David's discovery of some hitherto unknown statute or decision exculpating him. As with almost everything I have written, Arthur Schlesinger read, challenged and corrected. No one else does so out of such a rich store of information and judgment. The errors that remain are all mine. My friend and assistant, Emeline Davis, typed, retyped and corrected the manuscript and generally managed its progress toward the printer. Nanny Bers helped her and me. And as in the case of everything I've done for years, all questions of adequacy of explanation, editing, style and elementary good taste were subject to the unfailing eye and implacable authority of Andrea Williams. To all, all thanks.

Contents

MONEY

Whence It Came,
Where It Went

CHAPTER I

Money

"Mrs. Bold has twelve hundred a year of her own, and
I suppose Mr. Harding means to live with her."

"Twelve hundred a year of her own!" said Slope;—
and very shortly afterwards took his leave . . . Twelve
hundred a year, said he to himself, as he rode slowly
home. If it were the fact that Mrs. Bold had twelve
hundred a year of her own, what a fool would he be
to oppose her father's return to his old place. The
train of Mr. Slope's ideas will probably be plain to all
my readers . . . twelve hundred a year . . .

Anthony Trollope, *Barchester Towers*

NOT VERY LONG AGO one of the investigations into the
typically intricate affairs of the 37th President of the
United States turned up a more than normally interesting transaction. Mr. Charles G. Rebozo, Mr.
Nixon's good and reticent friend, had received for the
then President's benefit, political or personal, $100,-
000 from the even more reticent entrepreneur, Mr.
Howard Hughes. This considerable sum, it was
claimed, had thereafter been kept in cash in a safe-
deposit box for rather more than three years before
being returned to Mr. Hughes. The curiosity concerning this transaction was not over why anyone should
return money to Mr. Hughes, which is something like
returning salt tears to the ocean. Rather it was why
anyone should leave so much money in storage. So

left, as everyone knew, it lost radically in value—a dollar of 1967 had the purchasing power of only 91 cents in 1969, the year Mr. Rebozo resorted to storage, and of less than 80 cents when he retrieved and returned the money. (In early 1975, it was down to 64 cents.) The impact of this trend could not have been lost on the two gentlemen. The partial compensation for this loss in the form of interest, dividends or, one might even hope, capital gains, which a minimally prudent man would have been expected to collect, was forgone. The most retarded of the borrowers in the Parable of the Talents had incurred rebuke for coming back with only the original advance. Neither Mr. Nixon nor Mr. Rebozo was thought indifferent to pecuniary concern; both had fallen well below the Biblical minimum for financial performance. There was general disbelief and shaking of heads that they should have been so bad.

There was in this episode a quite remarkable demonstration of what has happened to attitudes toward money. Everyone expects it to depreciate in value. No one suggested that the President, who was ultimately responsible for maintaining the value of the currency, had been so rash as to bet personally on his ability to do so. Like everyone else he was thought to need a strategy for offsetting its deterioration, although with no expectation that it would be successful. Nor was there any country in the nonsocialist world whose leader would have reposed more confidence in his ability to maintain the value of the currency than the President of the United States. Everywhere the tendency in these years was the same—for prices to rise, the purchasing power of money to decline and at an uncertain, erratic rate. Nothing is forever, not excepting inflation. But to many it must have seemed that this tendency was distressingly persistent.

Nor were those who carelessly stored $100,000 in

bills the major victims. Far more disenchanting was the position of those whose small wealth and income were fixed in dollars, pounds, marks, francs or other coin and who could not tell what these would buy in the future, only that it would be less. In the last century in the industrial countries there was much uncertainty as to whether a man could get money but very little as to what it would do for him once he had it. In this century the problem of getting money, though it remains considerable, has diminished. In its place has come a new uncertainty as to what money, however acquired and accumulated, will be worth. Once, to have an income reliably denominated in money was thought, as by Mr. Slope, to be very comfortable. Of late, to have a fixed income is to be thought liable to impoverishment that may not be slow. What has happened to money?

It has long been fashionable for historians, except in the secret recesses of their belief, to be modest about the lessons of history. Perhaps it teaches only that it teaches little. Where money is concerned, this restraint is unwarranted. The history of money teaches much or it can be made to teach much. It is, indeed, exceedingly doubtful if much that is durable can be learned about money in any other way. Attitudes toward money proceed in long cyclical swings. When money is bad, people want it to be better. When it is good, they think of other things. Only as matters are examined over time can we see how people who are experiencing inflation yearn for stable money and how those who are accepting the discipline and the costs of stability come to accept the risks of inflation. It is this cycle that teaches us that nothing, not even inflation, is permanent. We learn also that the fear of inflation which inflation leaves in its wake can be as damaging as the inflation itself. From the history we can also see, more vividly than in any other way, how money and the techniques for its management and mismanagement were evolved and how they now serve or fail to serve. It is from the past that we see how new institutions—corporations, trade unions, the welfare state—have altered the problem of maintaining price stability in the present and how changing circumstances—movement to a class structure in which fewer and fewer people are successfully taught to take less, the changing political interest of the affluent—have greatly complicated the task.

It is with the lessons of history, rather than the history itself, that this book is concerned. Its purpose is didactic and expository, less in relation to the past than to the present. But its purpose is also less than completely solemn. There is much in the history of money that is fascinating. There is more that richly illuminates human behavior and human folly. That the love of money is the root of all evil can, conceivably, be disputed. Adam Smith, for many a prophet of only slightly less than scriptural authority, thought in 1776 that of all the occupations on which man had to that time engaged—war, politics, religion, violent recreation, unrequited sadism—the making of money was socially the least damaging. What is not in doubt is that the pursuit of money, or any enduring association with it, is capable of inducing not alone bizarre but ripely perverse behavior.

There are good reasons. Men possessed of money, like men earlier favored by noble birth and great title, have infallibly imagined that the awe and admiration that money inspires were really owing to their own wisdom or personality. The contrast between their view of themselves, as so enhanced, and the frequently ridiculous or depraved reality has ever been a source of wonder and rich amusement. Similarly there has always been pleasure of a low sort in the speed with which the awe and admiration evaporate when something happens to the individual's money.

Money bemuses in another way. Recurrently over the centuries men have supposed that they have mastered the secret of its infinite amplification. And as reliably as they have persuaded themselves of this, they have also persuaded others. Invariably it involves the rediscovery, perhaps in slightly novel form, of some infinitely ancient fraud. The span of time between the transcendental heights of the financial genius and the nadir of the ensuing collapse—from being John Law the savior of the French Regency to being John Law the penitent in Venice, from being Nicholas Biddle the first master of American finance and a fearsome figure to Presidents to being Nicholas Biddle the most distinguished of Philadelphia bankrupts, from being Bernard Cornfeld of the jet planes and sad-eyed concubines to being Bernard Cornfeld of the prison of St. Antoine—is often only a few months, at most only a few years. There is wonder and a certain wicked pleasure in these giddy ascents and terrible falls, especially as they happen to other people. Here, no doubt, it is the story and not the meaning that is important.

A word must be said about the frame of mind in which one wishes the reader to approach a book such as this. Much discussion of money involves a heavy overlay of priestly incantation. Some of this is deliberate. Those who talk of money and teach about it and make their living by it gain prestige, esteem and pecuniary return, as does a doctor or a witch doctor, from cultivating the belief that they are in privileged association with the occult—that they have insights that are nowise available to the ordinary person. Though professionally rewarding and personally profitable, this too is a well-established form of fraud.

There is nothing about money that cannot be understood by the person of reasonable curiosity, diligence and intelligence. There is nothing on the following pages that cannot be so understood. And whatever errors of interpretation or of fact this history may contain, there are, the reader may be confident, none that proceed from simplification. The study of money, above all other fields in economics, is the one in which complexity is used to disguise truth or to evade truth, not to reveal it. Most things in life—automobiles, mistresses, cancer—are important only to those who have them. Money, in contrast, is equally important to those who have it and those who don't. Both, accordingly, have a concern for understanding it. Both should proceed in the full confidence that they can.

It will be asked in this connection if a book on the history of money should not begin with some definition of what money really is. What makes this strip of intrinsically worthless paper useful in exchange, leaves another piece of similar size without any such worth? The precedents for such effort are not encouraging. Television interviewers with a reputation for penetrating thought regularly begin interviews with economists with the question: "Now tell me, just what is money anyway?" The answers are invariably incoherent. Teachers of elementary economics or money and banking begin with definitions of genuine subtlety. These are then carefully transcribed, painfully memorized and mercifully forgotten. The reader should proceed in these pages in the knowledge that money is nothing more or less than what he or she always thought it was—what is commonly offered or received for the purchase or sale of goods, services or other things. The several forms of money and what determines what they will buy are something else again. But that is the purpose of the pages following to reveal.

A final word. This is a history of money; it is considerably less than a history of all money during all time—something with which no historian is likely soon to offend. So at all periods there had to be selection. The selection was based on what (as in the case of the Bank of England) most shaped the development of money; or (as in the case of the struggle between Jackson and Biddle) best illuminated the forces contending for its control; or (as in the work of Keynes and the recent history) contributed most to our present understanding. More prejudicially, some of the selection, no doubt, also resulted from what most interested the author.

In the later chapters, as will be evident, the selection converges strongly on the dollar. Here art, real or alleged, merely imitates life. It is to the dollar that the history of money comes. It is with the dollar that, for the moment, the history of money ends.

CHAPTER II

Of Coins and Treasure

MONEY is a very old convenience but the notion that it is a reliable artifact to be accepted without scrutiny or question is, in all respects, a very occasional thing—mostly a circumstance of the last century. For some four thousand earlier years there had been agreement on the use of one or more of three metals for purposes of exchange, these being silver, copper and gold, with silver and gold being also once used in the natural combination called electrum. For most of these many years silver was pre-eminent; for lesser periods, as under the Mycenaeans or in Constantinople after the division of the Roman Empire, gold had prior place.[1] It has always been thought derogatory that Judas delivered up Jesus for 30 pieces of silver. That it was silver suggests only that it was a normal commercial transaction; had it been three pieces of gold, a plausible early ratio, the deal would have been somewhat exceptional. On occasion, in the extent of use, gold ranked below copper. For brief periods, it should be noted, iron also intruded. And

---

[1] On the use of different metals there is less than agreement. The above follows the standard view as given by Keynes. Cf. John Maynard Keynes, *Essays in Persuasion* (New York: Harcourt, Brace & Co., 1932), pp. 181–182. An interesting general sketch of the early development of metals and money is in Fernand Braudel, *Capitalism and Material Life 1400–1800* (New York: Harper & Row, 1967), pp. 325–372.

much later tobacco, as will be told, had a limited but notable run. More awkward or exotic items such as cattle, shells, whiskey and stones, though greatly relished by teachers on money, have never been durably important for people much removed from primitive rural existence. The historical association between money and metal is more than close; for all practical purposes, for most of time, money has been a more or less precious metal.

Metal was an inconvenient thing to accept, weigh, divide, assess as to quality in powder or chunks, although more convenient in this regard than cattle. Accordingly, from the earliest known times and more likely somewhat before, metal was made into coins of predetermined weight. This innovation is attributed by Herodotus to the kings of Lydia, presumably in the latter part of the eighth century B.C.:

> All the young women of Lydia prostitute themselves, by which they procure their marriage portion; this, with their persons, they afterwards dispose of as they think proper . . .
> . . . The manners and customs of the Lydians do not essentially vary from those of Greece, except in this prostitution of the young women. They are the first people on record who coined gold and silver into money, and traded in retail.[2]

It seems possible, based on references in the Hindu epics, that coins, including a decimal division, were, in fact, in use in India some hundreds of years earlier.[3] Coinage after the Lydians developed greatly in the Greek cities and in their colonies in Sicily and Italy to become a major art form. Some surviv-

[2]Herodotus, Book I, *Clio*. Rev. William Beloe, trans. (Philadelphia: M'Carty and Davis, 1844), p. 31.
[3]Alexander Del Mar, *History of Monetary Systems* (London: Effingham Wilson, 1895; New York: Augustus M. Kelley, 1969), pp.1–2.

ing specimens cannot be viewed without a quick intake of breath at their beauty. After Alexander the Great the custom was established of depicting the head of the sovereign on the coin, less, it has been suggested, as a guarantee of the weight and fineness of the metal than as a thoughtful personal gesture by the ruler to himself. It was one that could work in reverse. According to Suetonius, after the death of Caligula his money was called in and melted down so that not only the name but the features of the tyrant might be forgotten.

Coinage was a notable convenience. It was also an invitation to major public and minor private fraud. For profligate or hard-pressed rulers, and these, over time, have been a clear majority of their class, it regularly appeared as a flash of revelation that they could reduce the amount of metal in their coins or run in some cheaper brass and hope, in effect, that no one would notice, at least soon. Thus a smaller amount of silver or gold would buy as much as before, or the same pure weight that much more. And it occurred equally to private entrepreneurs, after concluding a bargain, that they could clip or shave a few micromilligrams from the coins they had agreed to pay. This, over time, would add marginally but agreeably to the profits. Counterfeiting was also an early innovation. As early as 540 B.C., Polycrates of Samos is said to have cheated the Spartans with coins of simulated gold.

With the passage of time and depending on the financial needs of rulers, their capacity for resisting temptation, which was generally modest, and the private development of the peculative arts, coinage had a highly reliable tendency to get worse. The Greeks, notably the Athenians, seem to have resisted debasement out of a rather clear understanding that this was a short-run and self-defeating expedient and that honesty was, at a minimum, good commercial policy. After the division of the Roman Empire and the reassertion of Greek influence at Constantinople the bezant was for several centuries the world symbol of sound money, everywhere as acceptable as the gold it contained.

By contrast, the history of the highly developed coinage of Rome itself, as legend has sufficiently established, was one of steady debasement, beginning, it is commonly supposed, in consequence of the financial pressures of the Punic Wars. In time, this had the effect of converting the empire from a gold and silver to a copper monetary standard. By the time of Aurelian the basic *silver* coin was around 95 percent copper. Later its silver content was brought down to 2 percent.[4] Modern coin collectors, it has been suggested, now own the good gold and silver coins that were held back in hoards and which, with the slaughter, urgently compelled departure or normal demise of their owners, were then orphaned and forgotten.[5] In time it would be asserted that the debauchment of the currency caused the downfall of Rome. This historiography—the tendency to attach vast adverse consequences to monetary behavior of which the observer happens to disapprove—is one which we will find frequently to recur. It should, needless to say, be regarded with the utmost suspicion.

In the ancient and medieval world the coins of different jurisdictions converged at the major trading cities. If there were any disposition to accept coin on

---

[4]Norman Angell, *The Story of Money* (New York: Frederick A. Stokes Co., 1929), pp. 116–117.
[5]Angell, pp. 117–118.

faith, it was inevitably the bad coins that were prof-
fered, the good ones that were retained. Out of this
precaution came, in 1558, the enduring observation
of Sir Thomas Gresham, previously made by Ores-
me and Copernicus and reflected in the hoarding of
the good Roman coin, that bad money always drives
out good. It is perhaps the only economic law that has
never been challenged, and for the reason that there
has never been a serious exception. Human nature
may be an infinitely variant thing. But it has constants.
One is that, given a choice, people keep what is the
best for themselves, i.e., for those whom they love
the most.

With numerous coins in circulation variously adul-
terated, clipped, filed, sweated, trimmed, and with
the worst being offered first, coins became a problem. The path was now open for the next great reform, which was to go back to weighing. This decisive step was taken by the City of Amsterdam in 1609
—a step that joins the history of money to the history
of banking. It was a step especially occasioned by the
large trade of Amsterdam. That, in turn, was associated with one of the most pervasively influential
events in the history of money—the voyages of Columbus and the effect on Europe of the ensuing conquest and development of Spanish America.

There were many in Europe after 1493 who knew
only distantly of the discovery and conquest of lands
beyond the ocean seas, or to whom this knowledge
was not imparted at all. There were few, it can safely
be said, who did not feel one of its principal consequences. Discovery and conquest set in motion a vast
flow of precious metal from America to Europe, and
the result was a huge rise in prices—an inflation
occasioned by an increase in the supply of the hardest of hard money. Almost no one in Europe was so

removed from market influences that he did not feel some consequence in his wage, in what he sold, in whatever trifling thing he had to buy. The price increases occurred first in Spain where the metals first arrived; then, as they were carried by trade (or perhaps in lesser measure by smuggling or for conquest) to France, the Low Countries and England, inflation followed there. In Andalusia, between 1500 and 1600, prices rose perhaps fivefold. In England, if prices during the last half of the fifteenth century, i.e., before Columbus, are taken as 100, by the last decade of the sixteenth century they were roughly at 250; eighty years later, by the decade of 1673 through 1682, they were at around 350, up by three-and-a-half times from the level before Columbus, Cortez and the Pizarros. After 1680, they leveled off and subsided, as much earlier they had fallen in Spain.[6]

As noted, these prices, not the tales of the conquistadores, were the message to most Europeans that

---

[6]Much of the modern knowledge of this period derives from the diligent, indeed phenomenal, researches of Earl J. Hamilton, early on of Duke University and later of the University of Chicago, to whom Keynes, along with many others, paid warm tribute—work "of high historical importance." Professor Hamilton spent thousands of youthful hours on the account books and records of Spanish hospitals, convents and other institutions, building up price indexes, and similarly in the Spanish archives (including that marvelous monument to the bureaucrat's affection for paper, the Archivo General de Indias) establishing the source, kind and quantities of American treasures reaching Spain. Cf. in particular his *American Treasure and the Price Revolution in Spain, 1501–1650,* Harvard Economic Studies, Vol. XLIII (Cambridge: Harvard University Press, 1934), and "American Treasure and the Rise of Capitalism (1500–1700)", *Economica,* Vol. IX, No. 27 (November 1929), from which I have taken the price indexes herewith. The English index numbers cited here, with some rounding off, are the work of the German historian Georg Wiebe. His calculations, first published in 1895, are corrected in details but not in orders of magnitude in Abbott Payson Usher's "Prices of Wheat and Commodity Price Indexes for England, 1259–1930," *The Review of Economic Statistics,* Vol. XIII, No. 1 (February 1931), p. 103 et seq.

America had been discovered. At work in a primitive but unmistakable fashion was the central proposition concerning the relation of money to prices—the quantity theory of money. This holds, in its most elementary form, that, other things equal, prices vary directly with the quantity of money in circulation. In the sixteenth and early seventeenth centuries prices varied upward and greatly with the vast increase in the supply of precious metals available for coinage from across the Atlantic. There will be occasion later in this history to look at the quantity theory in its modern and more sophisticated form. By then, enough knowledge will have been gleaned from the record of monetary experience so it can be rather readily understood and, what is more important, not misunderstood.

The message from the Americas was not one that brought uniform joy. In Spain the new wealth led also to a bidding up of wages; there wages seem to have kept pace, more or less, with prices. Elsewhere in Europe they lagged far behind, differences in population growth being a possible influence. The figures available show only orders of magnitude. Also, in those times, workers, and most notably the many in agriculture, had income that was not part of their money wage. Nevertheless, in England, in the decade from 1673 through 1682, when prices were around three-and-a-half times the pre-Columbian level, it seems probable that wages were only about twice as high. There was a similar discrepancy in France and, it may be assumed, also in the trading cities of the Low Countries and northern Europe.

Not for the last time—and probably not for the first—inflation had a profound effect on the distribution of income, with a particular tendency to punish most those who had least. The loss of those who received the lagging wages was in turn the gain of those who paid them and received the high and increasing prices. The result was high profits,[7] and the further result was a general quickening of commercial and, in more elementary manifestation, industrial capitalism. Historians have for long talked, often with more grandeur than personal comprehension, of how the American treasure financed, lubricated, stimulated or otherwise enhanced the early development of European capitalism. In one view it was the gold and silver *per se* that nurtured that capitalism. In fact, it was not the metal but its consequences, and these were not at all mysterious. The high prices and low wages meant high profits. From the high profits came high savings and a strong incentive to their investment. Additionally the rising prices made it easy to make money; to the natural rewards of shrewd trading or efficient manufacture was added the gain, with the passage of time, from the ability to sell the same thing for more. Inflation does lubricate trade but by rescuing traders from their errors of optimism or stupidity. Finally it may be assumed that the easy profits gave easier opportunity to new entrepreneurs who were, as is often the case, more energetic, aggressive or imaginative or less deterred by the impossible than those already in the field. It was thus that American money and the resulting inflation assisted at the birth of European capitalism. Doubtless it would have been born anyway. But there can be no doubt that the assistance was real.

Where Spain is concerned, legend regularly persists against the strong burden of fact. Possibly this is because Spanish historians, unlike those of other countries, have rarely been aroused by national conceit. They

---

[7] A distinction made by Keynes who spoke of profit inflation as opposed to income inflation. John Maynard Keynes, *A Treatise on Money* (New York: Harcourt, Brace & Co., 1930), Vol. II, p. 148 et seq.

have been content to assume the worst. The Holy Inquisition in Spain remains in the minds of all as the paramount example of public cruelty, at least until Hitler. It is not something one would wish to praise. But the number of Jews, Marranos and other heretics who fell victim to its professedly judicial procedures during the three centuries of its sway—a few thousand at most—were fewer than were, on occasion, slaughtered summarily in the Rhineland cities in a single year. The Spanish Armada remains to this day the classic case of overwhelming and pompous military power brought to defeat by an inferior but far more sanguinary and alert foe. Against this belief the truth has never made headway. It is that the English had a nearly equivalent tonnage of much better designed men-of-war which were much more heavily gunned and much better manned and thus made up an altogether superior force.[8]

Similarly the accepted view of the American treasure of Spain. The legend holds it to be gold looted from the temples of the Aztecs, extracted as a ransom by Francisco Pizarro for Atahualpa—the wonderful roomful of gold artifacts demanded by Pizarro for the Inca—or surrendered by the Indians after persuasion of a uniquely painful sort. This treasure was then conveyed to Spain by galleons, many of which fell victim to the hordes of pirates that patrolled the Spanish Main and who were justified at least partly in their theft by the yet greater criminality and avarice of the Spaniards.

The treasure looted from the temples or extracted from the Indians was, in fact, a trifling part of the total. The overwhelming part was mined. Nor was the trea-

---

[8]"[B]y 1588 Elizabeth I was the mistress of the most powerful navy Europe had ever seen . . . a fleet capable of outsailing and outmaneuvering any enemy in any weather, and at its chosen range . . . of outgunning him decisively." Garrett Mattingley, *The Armada* (Boston: Houghton Mifflin Co., 1959), pp. 195–196.

sure gold. Nearly all, after the first years, was silver. Beginning with the decade of 1531 through 1540, the weight of silver was never less than 85 percent of the total and from 1561 through 1570, never less than 97 percent.[9] San Luis Potosi, Guanajuato and the other rich silver mines of Mexico, some of which continue to operate to the present day, and their counterparts in Peru were the source of the American treasure. Finally, by far the greatest part of it was conveyed safely and routinely to Spain. Two or three bad years apart, the losses to piracy, righteous and otherwise, were slight. This continued to be the case until the 1630s, after which, the richest ore having been exploited, exports of silver declined.

The bullion coming officially into Spain was, according to law and mercantilist policy, coined at the Spanish mints. These coins then went on to the trading centers of northern Europe, which sold desired products or, being less affected by the inflow of money, had lower prices. Along with the coins went smuggled metal that had circumvented the Spanish mints or avoided Spain entirely. In the sixteenth century precious metal went in quantity to France and in the following century to the Low Countries to pay for Spanish armies operating there. War, it is well to recall, was an important occupation of the age, with a major claim on public revenue. (Max Weber estimated that in this period about 70 percent of Spanish revenues and around two-thirds of the revenues of other European countries were so

---

[9] Hamilton, *American Treasure and the Price Revolution in Spain, 1501–1650*, p. 40. Thorold Rogers, in his classic study of English prices made in the last century, speaks of the large effect of new silver and the slight effect of new gold. *A History of Agriculture and Prices in England*, Vol. V, 1583–1702 (Oxford: Clarendon Press, 1887), p. 779.

employed.[10]) A not inconsiderable part of this flow converged on Amsterdam, to which we now return.

Not only did the American treasure enhance profits and stimulate commerce and industry, it also enlarged the opportunity of all who saw money as a way of making money. The silver coinage of the time contained some copper. It was not difficult for counterfeiters to produce an excellent imitation that contained a little, or even a great deal, more. They were assisted by the fact that the minting of money, even if as in Spain closely regulated, was still extensively a form of private enterprise. The merchants of Amsterdam at the end of the sixteenth century—a hundred years after the great flow of silver had started—were the recipients of a notably diverse collection of coins, extensively debased as to gold or silver content in various innovative ways. A manual for money changers issued by the Dutch parliament in 1606 listed 341 silver and 505 gold coins.[11] Within the Dutch Republic no fewer than fourteen mints were then busy turning out money; there was, as ever, a marked advantage in substituting plausibility for quality. For each merchant to weigh the coins he received was a bother; the scales were also deeply and justifiably suspect. Adam Smith told, 170 years later, of the solution: "In order to remedy [the aforementioned] inconveniences, a bank was established in 1609 under the guarantee of the City. This bank received both foreign coin, and the light worn [and other debased] coin of the country at its real intrinsic value in the good standard money of the country, deducting

---

[10]As cited in Hamilton, "American Treasure and the Rise of Capitalism (1500–1700)," p. 340.
[11]Richard Van Der Borght, "A History of Banking in the Netherlands," *A History of Banking* (New York, The Journal of Commerce and Commercial Bulletin, 1896), Vol. IV, p. 192.

only so much as was necessary for defraying the expense of coinage, and the other necessary expense of management. For the value which remained, after this small deduction was made, it gave a credit on its books."[12] Thus appeared, to regulate and limit abuse of the currency, the first notable public bank.[13] Similar institutions were soon established in Rotterdam, Delft and the then important trading town of Middlebourg. In time, guardian banks appeared in other countries.

With the rise of these banks the profits from sweating, adulterating and otherwise diminishing the coinage fell. At the public bank it was only the valid metal that counted. And, equally or more important, with the rise of national states coins became fewer and better minted. So coinage ceased to attract the attention of men of peculative instinct. The returns from such ingenuity were now low or derisory. The problems associated with money ceased to be those of coinage; they became, instead, those of banks and exchequers, not excluding those of the institutions that had been established to safeguard the coinage. A constant in the history of money is that every remedy is reliably a source of new abuse.

Such was true of the Bank of Amsterdam, on which a word should be added by way of completing the story. For a century after its founding it functioned usefully and with notably strict rectitude. Deposits were deposits, and initially the metal remained in storage for the man who owned it until he transferred it to another. None was loaned out. In 1672, when the armies of Louis XIV approached Amsterdam, there was grave alarm. Merchants besieged the Bank, some in the

---

[12]Adam Smith, *Wealth of Nations* (London: T. Nelson and Sons, 1884), Book IV, Ch. III, p. 196.
[13]There was at least one short-lived Venetian precursor. The proper reference is to a public bank rather than to a central bank. The Bank of Amsterdam had little of the character and few of the functions later associated with central banking.

suspicion that their wealth might not be there. All who sought their money were paid, and when they found this to be so, they did not want payment. As was often to be observed in the future, however desperately people want their money from a bank, when they are assured they can get it, they no longer want it.

In time, however, there came a turn for the worse. A companionable relationship had always existed between the mayor and members of the Senate of the City of Amsterdam which, more than incidentally, owned the Bank, and the directors of the Dutch East India Company. Often they were the same men. In the seventeenth century the Company had been an exceedingly solid enterprise, although it often needed short-run accommodation for outfitting ships or until the ships came in. Such loans the Bank came to provide out of the funds on deposit to the account of others. This was a small step toward what, for the modern, everyday commercial bank, is the most orthodox of operations. Then, toward the end of the seventeenth century, the East India Company began to do less well. Its deficits and debts increased, and in the eighteenth century things got even worse. In 1780, the war with England brought heavy losses of ships and cargos, and the Bank became yet slower to pay. The City government also began hitting the Bank for loans. Now, were all depositors to come at once for their money, all could not be satisfied. Some of the money would be away in uncollected or uncollectible loans to the Company or City. Previously merchants, accepting payment for goods and debts, had taken bank deposits at a premium over the more dubious coin that was the alternative. Now, suspecting trouble at the Bank, they took payment by transfer of a bank deposit only at a discount. And presently the Bank began to limit the amount of coin that could be withdrawn or transferred to another bank. Refusal or inability to make good in coin on deposits was, in days to come, to be the certain signal that a bank was in trouble—that, however the action might be explained, the end was in sight. For the Bank of Amsterdam the end came in 1819. After two centuries and a few odd years of service its affairs were wound up.

CHAPTER III

Banks

THERE ARE THREE progenitors of money: mints; treasury secretaries or finance ministers, these being the source of paper money; and banks of one description or another. In their claim to precedence banks come next after mints and are likewise an exceedingly old idea. Banking had a substantial existence in Roman times, then declined during the Middle Ages as trade became more hazardous and lending came into conflict with the religious objection to usury. With the Renaissance it revived as trade revived and religious scruples yielded in normal fashion to pecuniary advantage. So far as any business can be given ethnic association, banking belongs to the Italians.[1] Both the decline and revival were in Italy; no bankers since, not even the Rothschilds or J. Pierpont Morgan, have equaled the Medicis in grandeur, the grandeur being substantially enhanced by their being the fiscal agent of the Holy See. The banking houses of Venice[2] and Genoa

---

[1] See Abbott Payson Usher, "The Origins of Banking: The Primitive Bank of Deposit, 1200–1600," *The Economic History Review*, Vol. IV, No. 4, (April 1934), p. 399 et seq. Professor Usher suggests a possible connection between Roman and later Italian banking but concludes that "there is nothing in evidence now available to indicate any direct continuity in practice." (P. 402.)

[2] A pioneer and exceedingly interesting study of early practice is Charles F. Dunbar's "The Bank of Venice," *The Quarterly Journal of Economics*, Vol. VI, No. 3 (April 1892). Banks of deposit to the number of a hundred or more came into existence in Venice in

are the recognized precursors of modern, everyday, commercial banks. Almost as advanced were those of the Po valley, and, as money lending developed in London, it was natural that the street on which it settled should be named for the Lombards.

The process by which banks create money is so simple that the mind is repelled. Where something so important is involved, a deeper mystery seems only decent. The deposits of the Bank of Amsterdam just mentioned were, according to the instruction of the owner, subject to transfer to others in settlement of accounts. (This had long been a convenience provided by the Bank's private precursors.) The coin on deposit served no less as money by being in a bank and being subject to transfer by the stroke of a primitive pen.

Inevitably it was discovered—as it was by the conservative burghers of Amsterdam as they reflected incestuously on their own needs as directors of the Dutch East India Company—that another stroke of the pen would give a borrower from the bank, as distinct from a creditor of the original depositor, a loan from the original and idle deposit. It was not a detail that the bank would have the interest on the loan so made. The original depositor could be told that his deposit was

---

the thirteenth, fourteenth and fifteenth centuries. A very considerable number also failed with varying degrees of resonance. Numerous efforts were made by the Senate at regulation, including such details as the hours that banks were required to be open and their obligation to count out the depositor's cash in his full view. The results of the regulation were less than perfect. A sixteenth-century senator, one Tommaso Contarini, told in a speech of the difficulties. As paraphrased by Dunbar, he noted that a banker ". . . can accommodate his friends without the payment of money, merely by writing a brief entry of credit. The banker can satisfy his own desires for fine furniture and jewels by merely writing two lines in his books, and can buy estates or endow a child without any actual disbursement." (P. 316). See also Frederic C. Lane, "Venetian Bankers, 1496–1533: A Study in the Early Stages of Deposit Banking," *The Journal of Political Economy*, Vol. XLV, No. 2 (April 1937), p. 187 et seq.

subject to such use—and perhaps be paid for it. The original deposit still stood to the credit of the original depositor. But there was now also a new deposit from the proceeds of the loan. Both deposits could be used to make payments, be used as money. Money had thus been created. The discovery that banks could so create money came very early in the development of banking. There was that interest to be earned. Where such reward is waiting, men have a natural instinct for innovation.

There was an alternative opportunity involving bank notes, one that was to be wonderfully exploited in the eventual American Republic. That was to give the borrower not a deposit but a note redeemable in the hard currency that had been placed in the bank as capital or as a sedentary deposit. With this note the borrower could make his payment; the recipient of such payment might, instead of redeeming the note for cash, use it for his payments, and so on *ad infinitum*. Meanwhile back at the bank interest was being received on the original loan. One day, perhaps, the note would be returned and redeemed for the hard cash of the original deposit. But by then the borrower would have repaid his loan, also in hard money. All would be well, and interest would have been earned. There was a chance also that the note would continue its passage from hand to hand and to yet further hands and never be returned for collection. The loan which led to its emission would earn interest and in due course be repaid. The note meanwhile would continue its rounds. Against the original coin that allowed of the original loan, no claim would ever be entered. In the 1960s, Mr. George W. Ball, an eminently successful lawyer, politician and diplomat, left public office to become a partner of the great Wall Street house of Lehman Brothers. "Why," he was heard to ask a little later, "didn't someone tell me about banking before?"

Writing in the middle of the last century, John Stuart Mill disposed of the factors determining the value of money—what it will buy—in a few sentences:

> The value or purchasing power of money depends, in the first instance, on demand and supply . . . The supply of money . . . is all the money in *circulation* at the time . . . The demand for money, again, consists of all the goods offered for sale.[3]

The explanation was fully adequate for the time. And it tells what the banks could do to the money. From an original deposit of hard currency, loans could be made. New notes or new deposits usable as money would result. The supply of goods remaining unchanged, prices would be higher and money would be worth less. Were the banks avaricious, competitive or both and borrowers suitably euphoric, the expansion of loans with resulting interest and in consequence of deposits or notes could be great. So could be the increase in prices or the decrease in the value or purchasing power of money.

This increase in price was a flaw from the standpoint of the public or, in any case, for those who paid but did not receive it. For the banks there was also a serpent. That was the possibility that depositors and noteholders might, more or less simultaneously, come for their money. The original depositor could get his money, for it was still there. So, alternatively, could the man to whom the deposit was lent. Both could not. The marvel of banks in relation to money—the wonder of creating deposits or issuing notes that so served—was suspended on one silken thread. That was the requirement that depositors or noteholders come in decently small numbers for the hard currency that the bank was

---

[3]John Stuart Mill, *Principles of Political Economy* (London: John W. Parker and Son, 1852), Vol. II, Book III, Ch. VIII, pp. 12–13.

under obligation to pay. If all came at once, the bank could not pay. And when the thought spread that the bank could not pay, then, often in much haste, all came. When that occurred, the deposits or notes serving previously as money ceased to be serviceable. The deposits and notes of the firstcomers could be cashed; for the deposits or notes of the latecomers there would be nothing. Theirs were the worthless deposits or the worthless paper of what was now a failed bank. As such, it was money no longer. The miracle of the earlier creation of money was now matched by the despair of its sudden erasure from existence.

There being less money to buy things, prices would fall. The fall might be fast and ruinous to those with goods to sell or debts to meet. This was the depression or panic, the natural counterpart of the earlier euphoria. Again a rather simple thing.

As banking developed from the seventeenth century on, so, with the support of other circumstance, did the cycles of euphoria and panic. Their length came to accord roughly with the time it took people to forget the last disaster—for the financial geniuses of one generation to die in disrepute and be replaced by new craftsmen who the gullible and the gulled could believe had, this time but truly, the Midas touch. The cycles of euphoria and awakening span a full two hundred and fifty years to connect John Law with Bernard Cornfeld and with the Equity Funding Corporation of America. Since John Law showed, perhaps better than any man since, what a bank could do with and to money, he calls for a special glance. Also, since they were in Paris, his operations had a style and *panache* that would not have been manifested in more prosaic financial precincts. They had also a remarkable clarity of line.

Law arrived in France in 1716 with credentials that some must even then have thought less than reassuring.

Originally from Scotland, a detail for later attention, he was in flight from a murder charge in England where he had been unduly successful in a duel. Having run through a considerable inheritance, he had made his living for some years as a gambler. The Duc de Saint-Simon, to whose memoirs we are indebted for an extended comment on Law's operations—and who was one of the few French noblemen who knew Law and was not financially reduced by the acquaintance—described him as "the kind of man who, without ever cheating, continually won at cards by the consummate art (that seemed incredible to me) of his methods of play."[4] Previously, in Scotland, Holland and Italy Law had sought to sell his great idea, which was for a land bank that would issue notes to borrowers against the security of the land of the country. It was a revelation that was to recur in numerous later forms—in Germany as late as 1923. However, Law encountered difficulties with the unimaginative Scotch and Dutch.

France, however, was fertile ground, although here Law offered a variant based on more distant real estate. Louis XIV, having lived too long, had died the year before Law's arrival. The financial condition of the kingdom was appalling: Expenditures were twice receipts, the treasury was chronically empty, the farmers-general of the taxes and their horde of subordinate *maltôtiers* were competent principally in the service of their own rapacity. The Duc de Saint-Simon, though not always the most reliable counsel, had recently suggested that the straightforward solution was to declare national bankruptcy—repudiate all debt and start over. Philippe, Duc d'Orléans, the Regent for the seven-year-old Louis XV, was largely incapable of thought or action. Then came Law. Some years earlier, it is said, he had met Philippe in a gambling den. The latter "had

---

[4]Duc de Saint-Simon, *Memoirs,* Lucy Norton, ed. and trans. (London: Hamish Hamilton, 1972), Vol. III, p. 299.

been impressed with the Scotsman's financial genius."[5]

Under a royal edict of the second of May, 1716, Law, with his brother, was given the right to establish a bank with capital of six million livres, about 250,000 English pounds. The bank was authorized to issue notes. This it did in the form of loans, and, as might be imagined, the principal borrower was the state. The government used the notes in turn to pay its expenses and pay off its creditors. The notes were declared legal tender for payment of taxes.

Initially the notes were eminently acceptable not only for taxes but for all purposes. This was because Law, apart from holding that any banker who did not keep a sufficient reserve in good coin to redeem his paper was deserving of death, promised redemption in the currency of the weight of metal it contained at the date of issue of the paper. The kings of France, in accordance with long-established practice, had been steadily reducing the weight of the metal in the French currency, hoping as always that less gold or silver would do the work of more. Accordingly, Law seemed to be providing security against royal malversation. For a while, as compared with the coins of the same denominated value, Law's notes commanded a premium.

In these first months, there can be no doubt, John Law had done a useful thing. The financial position of the government was eased. The bank notes loaned to the government and paid out by it for its needs, as well as those loaned to private entrepreneurs, raised prices in accordance with Mill's formulation. And the rising prices, abetted by the optimism engendered by the death of Louis and the ancient and enduring ability of the French economy to survive and even improve in face of all difficulties, brought a substantial business re-

---

[5]Elgin Groseclose, *Money and Man* (New York: Frederick Ungar Publishing Co., 1961), p. 129.

vival. Law opened branches of his bank in Lyons, La Rochelle, Tours, Amiens and Orléans; presently, in the approximate modern language, he went public. His bank became a publicly chartered company, the Banque Royale. Had Law stopped at this point, he would be remembered for a modest contribution to the history of banking. The capital in hard cash subscribed by the stockholders would have sufficed to satisfy any holders of notes who sought to have them redeemed. Redemption being assured, not many would have sought it. It is possible that no man, having made such a promising start, could have stopped.

The first loans and the resulting note issue having been visibly beneficial—and also a source of much personal relief—the Regent proposed an additional issue. If something does good, more must do better. Law acquiesced. Sensing the need, he also devised a way of replenishing the reserves with which the Banque Royale backed up its growing volume of notes. Here he showed that he had not forgotten his original idea of a land bank. His idea was to create the Mississippi Company to exploit and bring to France the very large gold deposits which Louisiana was thought to have as subsoil. To the metal so obtained were also to be added the gains of trade. Early in 1719, the Mississippi Company (Compagnie d'Occident), later the Company of the Indies, was given exclusive trading privileges in India, China and the South Seas. Soon thereafter, as further sources of revenue, it received the tobacco monopoly, the right to coin money and the tax farm.

The next step was to place on the market the stock in what was now a primeval conglomerate. In 1719, this was done with a more visible, audible and at times violent response than ever before or possibly since. The jam of people seeking to buy the stock was dense; the din of the sale was deafening. Transactions were in the old bourse in the Rue Quincampoix. (Later they were moved to the Place Vendôme and finally to the grounds of the Hôtel Soissons.) The value of adjacent property rose sharply from the demand of people seeking to be close to the action. The shares rose phenomenally in value. Men who had invested a few thousands early in the year were worth millions in a matter of weeks or months. Those so transformed were called millionaires; it is to that year, evidently, that we owe this useful French word. As the year passed, more and more stock in the conglomerate was fed out to the investors.

Meanwhile the Banque Royale was also steadily increasing its loans and therewith the notes in which they were taken away. In the spring of 1719, it had some 100 million livres in notes outstanding; by midsummer there were 300 million more. In the last six months of 1719, another 800 million were issued.

The sale of stock, it might be assumed, was creating a vast fund for the development of the Louisiana wilderness. Alas, it was not. By a beneficial arrangement with the Regent, the proceeds of the sale of the Mississippi stock went not to the Mississippi but as loans to pay the expenses of the government of France. Only the interest on the loans was available for colonial development and to mine the gold that would go into the Banque Royale reserves. To simplify slightly, Law was lending notes of the Banque Royale to the government (or to private borrowers) which then passed them on to people in payment of government debts or expenses. These notes were then used by the recipients to buy stock in the Mississippi Company, the proceeds from which went to the government to pay expenses and pay off creditors who then used the notes to buy more stock, the proceeds from which were used to meet more government expenditures and pay off more public creditors. And so it continued, each cycle being larger than the one before.

That the government of France was an even more

unappealing investment than the Louisiana swamps or even that it and not Louisiana was the object of the investment went unnoticed by nearly all, that year. Law, whose name was converted in French speech to the better-sounding Lass, was by now the most highly regarded man in all France. Persuaded, as invariably happens with financial genius, by his own notices, he turned his attention to other economic and social reforms—most of them exceedingly sensible. He asked that the peasants be given the uncultivated lands of the clergy, that tolls be abolished, tariffs reduced, the grain trade freed of restraints. And he began systematically to finance public works and industry with his loans and resulting notes. He was ennobled by a grateful sovereign: He could not, without confusion with the Regent, be identified with New Orleans so he became the first, and as yet the only, Duc d'Arkansas.[6] On January 5, 1720, he received the ultimate recognition of his financial genius; he was made Comptroller General of France. The end was very near.

The notes, needless to say, were the problem. Early in 1720, the Prince de Conti, offended it is said by his inability to buy stock at a price he considered right, sent a bunch of the notes to the Banque Royale to be redeemed in hard currency. They were a sizable package; three wagons were sent to carry back the gold and silver. Law appealed to the Regent, who ordered the Prince to turn back a considerable share of the metal he had thus received in exchange. But others, acting out of a deeper insight, were busy getting Law's paper into metal and the metal into England and Holland. One, a jobber named Vermalet, "procured gold and silver coin to the amount of nearly a million of livres, which he packed in a farmer's cart, and covered with hay and cow-dung. He then disguised

---

[6]Norman Angell, *The Story of Money* (New York: Frederick A. Stokes Co., 1929), p. 247.

himself in the dirty smock-frock, or *blouse,* of a peas-
ant and drove his precious load in safety into Belgium."[7] Steps had to be taken to restore confidence.
One, not lacking in ingenuity, involved the impress-
ment of some thousand or more assorted mendicants
from the Paris slums. They were equipped with shovels
and other tools and marched in small groups along the
streets as though on their way to Louisiana to mine the
gold. All would know that the gold from their toil
would soon be pouring back into the Bank to back
up their notes. Having been sufficiently deployed and
displayed, the men were marched off to the ports. Unfortunately a large proportion escaped on the way to
the ships—perhaps were encouraged to do so. So, having meantime sold their tools, they were soon observed
back in their old haunts. The news that Paris had the
mendicants and not the gold had an unsettling effect
on investors and holders of the notes of the Banque
Royale. Presently it was necessary to restrict the payment of specie in return for the notes—the enduring
signal that the boom was over. Later Law took a further and far stronger step—in his new official capacity
he forbade, except in small quantities, the possession of
gold and silver and extended the prohibition to jewelry.
Informers were invited to share in any hoards they
might report. Meanwhile at the Banque Royale in Paris
there was now an even greater jam of people, these
wanting not securities or notes but hard money; on one
day in July 1720 so great was the crowd that fifteen
people were squeezed to death. Or so it was said. Law
was no longer a financial genius; exposed to the Paris
mob, it was now known, no sizable fragment of him

---

[7] Charles Mackay, *Memoirs of Extraordinary Popular Delusions and
the Madness of Crowds* (London: Richard Bentley, 1841; Boston:
L.C. Page and Co., 1932), p. 29. This is a vivid account of Law's
operations, as of numerous other episodes in popular dementia. It
would be too much to suppose that all of it would stand the test of
modern historical research, which is too bad for it is a fascinating
book.

would have remained. Accordingly, the Regent kept him out of sight, then got him out of France. He went to Venice and having for a decade "lived, in decent poverty, a quiet and virtuous life, died there in the Catholic faith, piously receiving the Sacraments of the Church."[8]

In France Law left broken fortunes, falling prices, depressed business and an exceptionally durable suspicion of banks and banking. As for the notes:

> Of all the nations in the world the French are the most renowned for singing over their grievances . . . the streets resounded with songs . . . one . . . in particular counselled the application of . . . [Law's] notes to the most ignoble use to which paper can be applied.[9]

The requiem of the Duc de Saint-Simon is also worthwhile:

> If to the solid merits of such a bank are added, as indeed they were, the mirage of a Mississippi scheme, a joint-stock company, a technical language, a trickster's method of extracting money from Peter in order to pay Paul, the entire establishment, possessing neither gold-mines nor the philosopher's stone, must necessarily end in ruin, leaving a tiny minority enriched by the total ruin of all the rest of the people. That, in fact, is what actually happened.[10]

In the further view of the Duc de Saint-Simon, Law's bank, except in France, might have been a good idea. The French only lacked the requisite restraint. It was, we shall see, an exceedingly doubtful point.

---

[8]Saint-Simon, p. 299.
[9]Mackay, p. 37.
[10]Saint-Simon, p. 269.

CHAPTER IV

The Bank

THE MIRACLE of money creation by a bank, as John Law showed in 1719, could stimulate industry and trade, give almost everyone a warm feeling of well-being. Parisians had never felt more prosperous than in that wonderful year. And, as Law also showed, the further result could be a terrible day of reckoning. Here, in the briefest form, was framed the problem that was to occupy men of financial genius or cupidity for the next two centuries: How to have the wonder without the reckoning?

Some did conclude that the one could not be had without the other. For a long time after Law, Frenchmen remained deeply suspicious of banks and bank notes, of any money that was not made of metal. That suspicion was reinforced during the Revolution by the experience with the assignats, of which there will be a later word. French peasants, in particular, developed a preference for having their wealth in hard coin, one that is not yet quite dead. In this they were not alone. In China and India silver and gold were also much preferred, and in India to this time it is thought prudent to have one's savings in silver or gold around the wrists and the neck or on the ears of one's wife. As a woman she is decently exempt from violence. So, therewith, is the family wealth. All jewelers have scales to reassure the investor as to the weight of the precious metal in the ornaments they sell. But the suspicion of banks and their money in their earliest manifestations was by no means confined to simple people alone. It was widely shared. Though he was willing to have banks for purposes of deposit, Thomas Jefferson strongly opposed their issue of notes. Writing to John Taylor in 1816, he agreed that banking establishments were more to be feared than standing armies. John Adams held that every bank bill issued in excess of the quantity of gold and silver in the vaults "represents nothing, and is therefore a cheat upon somebody."[1]

Against these austere views stood the circumstance of overriding power already mentioned: Gold and silver, when deposited at the bank, could be loaned at interest, and borrowers could pay the interest out of what they made from having the loan. And if, as described in the last chapter, more could be loaned than was on deposit—given the unlikelihood that all depositors would come for their hard money at once—yet more borrowers could be accommodated, yet more interest earned. Alas, then, for John Adams. From the intrinsic charm of this reward and the resulting improvement in community well-being came an overriding pressure to make the loans that increased the outstanding notes and deposits beyond the amount of gold and silver in the vault. Thus, more precisely, the problem of banking: How should lending be limited and other precautions taken against the day when depositors and noteholders would come for the precious metal that, in the nature of banking, wasn't there?

The solutions are three and, as regarded in retrospect, rather obvious. In practice, two or all three could be combined. Arrangements could be made to face bankers fairly systematically with their notes (or deposits) and require them to pay the supporting cash. Knowing that they would be so compelled, they

---

[1] Harry E. Miller, *Banking Theories in the United States Before 1860*, Harvard Economic Studies, Vol. XXX (Cambridge: Harvard University Press, 1927), p. 20.

would be cautious in their lending, would make sure that they always had reasonably ample reserves of metal on hand. Or the reserve of coin to be kept on hand could be specified by law, a solution favored later on in the United States. Or some special provision could be made against the day when everyone came for the metal that wasn't sufficiently there. If some higher source stood ready to provide hard cash on those occasions, then, as was observed when the armies of Louis approached Amsterdam, the desire to have it would dissolve.

In the two centuries after Law all of these solutions came into use, together with the further one of prohibiting banks from having borrowers take out their loans in notes as distinct from receiving deposits. The right of note issue, with the hope that the notes might continue to pass from hand to hand and never be presented for payment in hard money, was thought, correctly, to be especially subject to abuse. These remedies were rarely the result of ratiocination; all were a response to bitter experience. At all times men were torn between the immediate rewards and costs of excess and the ultimate rewards of restraint. It was only after the first were experienced that the second were legislated.

The pioneering instrument of reform was the Bank of England. Of all institutions concerned with economics none has for so long enjoyed such prestige. It is, in all respects, to money as St. Peter's is to the Faith. And the reputation is deserved, for most of the art as well as much of the mystery associated with the management of money originated there. The pride of other central banks has been either in their faithful imitation of the Bank of England or in the small variations from its method which were thought to show originality of mind or culture. In recent times central banking has become, as we shall see, a sadly pedestrian profession.

Governments keep their central banks on the shortest of leashes. This is true, with all others, of the Federal Reserve System in the United States, which enjoys the liturgy but not the reality of independence. Most functions have long since been reduced to a routine; by tradition even the research of a central bank must be noncontroversial, which is to say it must avoid important issues, for it is on these that opinion is likely to be divided. The best conclusions are those that thoughtfully affirm the obvious: "The pervasive role of petroleum products in overall industrial production implies that fuel price increases may intensify the strong inflationary pressures already in prospect for the months ahead."[2] Recognizing the relative innocuousness of the Federal Reserve Board, Presidents from both parties have on occasion used it as a place of deposit not alone for public funds but also for men who could not reliably be trusted to balance their own checkbooks. Miss Margaret Truman, in her highly agreeable recollections of her father, has left doubt that one of his appointees, Mr. Jake Vardaman, a onetime naval aide, could add. In the modern Bank of England, if a decision is thought important, it is *not* communicated to the outside directors until after it has been taken. This cannot be thought to enhance their power. The glow nonetheless remains. Some of the glow is what comes from any association, however routine, with money—it is what leads young men who are otherwise very intelligent to become vice-presidents of Chase Manhattan or to join the Prudential. But more of the glow is the legacy of the Bank of England. No head of a central bank of any distinction, as he pursues his dreary round of discussion on decisions that are not his to make, fails to dream that his day will come. Then, as it once did for the Governor of the

---

Bank of England, the whole financial world will wait on his word or gesture. Men will tremble at its impact even though they do not, in the slightest, know its meaning.

The origins of the Bank of England were not awesome. The founder, William Paterson, was a contemporary and fellow countryman from the Scottish Lowlands of John Law and with the same, possibly ethnic, instincts for fiduciary invention. While in America in the last years of the seventeenth century, Paterson became possessed of the idea of a great colony strategically situated on the Isthmus of Panama, which was then called Darien. Returning to Europe, he encountered initial difficulty in selling the idea, as did Law his land bank. But as Law later found the Regent in need of funds following Louis XIV, so Paterson found William of Orange in straits in consequence of his wars with the same monarch. Paterson likewise offered a solution: A banking company would be organized under a royal charter with a capital of £1,200,000. When subscribed, the whole sum would be lent to William; the government's promise to pay would be the security for a note issue of the same amount. The notes so authorized would go out as loans to worthy private borrowers. Interest would be earned both on these loans and on the loans to the government. Again the wonder of banking.

In 1694, it was agreed, and the Bank of England was born. Financial need overcame all objections including that of Tories who held, with some passion, that banks were republican by nature. Against the double-interest return the expenses must have been small; the initial table of organization consisted of the Court of Directors, Governor, Deputy-Governor, seventeen clerks and two doorkeepers, the latter at

£25 a year. Soon the Court did not include William Paterson, who had originally been retained at £2000. He quarreled with his colleagues after only a few months—recent writers suggest a conflict of interest. He was promoting a rival Orphans' Fund Bank.[3] In any case, he returned to Scotland and there now found an enthusiastic welcome for his Darien scheme. Frugal Scots rushed, as Frenchmen did later to the Banque Royale, to invest in the company that would develop Paterson's fever-ridden shore. All the investors who remained faithful to the enterprise lost their money. Nearly all of the 1200 colonists who set sail in the five ships, including Paterson's wife and child, lost their lives. Paterson narrowly survived. In later years his considerable contribution to financial history was recognized, and in reputation he was partly rehabilitated. He became an influential proponent of the union of England and Scotland.

In the fifteen years following the granting of the original charter the government continued in need, and more capital was subscribed by the Bank. In return, it was accorded a monopoly of joint-stock, i.e., corporate, banking under the Crown, one that lasted for nearly a century. In the beginning, the Bank saw itself merely as another, though privileged, banker. Similarly engaged in a less privileged way were the goldsmiths, who by then had emerged as receivers of deposits and sources of loans and whose operations depended rather more on the strength of their strongboxes than on the rectitude of their transactions. They strongly opposed the renewal of the Bank's charter. Their objection was overcome, and the charter was renewed. Soon, however, a new rival

---

[3]John Giuseppi, *The Bank of England* (London: Evans Brothers, 1966), p. 26. Earlier writers thought he had been unfairly removed from his great design.

appeared to challenge the Bank's position as banker for the government. This was the South Sea Company. In 1720, after some years of more routine existence, it came forward with a proposal for taking over the government debt in return for various concessions, including, it was hoped, trading privileges to the Spanish colonies, which, though it was little noticed at the time, required a highly improbable treaty with Spain. The Bank of England bid strenuously against the South Sea Company for the public debt but was completely outdone by the latter's generosity, as well as by the facilitating bribery by the South Sea Company of members of Parliament and the government. The rivalry between the two companies did not keep the Bank from being a generous source of loans for the South Sea venture. All in all, it was a narrow escape.[4]

For the enthusiasm following the success of the South Sea Company was extreme. In the same year that Law's operations were coming to their climax across the Channel, a wild speculation developed in South Sea stock, along with that in numerous other company promotions, including one for a wheel for perpetual motion, one for "repairing and rebuilding parsonage and vicarage houses" and the immortal company "for carrying on an undertaking of great advantage, but nobody to know what it is."[5] All eventually passed into nothing or something very near. In consequence of its largely accidental escape, the reputation of the Bank for prudence was greatly enhanced. As Frenchmen were left suspicious of banks, Englishmen were left suspicious of joint-stock

---

[4]Details are in R. D. Richards, "The Bank of England and the South Sea Company," *Economic History* (A Supplement of *The Economic Journal*), Vol. II, No. 7 (January 1932), p. 348 et seq.

[5]Charles Mackay, *Memoirs of Extraordinary Popular Delusions and the Madness of Crowds* (London: Richard Bentley, 1841; Boston: L. C. Page and Co., 1932), p. 55.

companies. The Bubble Acts (named for the South Sea Bubble) were enacted and for a century or more kept such enterprises under the closest interdict.

From 1720 to 1780, the Bank of England gradually emerged as the guardian of the money supply as well as of the financial concerns of the government of England. Bank of England notes were readily and promptly redeemed in hard coin and, in consequence, were not presented for redemption. The notes of its smaller private competitors inspired no such confidence and were regularly cashed in or, on occasion, orphaned. By around 1770, the Bank of England had become the nearly sole source of paper money in London, although the note issues of country banks lasted well into the following century. The private banks became, instead, places of deposit. When they made loans, it was deposits, not note circulation, that expanded, and, as a convenient detail, checks now came into use.

The prestige of the Bank was by now very great. In 1780, when Lord George Gordon led his mob through lishment. For so long as the Catholic Relief Acts, the Bank was a principal target. It signified the Establishment. For so long as the Catholic districts of London were being pillaged, the authorities were slow to react. When the siege of the Bank began, things were thought more serious. Troops intervened, and ever since soldiers have been sent to guard the Bank by night.

As noted, by the end of the eighteenth century the Bank of England had eliminated the notes of its smaller London rivals. Abuse from excessive issue of bank notes had thus been eliminated, at least in the City. But the other main tasks of a central bank had yet to be mastered. In times of optimism or speculative euphoria the lesser banks could expand their loans and deposits without restraint and thus invite the ensuing collapse and contraction of the supply of deposit money. And there was still no protection against the day when, for whatever reason, depositors came for the hard cash that by nature was not there. There was also a further need—by no means peculiar to banks and money. That was for a mechanism to regulate the regulator. For the Bank itself, under pressure of optimism or public need, could succumb and expand too prodigiously its own loans, notes and deposits. This problem was the first to obtrude.

Over the end of the century Britain was at war alternately on two fronts—first with the American colonies (with which, incidentally, differences of view over issuing money were an important cause of friction), then with Napoleon and then again with the new Republic. War had its usual consequences. Money was needed for sustaining the armies in the field, for the fleet and for the subsidies to allies that reflected the (for Britain) humane policy of contributing from more abundant wealth as allies contributed from more abundant manpower. Pitt was relentless and many thought ruthless in his demands on the Bank for loans. Though taxes were increased, and an income tax, also called a property tax, was levied against heavy resistance, the need continued. In the closing years of the century Bank reserves dwindled, and there were occasional runs. Finally, in 1797, under conditions of great tension which included the thought that the French might soon be landing, the Bank suspended the right of redemption of its notes and deposits in gold and silver. The principal immediate consequence was the prompt disappearance of gold and silver coins and a shortage of coins for modest transactions. People passed on the notes and kept the metal. Gresham again. The Bank hurriedly printed one- and two-pound notes, and it also redeemed from its vaults a store of plundered Spanish pieces of eight. The head of George III was stamped over the head of the Spanish monarch, inspiring an anonymous but notably anti-Establishment poet to write:

> The Bank, to make their Spanish dollars pass,
> Stamped the head of a fool on the neck of an ass.[6]

The needs of the government continued to press. Loans and the resulting note issues continued to increase. And now so did prices and the price of gold. Wheat, which was six shillings, ninepence a bushel at Michaelmas in 1797 and at the same level a year later, went to above eleven shillings in 1799 and to sixteen shillings the following year.[7] Bread went up accordingly. The price of uncoined gold bullion advanced substantially in the same period. In the next few years prices receded somewhat, only to rise sharply again. All this was a matter of much concern, and, in reflection of the distribution of power in the British polity of the day, the concern was focused not on the price of food but on the price of gold. In consequence, in 1810, the House of Commons impaneled a committee to inquire into the matter—the Select Committee on the High Price of Gold Bullion. Its principal task, which many would think involved a different phrasing of the same question, was to ascertain whether Bank of England notes, the basic money, had fallen or the price of gold had risen. The committee deliberated and duly found against the notes. Gold had increased in price because of an overissue of the still irredeemable Bank of England notes. The committee proposed that, after a two-year period, the

---

[6]Giuseppi, p. 76.
[7]T. S. Ashton, *Economic Fluctuations in England, 1700–1800* (Oxford: Oxford University Press, 1959), p. 181.

Bank make its notes fully convertible into specie once more. Thus convertible, there could be no increase in the price of metal.

There followed in 1811 a famous debate on the nature of money and its management, the most famous indeed in all history. Parliamentarians took part, and monetary experts came forward to offer their views. Then, as since, it was uncertain what made a man a monetary expert. Thenceforth, however, they were to be a fixed feature of the monetary scene.

In the debate, indistinct but wholly recognizable, is a difference of opinion that continues to this day.[8] Where does economic change originate? Does it begin with those who are responsible for money—in this case with those who made loans and thus caused the supply of notes and deposits to increase? (From this then comes the effect on prices and production, including the stimulating effect of rising prices on production and trade.) Or does change begin with the production? Does it originate in business activity and prices with consequent effect on the demand for loans and thence on the supply of notes and deposits, which is to say the supply of money? In short, does money influence the economy or does money respond to the economy? The question is still asked. "Monetary doctrine has wavered over time in its assessment of money as cause or effect of economic conditions."[9]

The war years were ones of expanding business activity and, as noted, of rising prices. One party, including the great men of the Bank itself, held that business conditions (as affected by the war) were the decisive influence. The Bank and its loans and note

---

[8] As also in its recurrence a few years later in the discussion between the adherents of the so-called banking and currency principles of Bank policy.

[9] Sidney Weintraub and Hamid Habibagahi, "Money Supplies and Price-Output Indeterminateness: The Friedman Puzzle," *Journal of Economic Issues,* Vol. VI, Nos. 2 and 3 (June–September 1972), p. 1.

issues were a response. The price of gold had gone up under pressure of active trade. The opposing party held that the Bank, by its generosity and weakness of will in resisting the government, had allowed out the notes that had caused the increase. The price of gold had not risen; it was the notes of the Bank that, most assuredly, had depreciated. And there should be no doubt; it was the responsibility of the Bank to ensure that its notes did not depreciate. This view reinforced that of the Bullion Committee.

By far the most memorable participant in this debate was a London stockbroker of Jewish provenance who, unknown to himself or anyone else, was, by this discussion, launching one of the most famous careers in economic thought. Some would later count him the greatest of all economists. This was David Ricardo, and he was an uncompromising supporter of the Bullion Committee and of what soon was to be known over the world as the gold standard. "During the late discussions on the bullion question, it was most justly contended, that a currency, to be perfect, should be absolutely invariable in value."[10] After conceding that precious metals could not be counted upon to be quite so invariable and perfect ("they are themselves subject to greater variations than it is desirable a standard should be subject to. They are, however, the best with which we are acquainted."[11]), Ricardo went on to hold that, without such a standard, money "would be exposed to all the fluctuations to which the ignorance or the interests of the issuers might subject it."[12] He was not opposed to bank notes. He thought them economical and a great con-

---

[10]David Ricardo, *The Works and Correspondence of David Ricardo*, Vol. IV, *Pamphlets 1815–1823*, Piero Sraffa, ed. (Cambridge: Cambridge University Press, 1951), p. 58.

[11]Ricardo, *Pamphlets*, p. 62.

[12]Ricardo, *Pamphlets*, p. 59.

venience. But let them always be fully convertible into
the metal on demand.

Ricardo's was in a great tradition of economic
counsel—one that is superb in willing the ends, weak
in willing the means. Or, as a recent historian has
gently suggested, he was "as a theoretical economist,
apt to be blind to what was happening under his
nose—for example, the fact that the country was at
war."[13] To this detail Pitt, however, could not be
blind; whatever the effect on the price of bullion, he
had the problem of Napoleon. He continued to come
to the Bank for loans. Ricardo was triumphant in
principle, failed only as a matter of practical necessity.

But in the end he won also in practice. Reputable
opinion continued to be strongly on his side. In 1821,
with the war well over, full convertibility was restored
at the old rate of exchange between notes and gold.
Ricardo, on this as on other matters, had conquered
England "as completely as the Holy Inquisition conquered Spain."[14]

Not that all was yet well. The Bank was still thought
too compliant. In 1824, memories of the South Sea
Bubble having sufficiently dimmed, there was another
notable outbreak of company promotions and issues.
Many of these again reflected the fatal attraction to
South America, although there was an encouraging
response to a company "to drain the Red Sea with
a view to recovering the treasure abandoned by the
Egyptians after the crossing of the Jews."[15] An easy-
going policy by the Bank was thought, though only
after the later collapse, to have encouraged the boom.

---

[13]Giuseppi, p. 79.
[14]John Maynard Keynes, *The General Theory of Employment Interest
and Money* (New York: Harcourt, Brace & Co., 1936), p. 32.
[15]A. Andreades, *History of the Bank of England* (London: P. S. King
and Son, 1909), p. 250, citing Juglar, *Les crises économiques*, p. 334.

A decade later there was another expansion of loans, another boom, then a heavy run on reserves. These approached exhaustion, and the Bank faced either a new suspension or bankruptcy. This time it was saved by a consortium of French bankers. They advanced gold to the Bank of England which they in turn drew from the Banque de France, the arrangement serving, among other things, somewhat to disguise the indignity of the rescue of the Bank of England by the Banque de France. In 1844, after an intense discussion of the respective roles of currency and banking in monetary management, Sir Robert Peel put the Bank firmly in a straitjacket— what Walter Bagehot, thirty years later, was to call the "cast-iron" system.[16] The Bank Charter Act of that year fixed the note issue of the Bank of England at £14 million. This amount was to be secured by government bonds. Beyond that, more notes could be issued only as there was gold and silver (no more than one-fourth the latter) in the vault. The cast-iron system was much too rigorous for another of the previously mentioned functions that the Bank was by now acquiring—that of supplying funds when people came in distressing numbers for their deposits in the lesser banks. This fault was remedied by suspending the law whenever it proved unduly inconvenient.

In these years the Bank moved to bring the operations of the subordinate or commercial banks under its control. In doing so, it brought into use the two historic instruments of central bank policy—open-market operations and the bank rate.

A rapid expansion of commercial bank loans and resulting deposits and the spending of the latter

---

[16]Walter Bagehot, *Lombard Street* (New York: Scribner, Armstrong and Co., 1876), p. 25.

would, as we have seen, cause prices to rise. The effect in England, exposed as it was to the full force of foreign competition, was to encourage purchases from abroad. And it made England a more costly market from which to buy. A signal of an unduly rapid expansion of bank lending, accordingly, was an outflow of gold for overseas purchases or for investment in supplying them. This the Bank now anticipated and forestalled by raising the bank rate—the rate at which, in one manner or another, it loaned funds to other banks or at which it accepted credit instruments from those seeking funds to finance commercial transactions. (This action had been facilitated in 1833 by legislation in effect exempting the Bank from the usury laws.) Such an increase in the bank rate now became a signal to the banks that they should restrict their lending. In case the signal was missed, the Bank of England could sell government securities in the open market and allow its other investments, including its commercial paper, to expire and be collected. So instead of an investment portfolio it now had cash. And this cash not being in the other banks, they had fewer reserves against their deposits and were thus forced to be more restrained in making new loans. They could replenish their cash by borrowing from the Bank of England. But here the bank rate entered. Having been increased, this discouraged such borrowing—and discouraged borrowing by ultimate customers when passed on to them. Thus did the Bank of England come to regulate the lending—and therewith the making of deposits and money—by the banking system as a whole.

Few phrases have ever been endowed with such mystery as open-market operations, the bank rate, the rediscount rate. This is because economists and bankers have been proud of their access to knowledge that even the most percipient of other citizens believe beyond their intelligence. Open-market operations are the sale of securities just mentioned by the central bank which removes the loanable cash or reserves from the commercial or ordinary banks. The bank rate and the rediscount rate are the same; they are what prevent the banks from too painlessly recouping their cash by borrowing from the central bank. This is it. Viewed in the context of their development in the last century, it is hard to regard these mysteries as anything but a simple, even obvious, accommodation to circumstance.

And so too was the final service of a central bank—the provision of a reliable supply of wholly acceptable money when, for whatever reason, people wished to turn their deposits in the commercial banks into the cash which, by the nature of deposit creation, was not there. In the crises of 1825 and 1833, there had been such a rush for gold. In the rest of the century it happened several times again. One of the more spectacular runs occurred in 1890 when the great banking house of Baring Brothers and Company suddenly found itself with £21 million in defaulted Argentine bonds on its hands and the prospect of bankruptcy ahead. (South America again.) For these emergencies there was also an established procedure. The Bank raised its rate high enough to discourage all unnecessary borrowing and to attract unattached investment funds from abroad. And then it met the needs of all solvent bankers who came for money. Their depositors were thus reassured. And so reassured, it was again as at Amsterdam. "The certainty that money could be got took away all desire to have it."[17] Beginning about 1825, the Bank of England recognized its responsibility to be "lender of last resort." This phrase is also much used by the *cognoscenti;* from it too history strips the mystery to leave a rather simple accommodation to circumstance.

---

[17] Andreades, p. 336.

In 1800, the lingering suspicions of the French of such institutions had yielded to the financial needs of Napoleon. There had emerged the Banque de France which, in the ensuing century, developed in rough parallel with the Bank of England. In 1875, the former Bank of Prussia became the Reichsbank. Other countries had acquired similar institutions or soon did. In 1867, in a relatively uncelebrated conference in Paris the representatives of the leading industrial countries of Europe decided that henceforth payment in specie would mean payment in gold alone. There will be occasion for later mention of this reform.

Within each country bank notes and deposits were freely transferable into gold at a fixed rate. Anyone so taking gold could exchange it for the currency of any other mature industrial state at a fixed rate. It followed that there was a fixed rate of exchange between the significant currencies. Accordingly, it was immaterial, except for a minor arithmetic calculation, in which currency a price was quoted, a contract entered or a loan agreed. The central banks—and by common agreement the Bank of England in particular—policed and protected the convertibility of currency into gold, and the armory of instruments for doing this was now complete. It seemed a very solid structure. It was less accepted in the United States than in Europe, as ensuing chapters will tell. But this seemed only a matter of time and understanding; such matters were bound to be difficult for a raw new democracy, and farmers, where money was concerned, were especially retarded. The trend in the United States was also very much in the right direction.

And in all countries there was a reinforcing morality. Those who supported sound money and the gold standard were good men. Those who did not were not. If they knew what they were about, they were only marginally better than thieves. If they did not, they were cranks. In neither case could they be admitted into the company of reputable citizens. This was not alone the morality of conservatives; it was also the virtue of intelligent and sophisticated men of the left. Socialists and, later, Communists, while they wished to be revolutionists, did not wish to be knaves.

In fact, the monetary achievement of the nineteenth century was a fragile thing. Thoughtful or anxious men had always posited one danger—that gold might become abundant and commonplace and the resulting rise in prices appalling. Perhaps then it would have to be abandoned for something with larger value and smaller bulk. It was not a totally academic thought. In but one year, 1850, following the rush of the adventurers, fortune seekers and optimists of the world to the Mother Lode, the new state of California produced as much gold as the whole world had in an average year of the preceding decade. At the same time in the Australian diggings fortunate men were picking up huge chunks when they could lift them—one of two hundred pounds was found reposing only a few inches under the surface. Then toward the end of the century came the discoveries on the Klondike and the Rand. There was still much distant and unexplored terrain on the planet. Who could tell what it might yield?

It would have been interesting to see what plethora would have done. Freud held that man's attachment to gold was deep in his subconscious. Accordingly, the prestige of the metal or some of it would have survived even had gold become like coal. The hypothesis was not tested, for the abundance did not develop. Enough gold *was* found to have an effect on prices. In the twenty-five years before 1848, when the specks were first seen in the race at John Augustus

Sutter's mill, prices in gold or its equivalent had been falling. In the next quarter-century they rose, although by modern standards the increase—by about 20 percent—was not very great. After South Africa, discoveries, on the whole, tapered off. Gold remained scarce. Keynes calculated in 1930 that an ocean liner could carry across the Atlantic all that had been mined, worked or dredged in the previous seven thousand years.[18] A modern supertanker would still be vastly more than adequate.

A greater danger to gold was war. The gold standard in the last century owed much to the intelligent management of the Bank of England—for a brief moment, central banking was an art. It owed much more to the British peace. In the next century warring governments would, as did that of Pitt, turn to their central banks for the money that they could not raise in taxes. And no bank, whatever its pretense to independence, would even think of resisting.

Most dangerous of all would be democracy. The Bank of England was the instrument of a ruling class. Among the powers the Bank derived from that ruling class was that of inflicting hardship. It could lower prices and wages, increase unemployment. These were the correctives when gold was being lost; euphoria was excessive. Few or none foresaw that farmers and workers would one day have the power that would make governments unwilling to impose these hardships even in so righteous a cause as defense of the currency.

However, it was early seen that the interests of the rich in these matters could differ from those of others. Writing in 1810, Ricardo observed that

---

[18]John Maynard Keynes, *A Treatise on Money* (New York: Harcourt, Brace & Co., 1930), Vol. II, p. 290. Keynes is also the source of Freud's observation.

The depreciation of the circulating medium has been more injurious to monied men . . . It may be laid down as a principle of universal application, that every man is injured or benefited by the variation of the value of the circulating medium in proportion as his property consists of money, or as the fixed demands on him in money exceed those fixed demands which he may have on others.[19]

Farmers, by contrast, were helped:

He, [the farmer] more than any other class of the community is benefited by the depreciation of money, and injured by the increase of its value.[20]

In England the triumph of Ricardo's monied class was complete or nearly so. In the United States, however, it was subject to the sharpest of challenges. In one form or another, this challenge was to dominate American politics for the first century and a half of the Republic. Only the politics of slavery would divide men more angrily than the politics of money.

[19]Ricardo, Vol. III, *Pamphlets and Papers, 1809–1811*, p. 136.
[20]Ricardo, *Pamphlets and Papers*, pp. 136–137.

CHAPTER V

Of Paper

IF THE HISTORY of commercial banking belongs to the Italians and of central banking to the British, that of paper money issued by a government belongs indubitably to the Americans. Bank paper and government paper have, of course, much in common. The notes loaned out by a bank retain full parity of purchasing power with the gold or silver to which they promise title so long as they can be exchanged for the metal. And they continue to retain this parity even though the notes outstanding substantially exceed in aggregate face value the metal available for their redemption. It is only important that the inadequacy of the underlying supply of metal not be demonstrated by all or too many coming for it at once.

Further, as British experience during the Napoleonic Wars showed, bank notes by no means lose all or even most of their value when convertibility into gold or silver is denied. The decisive factors, at first glance, are the number loaned out in relation to the general state of trade—more specifically, the volume of goods and services available for purchase—and the prospect for ultimate redemption. After the Treaty of Ghent and the victory at Waterloo, it became unlikely that the British government would much longer be pressing the Bank for loans and the resulting notes. And it seemed probable that the recommendations of the Bullion Committee for full convertibility would sooner or later be implemented. Accordingly, the Bank of England notes gained steadily in purchasing power and in relation to gold. This was in marked contrast with the opposite tendency of the vastly more abundant and infinitely less promising paper of the Banque Royale a century before.

Not much was changed when a government, instead of lodging its securities in its bank and taking the bank notes to pay its soldiers, sailors, servants and suppliers, issued its own notes directly to those who were waiting to be paid. The notes so issued were also a promise to pay gold or silver from the public treasury. Again the promise to pay usually—one may say all but invariably—exceeded in volume the metal available. But, as with bank notes, the esteem in which these government notes were held and the associated purchasing power remained high so long as they were fully convertible into gold or silver. How much their purchasing power diminished when they ceased to be convertible depended, likewise, on the volume of notes issued in relation to the volume of goods to be purchased and the prospect for ultimate redemption. Were the issue modest, the diminution in purchasing power might be slight and could remain so even though the promise of redemption, as was often the case, was infinitely postponed.

Government paper in its early manifestations often had the advantage of a rate of interest—a promise of a modest premium when turned in for redemption. It had also back of its promise of redemption the majesty and the integrity of the state, over much of history where money was concerned two exceedingly dubious assets. Usually, also, it was given a contrived or compelled value. It was declared that, when presented by a debtor to his creditor in adequate amount, the paper legally discharged the debt—it was legal tender. Thus debtors would seek and cherish the money for paying debts. Creditors could not resist. This reinforcement was invariably less potent than hoped.

A number of circumstances explain the pioneering role of the American colonies in the use of paper money. War, as always, forced financial innovation. Also paper money, like the Bank of England loans, was a substitute for taxation, and, where taxes were concerned, the colonists were exceptionally obdurate; they were opposed to taxation without representation, as greatly remarked, and they were also, a less celebrated quality, opposed to taxation with representation. "That a great reluctance to pay taxes existed in all the colonies, there can be no doubt. It was one of the marked characteristics of the American people long after their separation from England."[1] Paper money was also seen during colonial times, and not wrongly, as an antidote for economic discontent. Also the colonies were generally prevented by the mother country from sponsoring banks—thus bank notes, the obvious alternative to government notes, were excluded. And something must be credited to an instinct for monetary experiment—perhaps to the belief that, along with all of the other wonders of the New World, there existed also the possibility, original and unique in history, of creating money to make men rich.

The instinct for monetary experiment dates from the earliest days of settlement. The colonists, as every history tells, were endemically short of money. Almost all explanations attribute this shortage to the absence of any local source of gold and silver and to the commercial policy of the mother country

---

[1] G. S. Callender, *Selections from the Economic History of the United States, 1765–1860* (Boston: Ginn and Co., 1909), p. 123.

which, reflecting the mercantilist belief that all significant wealth consisted of gold and silver, insouciantly sucked these metals away from the settlers. Both explanations are improbable. Many countries or communities had gold and silver in comparative abundance without mines. Venice, Genoa, Bruges had no Mother Lode. (Nor today does Hong Kong or Singapore.) While the colonists were required to pay in hard coin for what they bought from Britain, they also had products—tobacco, pelts, ships, shipping services—for which British merchants would have been willing, and were quite free, to expend gold and silver. Much more plausibly, the shortage of hard money in the colonies was another manifestation of Gresham. From the very beginning the colonists experimented with substitutes for metal. The substitutes, being less well regarded than gold or silver, were passed on to others and thus were kept in circulation. The good gold or silver was kept by those receiving it or used for those purchases, including those in the mother country, for which the substitutes were unacceptable.

The first substitute was taken over from the Indians. From New England to Virginia in the first years of settlement, the wampum or shells used by the Indians became the accepted small coinage. In Massachusetts in 1641, it was made legal tender, subject to some limits as to the size of the transaction, at the rate of six shells to the penny. However, within a generation or two it began to lose favor. The shells came in two denominations, black and white, the first being double the value of the second. It required but small skill and a smaller amount of dye to convert the lower-denomination currency into the higher. Also the acceptability of wampum depended on its being redeemed by the Indians in pelts. The Indians, in effect, were the central bankers for the wampum monetary system, and beaver pelts were the reserve currency into which wampum could be converted. This convertibility sustained the purchasing power of the shells. As the seventeenth century passed and settlement expanded, the beavers receded to the ever more distant forests and streams. Pelts ceased to be available, wampum ceased, accordingly, to be convertible and thus, in line with expectation, it lost in purchasing power. Soon it disappeared from circulation except as small change.

Tobacco, although regionally more restricted, was far more important than wampum. It came into use as money in Virginia a dozen years after the first permanent settlement in Jamestown in 1607. Twenty-three years later, in 1642, it was made legal tender by the General Assembly of the colony by the interestingly inverse device of outlawing contracts that called for payment in gold or silver. The use of tobacco as money survived in Virginia for nearly two centuries and in Maryland for a century and a half— in both cases until the Constitution made money the concern solely of the Federal government. The gold standard, by the common calculation, lasted from 1879 until the cancellation of the final attenuated version by Richard Nixon in 1971. Viewing the whole span of American history, tobacco, though more confined as to region, had nearly twice as long a run as gold.

Initially the tobacco passed from hand to hand in the manner of paper and coins. Apart from being somewhat friable, it had two other characteristics of considerable importance. As a medium of exchange that was grown instead of mined, minted or printed, its supply was uniquely a matter not of luck, organization or state authority but of individual will. And it lent itself with exceptional readiness to depreciation in quality. Both characteristics of tobacco were energetically exploited. From the earliest days of the Virginia and Maryland settlements, colonial governments were concerned with arrangements for limiting the production of tobacco and thus sustaining its purchasing power. In 1666, a treaty was negotiated among Virginia, Maryland and Carolina (as it then was), agreeing to a one-year suspension of all tobacco production. In 1683, the failure of a similar effort sent bands roaming the countryside destroying tobacco plants and leading the Virginia Assembly to decree that, if such operations were conducted by eight or more marauders, the participants should be adjudged guilty of treason and suffer death.

Although high production brought a sharp inflation of prices as denoted in pounds of tobacco, tobacco as money had a marked charm for producers. The overproduction of farm products, their often inelastic demand and the resulting disastrous prices have regularly made it hard for farmers to meet interest or payments on mortgages or other debts. At low prices an excessive quantity of wheat, cotton or livestock was required. So long as tobacco was money, the same quantity serviced the given debt, for the debt was written in pounds of leaf. The law of 1642 forbidding contracts that called for gold and silver was a thoughtful concession by tobacco planters to themselves. Being troubled by creditors who, not wanting to be paid off in cheap tobacco, were contracting to receive something more substantial, notably gold or silver, the planters took the logical step of outlawing such a menace.

The price of tobacco in British currency was, *pari passu*, the rate of exchange between the money of Virginia and Maryland and sterling. When the price of tobacco was tenpence a pound, that was the rate of exchange; i.e., the Virginia or Maryland tobacco pound was worth tenpence sterling. When the price of tobacco dropped to fivepence, the rate of exchange was fivepence for one tobacco pound. As between price level and exchange rate there was thus an effortless and automatic accommodation with no lag. It was an early and exceptionally elegant manifestation of what is now called a floating exchange rate and by the *cognoscenti,* a float.

A pound of poor tobacco still being a pound of tobacco, there was obvious advantage in favoring that of lowest quality if it could be produced at lower cost. And this led Gresham's Law to operate with exceptional power on the resulting product. No one passed on good tobacco if scraps, stems or leaf of suffocating tendency were available instead. On the north shore of Lake Erie in Ontario, tobacco is an important crop. In my youth there a neighbor named Norman Griswold, whose farm was to the south of ours, sustained his nicotine addiction by odds and ends of leaf which were passed on to him from neighboring farmers and which he cured himself. Norman's approach, in a south wind, would be known a full fifteen minutes before he materialized. All authorities agree that such was the tobacco that the Virginia and Maryland planters put in circulation first.

It was, in fact, the counterpart of the clipped and sweated coins that the Amsterdam merchants had found so troublesome. And the eventual remedy was the same. Public warehouses, the counterpart of the Bank of Amsterdam, were established. There the tobacco was weighed and graded, and certificates representing a defined quality and quantity were then issued. These passed into circulation. In 1727, tobacco certificates or notes became full legal tender in Virginia and continued to serve until nearly the end of the century. So close was the association between tobacco and money that the paper currency of New

Jersey, not a tobacco-growing state, carried on its face a tobacco leaf as well as the exigent warning: "To counterfeit is *Death*."[2]

In South Carolina during the later colonial years rice, for a time, served as money in much the same fashion as tobacco in Virginia and Maryland. Elsewhere there were numerous lesser experiments with grain, cattle, whiskey and brandy, all of which at one time or another were declared legal tender for debts. The use of whiskey and brandy as money makes exceptionally poignant the injunctions, common through American history, against drinking up one's fortune. None of these substitutes was important as compared with paper money.

The first issue of paper money was by the Massachusetts Bay Colony in 1690; it has been described as "not only the origin of paper money in America, but also in the British Empire, and almost in the Christian world."[3] It was occasioned, as noted, by war. In 1690, Sir William Phips—a man whose own fortune and position had been founded on the gold and silver retrieved from a wrecked Spanish galleon near the shores of what is now Haiti and the Dominican Republic—led an expedition of Massachusetts irregulars against Quebec.[4] The loot from the fall of

---

[2]Reproduced in Norman Angell, *The Story of Money* (New York: Frederick A. Stokes Co., 1929), following p. 86.

[3]Ernest Ludlow Bogart, *Economic History of the American People* (New York: Longmans, Green and Co., 1930), p. 172.

[4]Whose intendants, at the time, were also making a most engaging contribution to the history of money. When hard money to pay the garrison and for other purposes was slow in arriving from France, promises to pay were inscribed on playing cards and issued to the soldiers and other creditors. The playing-card currency continued in use for some sixty years. Versailles initially disapproved, later went along. In 1711, there was a 100-livres issue in spades and clubs, a 50-livres issue in hearts and diamonds. By the time of Wolfe and Montcalm the issue was sadly inflated. With the fall of New France

the fortress was intended to pay for the expedition. The fortress did not fall. The American colonies were operating on negligible budgets—Adam Smith noted that the civil government of Massachusetts just before the Revolution cost £18,000 a year, those of New York and Pennsylvania around £4500 and that of New Jersey a mere £1200[5]—and there was no enthusiasm for levying taxes to pay the defeated heroes. So notes were issued to the soldiers promising eventual payment in hard coin. Redemption in gold or silver, as these were returned in taxes, was promised, although presently the notes were also made legal tender for taxes. For the next twenty years the notes circulated side by side with gold and silver of equivalent denomination. Notes and metal being interchangeable, there was, *pro tanto,* no depreciation.

Inevitably, however, it occurred to the colonists that the notes were not a temporary, onetime expedient but a general-purpose alternative to taxation. More were issued as occasion seemed to require, and the promised redemption was repeatedly postponed. Prices specified in the notes now rose; so, therewith, did the price of gold and silver. By the middle of the eighteenth century the amount of silver or gold for which a note could be exchanged was only about a tenth of what it had been fifty years before. Ultimately the notes were redeemed at a few shillings to the pound from gold sent over to pay for the colonial contribution to Queen Anne's War.

Meanwhile the other New England colonies and South Carolina had also discovered paper money. And some of them, notably South Carolina and Rhode

---

the experiment came to an end. Herbert Heaton, "The Playing Card Currency of French Canada," *The American Economic Review,* Vol. LVIII, No. 4 (December 1928), p. 649 et seq.

[5]Adam Smith, *Wealth of Nations* (London: T. Nelson and Sons, 1884), Book IV, Chapter VII, p. 235.

Island, were vastly more abandoned in their issues. The Rhode Island paper was so voluminous that it was regarded with alarm even in Massachusetts. A Massachusetts commentator complained in 1740 that "Rhode Island purchases from . . . Massachusetts-Bay all Sorts of British and Foreign Goods with this Paper Manufacture which costs nothing, which enables them to rival us in Trade."[6] These issues eventually became worthless or virtually so.

Samuel Eliot Morison has said of the notes issued by Massachusetts to pay off the soldiers back from Quebec that they were "a new device in the English-speaking world which undermined credit and increased poverty."[7] Other and less judicious historians have reflected the same view. But it is also known that rising prices stimulate the spirits of entrepreneurs and encourage economic activity just as falling prices depress both. Were only so much paper money issued by a government as to keep prices from falling or, at most, cause a moderate increase, its use could be beneficial. Not impoverishment but an increased affluence would be the result. The question, obviously, is whether there could be restraint, whether the ultimate and impoverishing collapse could be so avoided. The Law syllogism comes ominously to mind: If some is good, more must be better.

Restraint was clearly not available in Rhode Island or South Carolina or even in Massachusetts. Else-

---

[6] William Douglas, "A Discourse Concerning the Currencies of the British Plantations in America" (Boston, 1740). Cited in Richard A. Lester, *Monetary Experiments* (Princeton: Princeton University Press, 1939), p. 9. My debt to Professor Lester, an old friend whose book corrected in decisive fashion the view of colonial monetary history, is very great.

[7] Samuel Eliot Morison, *The Oxford History of the American People* (New York: Oxford University Press, 1965), p. 124.

where, however, it was present to a surprising extent. The Middle Colonies handled paper money with what must now be regarded as astonishing skill and prudence. A difference in degree which can become a difference in kind must here be noticed. It is between preventing or redressing falling prices and engineering a general increase—having inflation. The leaders of the Middle Colonies, like many after them, sought to do the first. They did not wish the second.

The first issue of paper money there was by Pennsylvania in 1723. Prices were falling at the time, and trade was depressed. Both recovered, and the issue was stopped. There appear to have been similar benefits from a second issue in 1729; the course of business and prices in England in the same years suggests that, in the absence of such action, prices would have continued down. Similar issues produced similarly satisfactory results in New York, New Jersey, Delaware and Maryland. As in Pennsylvania, all knew the virtue of moderation.

The most engaging experiment was in Maryland. Elsewhere the notes were put into circulation by the simple device of using them to pay public expenses. Maryland, in contrast, declared a dividend of thirty shillings to each taxable citizen and, in addition, established a loan office where worthy farmers and businessmen could obtain an added supply which they were required to repay. Remarkably the dividend was a onetime thing; as in the other Middle Colonies the notes so issued were ultimately redeemed in hard money. A near-contemporary historian with a near-gift for metaphor credited the experiment with "feeding the flame of industry that began to kindle."[8] A much later student has con-

---

[8] George Chalmers, *Introduction to the History of the Revolt of the American Colonies,* Vol. II, p. 160. Cited in Lester, p. 148.

cluded that "this was the most successful paper money issued by any of the colonies."[9] Two centuries later during the Great Depression a British soldier turned economic prophet, Major C. H. Douglas, made very nearly the same proposal. This was Social Credit. Save in such distant precincts as the Canadian prairies, he acquired general disesteem as a monetary crank. He was two hundred years too late.

The monetary experiments of Pennsylvania and its neighbors were by no means an unconsidered reaction to circumstance. They were extensively debated and had the energetic support of Benjamin Franklin, the most intelligent political man in the colonies and an ardent exponent of paper money. In 1729, he published his *A Modest Enquiry into the Nature and Necessity of a Paper Currency,* a brief on behalf of a paper currency, and in ensuing years aided the cause in an even more practical way. In 1736, Franklin's *Pennsylvania Gazette* printed an apology for its irregular appearance because its printer was "with the Press, labouring for the publick Good, to make Money more plentiful."[10] The press was busy printing money.

Toward the end of the nineteenth century expanding university faculties, an increased interest in the past and a pressing need for subjects on which to do doctoral theses and other scholarly research all led to a greatly expanded exploration of colonial economic history. By then, among historians and economists, the gold standard had become an article of the highest faith. Their research did not subordinate that faith to fact. By what amounted to a tacit understanding between right-thinking men the abandoned

[9]C. P. Gould, *Money and Transportation in Maryland, 1720–1765,* Johns Hopkins University Studies, Vol. XXXIII, 1915, p. 89. Cited in Lester, p. 151.
[10]*The Papers of Benjamin Franklin,* Vol. 2, 1735–1744, Leonard W. Labaree, ed. (New Haven: Yale University Press, 1960), p. 159.

tendencies of Rhode Island, Massachusetts and South Carolina were taken to epitomize the colonial monetary experience. The different experience of the Middle Colonies was simply ignored. A leading modern student of colonial monetary experience has noted that: "One looks in vain for any discussion of these satisfactory currency experiments in the standard works on American monetary and financial history."[11] Another has concluded that ". . . generations of historical scholarship have fostered a mistaken impression of the monetary practices of the colonies."[12]

The young have always learned that Benjamin Franklin was the prophet of thrift and the exponent of scientific experiment. They have but rarely been told that he was the advocate of the use of the printing press for anything except the diffusion of knowledge.

The colonial monetary experiments aroused no admiration in the mother country. They were proof of the abandoned tendencies of the colonists. In 1751, accordingly, Parliament forbade the issue of further paper money in New England and thirteen years later extended the ban to the rest of the colonies. A tactless exception was made for paper issued for the King's purposes, that is to say for war. There was strong protest in the colonies. In 1766, Franklin carried his case for paper money to the House of Commons in person. It was an eloquent effort but without effect. The ban became a serious source of tension between Britain and the colonies. It has been less celebrated than it deserves because, on this,

---

[11]Lester, p. 141.
[12]E. James Ferguson, "Currency Finance: An Interpretation of Colonial Monetary Practices" in *Issues in American Economic History*, Gerald D. Nash, ed. (Boston: D.C. Heath & Co., 1964), p. 85.

many reputable historians have believed that Parliament was superbly right. Writing in 1900, Charles J. Bullock, soon to become a Harvard professor and a respected authority on colonial finance, described the colonial monetary experience as a "carnival of fraud and corruption," a "dark and disgraceful picture." The action of Parliament putting an end to the issues he described as "wholesome." The objections of the colonists, he makes clear, were wholly wrongheaded. Independence itself had no merit, were it a license for monetary insanity.[13]

Some colonists shared the thought that independence was not worth the risk of the monetary experiment that it would allow: ". . . there was a substantial element of the population, particularly in the larger cities in the East, which stood aloof from the revolt against England, not so much out of opposition as because of the fear that independence would bring excessive issues of paper money with all its consequent derangement to business affairs."[14]

Given their instinct for experiment in monetary matters, it would have been surprising if the colonists had not discovered or invented banks. They did, and their enthusiasm for this innovation would have been great had it not also been systematically curbed. In the first half of the eighteenth century the New England colonies, along with Virginia and South Carolina, authorized banking institutions. The most

---

[13]Charles J. Bullock, *Essays on the Monetary History of the United States* (New York: Macmillan Co., 1900; Greenwood Press, 1969), p. 43 et seq. At the time of these essays Professor Bullock was teaching at Williams College. Over a long career at Harvard he acquired a not unjustified reputation as a pre-Renaissance, some held Mesozoic, figure. This later reputation does not at all detract from the respect accorded to his views on colonial finance.
[14]Davis Rich Dewey, *Financial History of the United States* (New York: Longmans, Green and Co., 1903), p. 43.

famous, as also the most controversial of these, was the magnificently named Land Bank Manufactory Scheme of Massachusetts which, very possibly, owed something to the ideas of John Law. The Manufactory authorized the issue of bank notes at nominal interest to subscribers to its capital stock—the notes to be secured, more or less, by the real property of the stockholders. The same notes could be used to pay back the loan that their issue had incurred. This debt could also be repaid in manufactured goods or produce, including that brought into existence by the credit so granted. The Manufactory precipitated a bitter dispute in the colony. The General Court was favorable, a predisposition that was unquestionably enhanced by the award of stock to numerous of the legislators. Merchants were opposed. In the end, the dispute was carried to London. In 1741, the Bubble Acts—the British response, as noted, to the South Sea Company and associated promotions and which outlawed joint-stock companies not specifically authorized by law—were declared to apply to the colonies. It was an outrageous exercise in *ex post facto* legislation, one that helped inspire the Constitutional prohibition against such laws. However, it effectively ended the colonial banks.

The history of money reveals two highly reliable tendencies. Having recent experience of inflation, people cherish stable prices, and having long experience of stable prices, they become indifferent to the risk of inflation. And, on the whole, older communities are less inclined to monetary experiment than newer ones. In the half-century before independence both of these factors were at work in the colonies. The inflation in New England in the first half of the eighteenth century led, in the second half, to a growing, if still less than decisive, interest in money with a relatively reliable, stable purchasing power. And as London once looked with horror on the monetary tendencies of Boston, so Boston would come in time to look with similar distaste on the seeming irresponsibility of Kentucky, Tennessee and Ohio. The partisans of hard money consisted no doubt in part of Ricardo's monied men—the legendary defenders of the currency whose defense is based firmly on their dislike for having their debts repaid in coin of lesser purchasing power. But merchants, so far as they represented a different interest, may have been more influential. They wanted the convenience of money that was readily acceptable abroad at a predictable rate of exchange and one which also would not diminish in purchasing power between the time goods were sold and the resulting bills were paid. It was Boston merchants, as just observed, who led the fight against the Manufactory.

CHAPTER VI

An Instrument of Revolution

WITH INDEPENDENCE the ban by Parliament on paper money became, in a notable modern phrase, inoperative. And however the colonies might have been moving toward more reliable money, there was now no alternative to government paper. It cannot be said that it was an alternative that was embraced with much reluctance. Before the First Continental Congress assembled, some of the colonies (including Massachusetts) had authorized note issues to pay for military operations. The Congress was without direct powers of taxation; one of its first acts was to authorize a note issue. More states now authorized more notes. It was by these notes that the American Revolution was financed. Between June 1775 and November 1779, there were *forty-two* currency issues by the Continental Congress with a total face value of $241,600,000. In the same years the states issued another $209,500,000. Domestic borrowing, much of it rendered in the notes just mentioned, brought in less than $100,000,000.[1] Reflecting the well-known distaste for such importunity, taxation was insignificant. Taxes levied in consequence of requisitions on the states produced only a few millions of dollars.

---

[1] These estimates vary as between different authorities. Those given here are from Davis Rich Dewey, *Financial History of the United States* (New York: Longmans, Green and Co., 1903), pp. 36, 46.

Robert Morris, to whom the historians have awarded the less than impeccable title of "Financier of the Revolution," obtained some six-and-a-half million dollars in loans from France, a few hundred thousand from Spain and later, after victory was in prospect, a little over a million from the Dutch. These amounts, too, were more symbolic than real. Overwhelmingly the Revolution was paid for with paper money.

Since the issues, Continental and state, were far in excess of any corresponding increase in trade, prices rose—at first slowly and then, after 1777, at a rapidly accelerating rate. Congress early took steps to stem the decay, resolving in 1776 that "any person who shall hereafter be so lost to all virtue and regard for his country, as to refuse to receive said bills in payment . . . shall be deemed, published and treated as an enemy in this country and precluded from all trade or intercourse with the inhabitants of these Colonies."[2] The results, as ever, were disappointing. The price increases continued unchecked. Eventually, in the common saying, "a wagon-load of money would scarcely purchase a wagon-load of provisions." Shoes in Virginia were $5000 a pair in the local notes, a full outfit of clothing upwards of a million. Creditors sheltered from their debtors like hunted things lest they be paid off in the worthless notes. "The widow who lived comfortably on the bequest of a deceased husband, experienced a frustration of all his well-meant tenderness. The laws of the country interposed, and compelled her to receive a shilling where a pound was her due. The blooming virgin who had grown up with an unquestionable title to a liberal patrimony was legally stripped of everything but her personal charms and virtues . . . The dreams of the golden age were realized to the poor man and the debtor, but unfortunately what these

---

[2]Norman Angell, *The Story of Money* (New York: Frederick A. Stokes Co., 1929), p. 255.

gained was just so much taken from others."[3] The phrase "not worth a Continental" won its enduring place in the American language. Even Benjamin Franklin became ironical:

> This Currency, as we manage it, is a wonderful machine. It performs its Office when we issue it; it pays and clothes Troops, and provides Victuals and Ammunition; and when we are obliged to issue a Quantity excessive, it pays itself off by Depreciation.[4]

Thus the United States came into existence on a full tide not of inflation but of hyper-inflation—the kind of inflation that ends only in the money becoming worthless. What is certain, however, is the absence of any alternative. Taxes, had they been authorized by willing legislators on willing people, would have been hard, perhaps impossible, to collect in a country of scattered population, no central government, not the slightest experience in fiscal matters, no tax-collection machinery and with its coasts and numerous of its ports and customs houses under enemy control. And people were far from willing. Taxes were disliked for their own sake and also identified with foreign oppression. A rigorous pay-as-you-go policy on the part of the Continental Congress and the states might well have caused the summer patriots (like the monetary conservatives) to have second thoughts about the advantages of independence. Nor was borrowing an alternative. Men of property, then the only domestic source, had no reason to think the country a good risk. The loans from France and Spain were motivated not by hope of

[3]David Ramsay, *History of the American Revolution* (London: Johnson and Stockdale, 1791), Vol. II, pp. 134, 136. Also in Angell, pp. 256–257.
[4]Letter to Samuel Cooper, April 22, 1779, in *The Writings of Benjamin Franklin,* Albert Henry Smyth, ed. (New York: Macmillan Co., 1906), Vol. VII, p. 294.

return but by malice toward an ancient enemy. So only the notes remained. By any rational calculation, it was the paper money that saved the day. Beside the Liberty Bell there might well be a tasteful replica of a Continental note.

It was not a thought to which later historians were attracted. As in the case of the colonial paper, the influential historians were men for whom hard money and the gold standard were matters not of economics but of morality. The exigent needs of the new country were secondary to what was right. Nor could either truth or an eclectic view of the problem faced by the new government be allowed to corrupt or mislead later students or politicians. The monetary experience of the Continental Congress "has furnished the stock example to nearly every writer on the subject of money. No criticism has been too severe."[5] Professor Bullock concluded that "the opposition which the revolutionary movement encountered from many of the most intelligent and respectable persons in America"[6] was a strong and honest response to their fear, wholly justified by the events, of a reckless use of paper money. To prevent such abuse, one concludes, it would have been worth keeping the British. Nor have all later scholars relented. A widely read economic history textbook of the post–World War II years concedes that "it is some-

---

[5]Dewey, p. 41. Professor Dewey's view of these matters was decidedly compassionate and broad-minded for his time: ". . . the question is not what might conceivably have been done, but what could be done in America during the Revolution by fallible statesmen. The nation was engaged in a struggle for existence; at such a time the rule of monetary art, like the ordinary rules and methods of civil procedure, must give way to the prime necessity of using all the resources available . . . war means a measure of disaster and loss . . . we cannot get much practical help for sound finance out of a general denunciation of the continental currency." Dewey, pp. 42–43.
[6]Charles J. Bullock, *Essays on the Monetary History of the United States* (New York: Macmillan Co., 1900; Greenwood Press, 1969), p. 63.

times urged that, since the [Continental] government was weak and the people hated taxes, paper money was the best device available and therefore justifiable." But the author responds: "To accept such reasoning is to assume an attitude toward economic problems that is fatalistic and subversive of social progress."[7]

In the last century few things more consistently troubled the conservative mind than the fear of paper money. No doubt this was primarily a matter of pecuniary interest—the fear of the creditor that he would be paid off in money of inferior purchasing power, the preference of the merchant for a widely acceptable coin, the ability of the man of means to look at his pile and know that it would persist, that he did not need a strategy for its preservation. But in the minds of some conservatives in this time there must also have been a lingering sense of the singular service that paper money had, in the recent past, rendered to revolution. Not only was the American Revolution so financed. So also was the socially far more therapeutic eruption in France. If the French citizens had been required to act within the canons of conventional finance, they could not, any more than the Americans, have acted at all. If paper had served revolutionaries before, might it not do so again—as it would in Russia after 1917 and in China after World War II?

Plausibly too we have here the explanation as to why the revolutionary role of paper money is so little celebrated. The American Revolution would immediately, and the French Revolution would eventually, acquire great respectability. School books would tell school-children of their wonders. But a line had to be drawn. It could not, either in decency or safety, be conceded

[7]Chester Whitney Wright, *Economic History of the United States* (New York: McGraw-Hill Book Co., 1949), p. 184.

that anything so wonderful was accomplished by anything so questionable as the Continental notes of the American Revolution or the assignats of the French Revolution.

As might be expected, the design by which the French brought paper to the support of revolution was, in all respects, more subtle, ingenious and logical than that of the Americans. So plausible, indeed, was the principle that there is a sense of disappointment in the discovery that the result was imperfect. But if the experience was flawed, the end was still served. "Expediency demanded paper money; the success of the people's Revolution was impossible without it."[8] For appreciating the assignats, a prefatory word, some of it by way of reminder, is essential.

There is very little in economics that invokes the supernatural. But by one phenomenon many have been tempted. In looking at a rectangular piece of paper, on frequent occasion of indifferent quality, featuring a national hero or monument or carrying a classical design with overtones of Peter Paul Rubens, Jacques Louis David or a particularly well stocked vegetable market and printed in green or brown ink, they have been assailed by the question: Why is anything intrinsically so valueless so obviously desirable? What, in contrast to a similar mass of fibers clipped from yesterday's newspaper, gives it the power to command goods, enlist service, induce cupidity, promote avarice,

[8]Seymour E. Harris, *The Assignats*, Harvard Economic Studies, Vol. XXXIII (Cambridge: Harvard University Press, 1930), p. 8. This book, originally a prize-winning Ph.D. thesis, is a remarkable document for its time. In a period of severe and well-enforced orthodoxy on monetary matters the author dealt sympathetically and eclectically with the problem of revolutionary money and finance. The accepted orthodoxy, which on the assignats is extensive, was examined with an informed and critical eye that foretold Professor Harris's later contribution to intelligent monetary and economic heresy.

invite to crime? Surely some magic is involved; certainly some metaphysical or extraterrestrial explanation of its value is required. The priestly reputation and tendency of people who make a profession of knowing about money have been noted. Partly it is because such people are thought to know why valueless paper has value.

The explanation is wholly secular; nor is magic involved. Writers on money have regularly distinguished between three types of currency: (1) that which owes its value, as do gold or silver, to an inherent desirability derived from well-established service to pride of possession, prestige of ownership, personal adornment, dinner service or dentistry; (2) that which can readily be exchanged for something of such inherent desirability or which carries the promise, like the early Massachusetts Bay notes, of eventual exchange; and (3) currency which is intrinsically worthless, carries no promise that it will be redeemed in anything useful or desirable and which is sustained, at most, by the fiat of the state that it be accepted. In fact, all three versions are variations on a single theme. John Stuart Mill, we have seen, made the value of money dependent on its supply in relation to the supply of things available for purchase. Were the money gold or silver, there was little chance, the plethora of San Luis Potosi and Sutter's Mill apart, for the amount to increase unduly. This inherent limit on supply was the security that, as money, it would be limited in amount and so retain its value. And the same assurance of limited supply held for paper money that was fully convertible into gold and silver. And it held for paper that could not be converted into anything for so long as the supply of such paper was limited. It was the fact of scarcity, not the fact of intrinsic worthlessness, that was important. The problem of paper was that, in the absence of convertibility, there was nothing to restrict its supply. Thus it was vulnerable to the unlimited increase that would diminish or destroy its value. The worthlessness of the paper is a detail. Rock quarried at random from the earth's surface and divided into units of a pound and upward would not serve very happily as currency. So great would be the potential supply that the weight of rock for even a minor transaction would be a burden. But rock quarried on the moon and moved to the earth, divided and with the chunks duly certified as to weight and source, though geologically indistinguishable from the earthbound substance, would be a distinct possibility, at least for so long as the trips were few and the moon rock retained the requisite scarcity.

The ingenuity of the assignats lay in the commodity into which they could be exchanged and which by its scarcity gave them value. It was not gold and silver; these were not available in plausible quantity, for, as might be expected, they were principally possessed by those at whom the Revolution was directed. Thus they had been secreted or sent or taken abroad. The supporting and restricting asset was land, the very thing that the Revolution was making available—which, in large measure, the Revolution was about. Land could not be hidden. And not even the most ingenious *émigré* could take it with him. It was also something that could not be increased in total amount. For this reason it was something that those who remained in France were as pleased to possess as gold itself.

The initial resource was the land not of the aristocracy but of the Church. This is usually estimated to have amounted to a fifth of all the land in France in 1789. The Estates-General had been summoned in consequence of the terrible fiscal straits of the realm. No more could be borrowed. There was no central bank which could be commanded to take up loans. All still depended on the existence of willing lenders or those who could be apprehended and impressed with their duty. The Third Estate could scarcely be expected to vote new or heavier levies when its members were principally concerned with the regressive harshness of those then being collected. In fact, on June 17, 1789, the National Assembly declared all taxes illegal, a breathtaking step softened by the provision that they might be collected on a temporary basis. Meanwhile memories of John Law kept Frenchmen acutely suspicious of ordinary paper money; during 1788, a proposal for an interest-bearing note issue provoked so much opposition that it had to be withdrawn. But a note issue that could be redeemed in actual land was something different. The clerical lands were an endowment by Heaven of the Revolution.

The decisive action was taken on December 19, 1789. An issue of 400 million livres was authorized; they would, it was promised, "pay off the public debt, animate agriculture and industry and have the lands better administered."[9] These notes, the assignats, were to be redeemed within five years from the sale of an equivalent value of the lands of the Church and the crown. The first assignats bore interest at 5 percent; anyone with an appropriate amount could use them directly in exchange for land. In the following summer when a new large issue was authorized, the interest was eliminated. Later still, small denominations were issued. There were misgivings. The memory of Law continued to be invoked. An anonymous American intervened with *Advice on the Assignats by a Citizen of the United States*. He warned the Assembly against the assignats out of the rich recent experience of his own country with the Continental notes. However, the initial response to the land-based currency was generally favorable.

Had it been possible to stop with the original issue or with that of 1790, the assignats would be celebrated as a remarkably interesting innovation. Here was not a gold, silver or tobacco standard but one based solidly and logically on the good soil of France. Purchasing

---

[9]Harris, p. 62.

power in the first years had stood up well. There was admiring talk of how the assignats had put land into circulation. And business had improved, employment had increased and sales of the Church and other public lands had been facilitated. On occasion, sales had been too good. In relation to annual income, the prices set were comparatively modest; speculators clutching large packages of the assignats had arrived to take advantage of the bargains.

However, in France, as earlier in America, the demands of revolution were insistent. Although the land was limited, the claims upon it could be increased. The large issue of 1790 was followed by others—especially after war broke out in 1792. Prices denominated in assignats now rose; their rate of exchange for gold and silver, dealing in which had been authorized by the Assembly, declined sharply. In 1793 and 1794, under the Convention and the management of Cambon, there was a period of stability. Prices were fixed with some success. What could have been more important, the supply of assignats was curtailed by the righteous device of repudiating those that had been issued under the king. In these years they retained a value of around 50 percent of their face amount when exchanged for gold or silver. Soon, however, need again asserted itself. More and more were printed. In an innovative step in economic warfare, Pitt, after 1793, allowed the royalist *émigrés* to manufacture assignats for export to France. This, it was hoped, would hasten the decay. In the end, the French presses were printing one day to supply the needs of the next. Soon the Directory halted the exchange of good real estate for the now nearly worthless paper—France went off the land standard. Creditors were also protected from having their debts paid in assignats. This saved them from the ignominy of having (as earlier in America) to hide out from their debtors. A new paper currency, the mandats territoriaux, also carrying an entitlement to land, met, not surprisingly, with an adverse response. In February 1797 (16 Pluvoise year V), the Directory returned to gold and silver. But by then the Revolution was an accomplished fact. It had been financed, and this the assignats had accomplished. They have at least as good a claim on memory as the guillotine.

Paper was similarly to serve the Soviets in and after the Russian Revolution. By 1920, around 85 percent of the state budget was being met by the manufacture of paper money. In that year or not long after, a Harvard graduate student in economics visited the Soviet Union. In accordance with the counsel of similar adventurers of the time he took in his pocket a pad of toilet paper. On a densely crowded streetcar in Moscow one day he felt the hand of a thief in his hip pocket. He noted with amusement and satisfaction that it was the pocket that contained not his money but the toilet paper. The latter the pickpocket deftly removed. Only later did the young scholar come to realize that the gentle product that was stolen was more valuable than the packet of notes in the other pocket. In the aftermath of the Revolution the Soviet Union, like the other Communist states, became a stern defender of stable prices and hard money. But the Russians, no less than the Americans or the French, owe their revolution to paper.

Not that the use of paper money is a guarantee of revolutionary success. In 1913, in the old Spanish town of Chihuahua City, Pancho Villa was carrying out his engaging combination of banditry and social reform. Soldiers were cleaning the streets, land was being given to the peons, children were being put in schools and Villa was printing paper money by the square yard. This money could not be exchanged for any better asset. It promised nothing. It was sustained by no residue of prestige or esteem. It was abundant. Its only claim to worth was Pancho Villa's signature. He gave this money to whosoever seemed to be in need or anyone else who struck his fancy. It did not bring him success, although he did, without question, enjoy a measure of popularity while it lasted. But the United States army pursued him; more orderly men intervened to persuade him to retire to a hacienda in Durango. There, a decade later, when he was suspected by some to be contemplating another foray into banditry, social reform and monetary policy, he was assassinated.

CHAPTER VII

The Money War

NOTHING, as has been noted, more reliably stirs an interest in stable prices and sound money than an experience of inflation. And this interest is notably enhanced after a complete collapse of the currency such as the one that occurred during the American Revolution or, a matter we will later discuss, in Germany in 1923. Accordingly,while the new American Republic came into existence on a flood of worthless money, its early years were marked by a strong and remorseful commitment to hard cash and to the means for ensuring against later backsliding.

The Constitution restricted the right of coinage to the Federal government. It expressly forbade the states to issue paper money. And, a far less convenient inhibition, it *also* forbade the national government to issue paper money as well. A motion to strike a clause permitting the government "to emit bills on the credit of the United States," this being the way paper money was then described, was specifically carried by the 1787 Convention. It was to be a lesson on the flexibility of the Constitution, and also of its defenders, where the urgencies of money are involved. The Constitutional ban was informally abrogated by Secretary of the Treasury Gallatin in the 1812–1814 war; under the usual wartime pressures he issued Treasury notes, most of them bearing interest at 5.4 percent but some bearing no interest at all and in denominations small enough, the smallest being $3.00, to pass from hand to hand as currency. These notes were not legal tender for debts. That, perhaps, was the thin thread of constitutionality on which they hung.

Then during the Civil War all pretense was dropped. There is some evidence that undue association with money cultivates self-righteousness, political obtuseness and an unattractively pompous manner. If so, Salmon P. Chase, to his deep personal regret Lincoln's Secretary of the Treasury for he believed he should be President, is useful evidence. After an initial display of reluctance he asked Congress to authorize repeated issues of greenbacks, these again in the absence of any alternative for paying pressing wartime bills. The greenbacks were paper money without cavil. Then, in 1870, as Chief Justice and speaking sternly for a majority of the Court, he held the greenbacks to be unconstitutional, and later still, in 1871, when a different Court reversed this stand, Chase was firmly in dissent.[1]

The Constitution, nonetheless, was a turning point. Government experiment with paper money, the Gallatin and greenback episodes apart, lost force. American innovative and inflationary instincts were not, however, stilled. Henceforth, with great enthusiasm and power, they were directed to banks.

Alexander Hamilton, in addition to assuming the debts of the states and the Continental Congress, made a gesture toward the Continental notes. They were redeemed from those who happened to be holding them at the time at the comparatively generous rate of one cent of hard money to the dollar. In response to another recommendation of Hamilton a mint was established in Philadelphia. That its gold and silver

---

[1]*Hepburn* v. *Griswold*, 8 Wallace 603 (1870); Legal Tender Cases—*Knox* v. *Lee* and *Parker* v. *Davis*, 12 Wallace 457 (1871).

coins would be the basic money of the country was widely agreed; the principal difference of opinion, indeed, was over whether the coins should carry the image of the goddess of liberty or of some appropriate contemporary politician.

The gold ten-dollar eagle was ordained to contain 24.75 grains of pure gold per dollar; the silver dollar 371.25 grains of pure silver. In the early years only silver came to the mint, for, by trading 24.75 grains of gold outside the mint, a few more than 371.25 grains of silver could be obtained. In consequence, a small but still rewarding number of extra cents could be made by taking silver instead of gold to the mint. Those who so profit are never known but always exist. In monetary language, gold was undervalued.

But soon silver did not come to the mint either. The dollar that was minted at Philadelphia was bright and shiny and a trifle lighter in weight than the Spanish silver dollar then in circulation in the Spanish colonies and from which the American dollar took its name. It was soon discovered by the Spanish colonists that the brighter and lighter United States dollar would pass just as well as the heavier and, in weight of silver, more valuable local coin. And North American traders discovered that Spanish dollars obtained from the Spanish colonists, presumably for a small premium, could be brought back to the United States, melted down and recoined into American dollars with a profit of a couple of dollars for each hundred so melted. So, having driven gold out of circulation in the United States, the United States dollar now drove the Spanish dollar out of circulation to the south. It was Gresham with double effect. Jefferson put a stop to this nonsense, as he evidently deemed it, by suspending the coinage of silver dollars. For a generation or more the new Republic got along with a currency consisting principally of a miscellany of foreign coins including, of course, pounds, shillings and pence. We turn now to the more important matter of banks, which, with independence, could thenceforth freely be formed.

Banks and their money were an even more compelling discovery for the citizens of the young Republic than paper money was for the colonists. Paper money might save the country from the horrors of taxation. And moderately used, as in colonial Pennsylvania, it might forestall deflation with its consequent depressing effect on business. These benefactions were, however, general in effect and required public action. The rewards of bank money were highly specific and within the will of the individual.

In particular, the notes of the bank went out to a borrower at an interest rate that duly and directly rewarded the owners of the bank. And the same notes allowed the borrower to possess the land, buildings, tools, raw materials and labor by which he became a farmer or manufacturer, or the stock of goods and buildings by which he became a merchant. The function of credit in a simple society is, in fact, remarkably egalitarian. It allows the man with energy and no money to participate in the economy more or less on a par with the man who has capital of his own. And the more casual the conditions under which credit is granted and hence the more impecunious those accommodated, the more egalitarian credit is. It is also that agreeable equalization which levels up, not down, or seems to do so. Thus the phenomenal urge in the United States, one that lasted through all of the last century and well into the present one, to create banks. And thus, also, the marked if unadmitted liking for bad banks. Bad banks, unlike good, loaned to the poor risk, which is another name for the poor man.

In telling of the Bank of England, it was said that a central bank has three primary functions in relation to the commercial banks: It counters the temptation to excessive loans and note issue by the ordinary banks by presenting their notes for redemption; it similarly restrains loan and resulting deposit expansion, perhaps by requiring the commercial banks to keep a specified proportion of their deposits in its vaults, perhaps by pulling loanable cash out of the banks by selling securities and holding the resulting cash itself; and its loans are a source of salvation when too many people come to the commercial banks for money. The first two of these functions were deeply inimical to the operation of the banks as the needy and ambitious in the new country wanted them to function. And were the first two functions not performed, the last one was also excluded. A bank could not be saved when too many people came for their money unless prior recklessness had been restrained.

Here was the setting of the great struggle over banking in the United States. It was to the pecuniary interest of some to have restraint, stable money and prices and a lender and savior of last resort. It was to the pecuniary interest of others to have no restraint either on what could be gained by lending or what could be made by borrowing. The consequences, however disastrous, were not as bad as the control. Though these were the essentials in the conflict, there were, as always where money is involved, numerous complicating circumstances, posturings, attitudes and misapprehensions.

Along with his proposals for assumption of the debt, the redemption (in a manner of speaking) of the Continental notes, his proposals for the coinage and his recommendations for stimulating manufactures, Alexander Hamilton also proposed a central bank. As with Napoleon's Banque de France a decade later; it was modeled on the Bank of England;

countries might fight the British but they did not scorn their financial institutions and pecuniary wisdom. The Bank of the United States was to be chartered for twenty years with an authorized capital of $10 million, of which the Federal government was to subscribe $2 million. No individual could hold more than a thousand of the twenty-five thousand shares; foreigners could own shares but not vote them. When the books were opened for subscription to the stock in July 1791, all was immediately taken up. Soon there was a sharp speculation in rights to buy the stock. However, numerous thrifty participants confined themselves to a modest down payment, and the bank began operations on around $675,000 in hard cash.

By its own standards the Bank of the United States was a marked success. In the next twenty years, along with its eight branches, it served as a place of deposit for government funds, as the instrument for their transfer from one part of the country to another (no detail, given the primitive communications of that time), in making public disbursements, as a source of government loans and as a source of private credit. Both the government and private borrowers took their loans, or some part, in notes of the Bank. These were exchangeable for gold or silver, circulated at par therewith and were well regarded by the public.

Other banks in these years were still fairly few in number—in 1805, there were an estimated seventy-five,[2] all in the eastern seaboard states. The United States Bank enforced (it would appear)[3] a substan-

---

[2] The figure is from the 1876 report of the Comptroller of the Currency and is cited in Paul Studenski and Herman E. Krooss, *Financial History of the United States* (New York: McGraw-Hill Book Co., 1952), p. 73.
[3] The evidence as to the general force of this restraint is somewhat subjective. It seems possible that some scholars have attributed actions of the Second Bank of the United States more or less automatically to the First. All who write on banking history must confess

tial measure of restraint on these banks by refusing
to accept the notes of those that did not pay out
specie on demand. With the example of the Bank
before them others would similarly refuse. Depositors
would then favor a bank whose notes would pass.
And all but the most mendicant of borrowers would
also seek out a bank whose notes would be taken by
their creditors. On occasion, the Bank of the United
States came to the assistance of good state banks that
were being besieged by their noteholders or other
creditors. So, besides enforcing restraint, it served
also as the lender of last resort. Thus in its short span
of life it went far to perceive and develop the basic
regulatory functions of a central bank. As will later
be noted, the Federal Reserve System, in its first
twenty years, did not do nearly as much. What the
Bank accomplished was precisely what many did not
want.

There was, to begin, suspicion of banks in general
and large ones in particular. As the British Tories
saw the Bank of England as inimical to traditional
authority and institutions, the entering wedge of
republicanism, the Virginia gentlemen saw the Bank of
the United States as the instrument of usurping financial power and of unwholesome urbanization. They
also considered banks a species of fraud, a means of
transferring wealth from those who did honest work
in the fields to those who lived by buying and selling
and thus profited from the work of others or to those
whose manufacturing enterprises were inimical to the
agrarian society they thought natural and right. In
1814, after he had returned to Monticello, forgotten
his earlier differences with John Adams and they had

their debt to Bray Hammond's massive *Banks and Politics in
America* (Princeton: Princeton University Press, 1957).

begun their famous correspondence, Jefferson expressed himself on both the malignity and the dishonesty of banks:

> I have ever been the enemy of banks; not of those discounting for cash; but of those foisting their own paper into circulation, and thus banishing our cash. My zeal against those institutions was so warm and open at the establishment of the bank of the U.S. that I was derided as a Maniac by the tribe of bank-mongers, who were seeking to filch from the public their swindling, and barren gains . . . Shall we build an altar to the old paper money of the revolution, which ruined individuals but saved the republic, and burn on that all the bank charters present and future, and their notes with them? For these are to ruin both republic and individuals. This cannot be done. The Mania is too strong. It has seized by its delusions and corruptions all the members of our governments, general, special, and individual.[4]

There was also more specific opposition from other banks, large and small. With these the Bank of the United States was a privileged competitor. It had the deposits of the Federal government, a very good thing; it was also in the same business as they as an ordinary commercial bank. But not only was the Bank a competitor, it was also a master. It imposed its discipline on the other banks, required them to make good on their notes with hard money. Operations would be much more relaxed without the Bank. It cannot be doubted that the resentment of the banks was communicated fully to customers—notably when they were being denied loans or were being required to repay them.

In the original vote establishing the Bank, the

---

[4]Letter to John Adams in *The Adams-Jefferson Letters*, Lester J. Cappon, ed. (New York: Simon and Schuster, 1971), Vol. II, p. 424.

Northeast was in favor, the less developed South
against. Age, by now, had made Massachusetts and
its neighbors the new bastions of conservative finance.[5] In 1810, the House of Representatives voted
comfortably (73–35) for renewal. Congress then ad-
journed, and the opponents of the Bank conducted
some urgent educational work on the errant legislators. On reconvening, the Senate voted. The result was
a 17–17 tie.

In recent times, in contrast to those of Defense or
State, the post of Secretary of the Treasury, unless
occupied by someone with exceptional access on
general policy to the President, has become one of
largely routine, ceremonial or delegated powers.
Lyndon Johnson, in seeking to persuade a subordinate to take the post, warned him that, in the event of
his refusal, he, Johnson, wasn't going to tolerate anyone with brains in the job. The position of Vice-
President has never been thought decisive in the affairs of the Republic, at least as long as the incumbent
is nonfelonious and the President not under threat of
impeachment or heart disease. In 1810, matters were
different. Jefferson had been opposed to the Bank, as
were most of his Cabinet members. Madison, who
succeeded him in 1809, though pliable, had earlier
argued that the Bank was unconstitutional. But Albert Gallatin was Secretary of the Treasury and
supported the Bank. Such was his independent power
that this was sufficient. He pressed for renewal but
when the Senate tied, Vice-President Clinton had *his*

---

[5]Bray Hammond has justly warned against a simplistic division between capitalists and agrarians on the bank issue. Both sides were
interested in making money; there were many defectors from the
regional pattern; and the specific objections of the state banks as
well as constitutional issues are to be emphasized. (Hammond,
p. 197 et seq.) Nonetheless, the broad tendency for easier banking
and easier money to associate themselves with the frontier and to be
moderated or contained with time seems to me absolutely inescapable.

moment. He rallied to the opposition, and the bill renewing the charter was defeated.

History may not repeat itself but the events of the ensuing twenty-five years are impressive testimony to the contrary. Free from the discipline of the Bank and encouraged by the War of 1812 and the postwar boom, the number of state banks now multiplied— from 88 in 1811 to 208 in 1815. Their note issue increased from an estimated $45 million in 1812 to $100 million in 1817.[6] The biggest expansion was in the new country in the Appalachians and the West.

Following the capture of Washington in 1814, and in many cases it must be supposed welcoming the excuse, the banks outside of New England suspended specie payment. The elimination of any need to redeem notes greatly facilitated their issue. It also led to a highly complicated set of discounts when the notes were forwarded for buying goods or paying debts. The notes of New England banks, since they were exchangeable into gold or silver, were accepted at par therewith. The slightly less promising notes of New York were subject to a discount of 10 percent. The distinctly more garish notes of Baltimore and Washington banks had a 20 percent discount. Numerous notes from west of the Appalachians were at a 50 percent discount. As a considerable further complication, all notes circulated in company with a mass of counterfeit paper.

In 1817, Pennsylvania chartered thirty-seven new banks in a single act of the legislature. In the years immediately following, there and elsewhere there

---

[6]The bank figures are from the Comptroller of the Currency, cited in Studenski and Krooss, p. 79. The estimates on bank-note circulation are from Ernest Ludlow Bogart, *Economic History of the American People* (New York: Longmans, Green and Co., 1931), pp. 370–371, and are almost certainly very rough estimates.

was a further increase. Every location large enough to have "a church, a tavern, or a blacksmith shop was deemed a suitable place for setting up a bank."[7] "Other corporations and tradesmen issued 'currency'. Even barbers and bartenders competed with the banks in this respect . . . nearly every citizen regarded it as his constitutional right to issue money."[8]

Once again disorder stimulated an interest in order, inflation in price stability. (To say that the notes of the western banks were at a 50 percent discount is, of course, to say that prices in these notes had doubled.) Also the Bank of the United States had disappeared at almost precisely the moment when its services—the purchase and marketing of government bonds and the important business of transferring and disbursing government funds—were much needed for the conduct of the War of 1812. So maladroit was the general management, military and otherwise, of this enterprise—unique, perhaps, until Vietnam—that monetary disorder could not have contributed much to the confusion. But, if only marginally, it helped.

Thus the replay. In 1814, financial leaders—Stephen Girard, David Parish, John Jacob Astor—formulated plans for a new United States Bank. In the next months they and others urged its need in Washington. In 1816, the Second Bank was chartered.[9] Save for being larger than its predecessor—a

---

[7]Norman Angell, *The Story of Money* (New York: Frederick A. Stokes Co., 1929), p. 279.

[8]A. Barton Hepburn, *A History of Currency in the United States* (New York: Macmillan Co., 1915), p. 102. He means to exaggerate.

[9]The historical literature on the Second Bank is so rich in detail that the problem of summary is formidable. On the efforts leading to the establishment of the Bank see Kenneth L. Brown, "Stephen Girard, Promoter of the Second Bank of the United States," *The Journal of Economic History,* Vol. II, No. 2 (November 1942), p. 125 et seq. and Raymond Walters, Jr., "The Origins of the Second Bank of the United States," *The Journal of Political Economy,* Vol. LIII, No. 2 (June 1945), p. 115 et seq. The standard earlier work

very large enterprise for its time—its authority and functions were very much the same.

Initially, as did the Bank of England a century before, the Second Bank showed powerfully the need for a regulator of the regulator. In 1816, the postwar boom was full on; there was especially active speculation in western lands. The new Bank joyously participated. It was particularly active in real estate loans. And, as though to emphasize its lax intentions, there was a wild speculation in the stock of the Bank itself. Nor did it press for restraint by others. Recalling, perhaps, the disfavor into which its predecessor had fallen in consequence of the practice, the Bank refrained from presenting the notes of the state banks for redemption. In 1818, the Baltimore branch of the Bank, its funds extensively lost in bad loans, went bankrupt, although, under the loose-jointed arrangements then prevailing, this did not bring down the Philadelphia parent.

In 1819, William Jones, a politician of questionable intelligence but proven bad judgment, was replaced as head of the Bank by Langdon Cheves, described by most historians as a notably insensitive man,[10] who may well have been what the occasion required. He instituted a drastic policy of loan contraction and foreclosure. Simultaneously, although mostly it would appear coincidentally, the boom collapsed, prices fell, debtors were closed out and bankruptcies went up. This was the first of the five great panics which, at intervals of around twenty years, marked the history of the century.

---

on the Bank is Ralph C. H. Catterall, *The Second Bank of the United States* (Chicago: University of Chicago Press, 1903).
[10] A characteristic that is open to some debate. The late David McCord Wright, on the basis of Cheves's *Papers,* has sought to retrieve Cheves's reputation as a reasonable man misportrayed by historians. See his "Langdon Cheves and Nicholas Biddle: New Data for a New Interpretation," *The Journal of Economic History,* Vol. XIII, No. 3 (Summer 1953), p. 305 et seq.

As Jones had been too easy, Cheves was, in the end, too austere. In 1823, he was followed by a much more interesting, intelligent and eclectic figure who had been declined a degree at the University of Pennsylvania when he graduated because, at thirteen, he was thought too young. This was Nicholas Biddle. Unlike his predecessors, Biddle had a clear perception of the role of the Bank. He wished it to be affirmative and useful in making loans and a positive force in the community in general. He saw clearly its function as a restraining force on the state banks. As compared with his predecessors or most men of his time, he was also appallingly more arrogant.

Under Biddle numerous new branches were established until there was a total of twenty-nine. Loans and investment in securities were expanded. Payments, including those accepted on behalf of the government, were accepted only in the notes of banks that redeemed them in gold or silver. The willingness and capacity of banks to do so were kept under current test by returning their notes promptly for redemption. The state banks, not surprisingly, responded to this importunity by turning in the notes of the Bank of the United States for specie. Each side, as it were, policed the other.

The note circulation of the Bank of the United States—and therewith the loans that put them in circulation—were initially limited as to amount, at least in small denominations, by a firm if accidental constraint. Under the charter of the Bank all notes had to be signed, without facsimile or forgery, by the president and cashier in person. With the primitive pens available, not more than 1500 notes[11] could be so signed in a day, and that left little time for other and more interesting duties. Congress was petitioned to mitigate this constraint by allowing the branches also

---

[11]The figure is given in Studenski and Krooss, p. 87.

to issue notes. It refused, and this led to one of the numerous acts by which Biddle aroused and infuriated his opposition. He arranged that an officer of a branch draw a check payable to another officer. The receiving officer then endorsed the check for payment in the name of the Bank. So improved, the check became a promise of the Bank to pay cash; it was no longer a check but a bank note. As such, it was accepted by borrowers and those to whom they passed it on.

Biddle's ingenuity in bending the law did not endear him to those who had refused to accommodate him with the legislation he had sought. Nor did his manner in general. He spoke appreciatively of his power as a banker and suggested on more than one occasion that it compared in authority with that of the President of the United States. He was also pleased to agree that his position gave him life-and-death authority over the state banks and praised the restraint and magnanimity with which he exercised this power. When asked by a Senate Committee if the Bank of the United States ever oppressed the state banks, he said, "Never. There are very few banks which might not have been destroyed by an exertion of the powers of the Bank. None has ever been injured."[12]. This led President Jackson to observe that "The president of the bank has told us that most of the State banks exist by its forbearance."[13] It has been suggested that association with money may encourage political obtuseness. Even more than Chase, Biddle is evidence in the case.

---

[12] Arthur M. Schlesinger, Jr., *The Age of Jackson* (Boston: Little, Brown and Co., 1946), p. 75.
[13] J. D. Richardson, *A Compilation of the Messages and Papers of the Presidents, 1789–1908*, Vol. II (Washington: Bureau of National Literature and Art, 1908), p. 581.

As Professor Schlesinger has emphasized, Biddle also had opposition from the Establishment and from the hard-money men. There were eastern bankers who resented his discipline. There was also concern in New York, how important as a practical matter cannot now be known, that the Bank was giving Philadelphia undue eminence in financial affairs. Certainly had the central bank survived there, Philadelphia would have been a major, perhaps the nation's major, financial center, and Wall Street could conceivably have been just another street. In these years the hard-money, anti-Bank views of Jefferson and now Jackson also found a sympathetic ear among workers, many of whom felt that paper money, whether issued by the government or a bank, was a device by which they were defrauded, through higher prices or the imposition of a discount, of some part of their just pay.[14]

However, there seems little question that, as in the case of the First Bank, the most severe opposition came from the smaller, newer and more ephemeral of the state banks and those citizens who sensed that their chance for economic advance depended on the existence of such institutions. Reflecting the general march of development, much of the South was now willing to accept the Bank and its regulation. The new settlements of the West, with their particular need for easy credit and easier creditors, were now the focus of opposition.

Although the charter of the Bank did not expire until 1836, the anticipating controversy started several years earlier. On occasion, it was acrimonious. In

---

[14]Schlesinger, p. 74 et seq. Along with everyone who has written of this period, I am greatly indebted to this superb book. It should be noted that my interpretation of some purely economic matters differs from the views held at the time of writing by the author.

1831, in distant St. Louis, Biddle's brother, the director of the local branch, became involved in an especially sharp dispute over the merits of the Bank, which he held to be great. A duel with pistols resulted, in which both of the duelists were killed. This double tragedy reflected less the quality of the marksmanship than the need to accommodate Major Biddle who was nearsighted. The duel was fought at the exceedingly compact range of five feet.

In 1832, the pro-Bank forces in Congress led by Henry Clay passed a bill renewing the Bank's charter. This Jackson vetoed in a stinging message, and the Bank became a major issue in the election later that year. Biddle was not without resources. In keeping with his belief that banking was the ultimate source of power, he had regularly advanced funds to members of Congress when delay on appropriations bills had held up their pay. Daniel Webster was, at various times, a director of the Bank and on retainer as its counsel. "I believe my retainer has not been renewed or *refreshed* as usual. If it be wished that my relation to the Bank should be continued, it may be well to send me the usual retainers."[15] Numerous other men of distinction had been accommodated, including members of the press. Among the prominent journalists so in hock was James Gordon Bennett, celebrated by Samuel Eliot Morison as the father of the American yellow press.[16] Jackson won the election, and more decisively than four years earlier. The fate of the Bank was thus sealed. So, for another eighty years, was that of the idea of central banking in the United States.

Back in office for another four years, Jackson moved promptly to remove the government deposits from the Bank. (Initially they were held in selected

---

[15]Letter from Webster to Biddle. Cited in Schlesinger, p. 84.
[16]Samuel Eliot Morison, *The Oxford History of the American People* (New York: Oxford University Press, 1965), p. 438.

or pet banks; later under the independent treasury system the government held its own deposits, became in effect the banker for itself.) There was opposition to the action from within the Cabinet. In an engaging pre-play of Richard Nixon's Saturday Night Massacre 140 years on, Jackson found it necessary to remove two Secretaries of the Treasury before he found one—Roger B. Taney, later Chief Justice—who would do as he was told. Biddle, still impressed by his omnipotence as a banker, responded by contracting his loans with a view to precipitating a crisis. "A minor recession was the result."[17] Mostly Biddle succeeded in crystallizing support for Jackson.

In the latter part of the last century and the early years of the present one, with the sound-money and gold-standard morality transcendent, Jackson's destruction of the Bank was all but universally regarded as a villainous action. Professor Wright of the University of Chicago, publishing, as earlier noted, in 1949, attributed the action to Jackson's violent hatred of the Bank, mourned that "the country's experiment with a great central bank was ended."[18]

In more recent times, however, as the conventional wisdom of bankers has come at least modestly into question and a heightened democratic ethos has ascribed both perception and virtue to the common man, Jackson's action has been viewed with contrasting warmth. He was ranging himself instinctively but indubitably with his constituents, speaking for the small, energetic and aspiring folk of the new states, the new farms and the frontier.

---

[17]Jacob P. Meerman, "The Climax of the Bank War: Biddle's Contraction 1833–34," *The Journal of Political Economy,* Vol. LXXI, No. 4 (August 1963), p. 388.
[18]Chester Whitney Wright, *Economic History of the United States* (New York: McGraw-Hill Book Co., 1949), p. 370.

He was, in an important respect, their accidental ally. He opposed the Bank as a monopoly—a monster which, as Biddle held, had power to rival that of the state. This power was inimical to the politics of democracy; it was also the power of his political enemies.[19] But he favored hard money—he was for currency consisting of gold and silver and for eschewing all paper as the instrument of the devil. In getting rid of the Bank, he got not hard money but the softest of all—an explosion of new banks, an avalanche of bank notes. But this, and the loans so allowed, were what his constituents most wanted. Had Andrew Jackson succeeded in establishing the hard money that he believed himself to want, his name would have been reviled by the aforementioned small, energetic and aspiring folk of the frontier. Had he accomplished this reform in his first term, they would not have voted for him again; had it happened in his second term, they might not have allowed him to come back to Tennessee. Historians, in pondering whether Jackson was right or wrong on financial matters, must allow for a third possibility, which is that he was confused.[20]

Or conceivably there was, in his case, a very loose nexus between speech and thought. According to legend, behind the cotton bales at the Battle of New Orleans as the British drew near, he had given the historic command: "Elevate them guns a little lower."

The further history of Biddle is a moral tale. His bank was rechartered by the Commonwealth of Pennsylvania, and, in consequence of speculation in cot-

---

[19]On the political aspects of the conflict, see especially Robert V. Remini, *Andrew Jackson and the Bank War* (New York: W. W. Norton & Co., 1967).

[20]"It was a battle involving arrogance, stupidity and confusion." Remini, p. 10.

ton and excessive advances to officers, it suspended
payments in 1839 and later was declared bankrupt.
Biddle was arrested and charged with fraud. The
Pennsylvania court found the evidence insufficient to
sustain the charge. Soon after, while still pursued by
civil litigation, he died.[21] His fate was that of
nearly all who have dealt in innovative fashion with
money. Law, it will be recalled, narrowly escaped
the Paris mob and died in reputable poverty in Venice. Paterson just missed death in the Darien disaster
by which he was ruined financially. Robert Morris,
from being the Financier of the Revolution, went
on to several years in a debtors' prison. Hamilton,
after suffering public indignity and abuse for his
liaison with the frightful Mrs. Reynolds and her
rapacious husband, was shot. Jay Cooke, who sold
the bonds that with the greenbacks paid for the Civil
War, failed later with a reverberating crash. Andrew
Mellon, once solemnly celebrated as Hamilton's
greatest successor, narrowly escaped an income tax
rap. Harry D. White and Lauchlin Currie, the two
men who with Marriner S. Eccles brought Keynesian
economics to Washington, were drummed out of
their jobs—in the one case to death and in the other
into exile—as Communist sympathizers. William Jennings Bryan, whose mighty voice trumpeted against
the cross of gold, was reduced at the end of life to
flacking Florida real estate. Challenged by Clarence
Darrow in Dayton to defend the literal truth of the
Bible, he upheld Jonah with certainty and aplomb.
But then he faltered and conceded that Noah had
not brought two of every living thing into the Ark.
Noah most likely had not taken in any fish. Bryan

[21]There was bitter division as to his guilt. Jacksonians thought he
escaped jail only because he was a banker and a Biddle. Cf. Bray
Hammond, "Jackson, Biddle and the Bank of the United States,"
The Journal of Economic History, Vol. VII, No. 1 (May 1947),
p. 15 et seq.

died a few days later. Finally, though only a modest figure in monetary history, there was John B. Connally. He joined Richard Nixon's Cabinet as Secretary of the Treasury, concluded the Smithsonian agreements in 1971 devaluing the dollar and, in the then normal course of events, was indicted. He, however, was more fortunate than most; he was acquitted.

CHAPTER VIII

The Great Compromise

IN THE ACCEPTED, and it must be added, far from inspired view of the monetary history of the United States, the years after 1832 were deplorable. Free banking, the resulting bank failures, then greenbacks, agitation for more greenbacks and the pressure, partly successful, for the coinage of cheap silver combined with the recurrent panics to make the financial system of the United States, as Andrew Carnegie held, "the worst in the civilized world."[1]

Yet not everything could have been wrong. For those who spoke most despairingly of the monetary aberrations of the United States in the last century spoke always admiringly and sometimes ecstatically of the nation's economic development. Nothing like it had ever been seen before. One of two things must be true. The monetary arrangements must have had some redeeming aspect. Or else they were exceptionally unimportant.

In a more serious and slightly deeper view, the hundred years from 1832 on were ones of basic compromise. There existed, in effect, a dual monetary system. Each of the parts fitted the needs or predilections of the part of the country or economy that it served. Between the parts was an uneasy coexistence

---

[1] Norman Angell, *The Story of Money* (New York: Frederick A. Stokes Co., 1929), p. 307.

interrupted by occasional conflict. Peace was based, in the main, on the inability of each side to destroy the system favored by the other. On each side this incapacity was the source of much righteous regret.

For the growing financial, trading and creditor community, mostly of the East but as always with the passing decades extending its influence west and south, the arrangement provided a basic hard money—gold and silver. And for this community, first under state, then under Federal regulation, there were increasingly reliable banks—banks with a firm disposition to redeem their notes and deposits in such hard money when asked. Bank notes and deposits had thus the full equivalent in purchasing power of gold and silver.

For the new parts of the country as they opened up, there was the right to create banks at will and therewith the notes and deposits that resulted from their loans. No central bank tested the ability of these banks to redeem their notes; while there were state regulations specifying the cash to be held in reserve against notes and deposits, these were enforced with a light and gracious hand. In consequence, as civilization, or some approximation, came to an Indiana or Michigan crossroads in the 1830s or 1840s, so did a bank. Its notes, when issued and loaned to a farmer to buy land, livestock, seed, feed, food or simple equipment, put him into business. If he and others prospered and paid off their loans, the bank survived. If he and others did not so prosper and pay, the bank failed, and someone—perhaps a local creditor, perhaps an eastern supplier—was left holding the worthless notes. But some borrowers from this bank were by now in business. Somewhere someone holding the notes had made an involuntary contribution to the winning of the West.

It was an arrangement which reputable bankers and merchants in the East viewed with extreme distaste.

Yet for them it was not intolerable. They had good money in which to do business with each other and with foreigners. And also good banks. With care they could distinguish between the good and the doubtful notes from the West and either refuse the latter or accept them at an appropriate discount. They had losses but they also had expanding sales. Men of economic wisdom, then as later expressing the views of the reputable business community, spoke of the anarchy of unstable banking. And they explained that the settlers, in their urge to get hold of bank notes and with their primitive view of economics, were confusing money with capital. The men of wisdom missed the point.

The anarchy served the frontier far better than a more orderly system that kept a tight hand on credit could have done. And no naïve confusion of capital and money was involved. For the settler the notes he got from the bank *were* capital, for they got him capital. It is not often that people misjudge their pecuniary interest on a large scale over a long time. The great westward movement in the last century was composed of those who did not. Those who suggested otherwise were showing that, then as still, what is called sound economics is very often what mirrors the needs of the respectably affluent.[2]

The compromise which followed the demise of the Second Bank of the United States had its price. Recurrently, and reflecting the euphoria stimulated by other causes, banks were created and loans were made with abandon. And then, for some precipitating reason, people came to the banks for their money. These were

---

[2]As Bray Hammond has noted—an important point—the Jacksonians were not less interested in making money than the people they attacked. They were a newer, more numerous generation of smaller entrepreneurs. Bray Hammond, *Banks and Politics in America* (Princeton: Princeton University Press, 1957), p. 326 et seq.

the panics. It will be convenient to look first at the history of this banking and then, in the next chapter, at the panics which were the price.

The end of the Second Bank, like the end of the First, left the field of banking—chartering and regulating—entirely to the states. And as the end of the First Bank was celebrated by a great increase in the number of state banks, so it was again. Only this time it was a stampede. Between 1830 and 1836, the number of banks more than doubled—the increase was from 330 to 713. Note circulation went up more or less in proportion—from $61 million to $140 million. Specie holdings—holdings of gold and silver—showed, as might be expected, a more modest gain—these increased only from $22 million to $40 million.[3]

The expansion in these years was facilitated by two new legal designs. One was the state-owned bank. This, since its immediate purpose was to make loans in its own newly printed notes, was palpably in conflict with the Constitutional prohibition on the issue of money by the states. As though to emphasize the point, the Kentucky legislature, in providing for such a bank, appropriated money only for printing plates, paper and some furniture. All else was to be paid for with the money then printed. However, as was now evident, where money is concerned the Constitution could be bent—it was subject to the yet higher laws that reflected public urgency and political need. In a preliminary proceeding Chief Justice John Marshall held

---

[3]Chester Whitney Wright, *Economic History of the United States* (New York: McGraw-Hill Book Co., 1949), p. 370. The figures on note circulation and specie holdings are, needless to say, rough estimates. Details of the development in individual states have been admirably studied by James Roger Sharp, *The Jacksonians versus the Banks* (New York: Columbia University Press, 1970).

the emission of "bills of credit" by state banks to be unconstitutional. But in 1837, following his death, the full Court upheld the right of the state banks to issue notes.

The other and more important new development was free banking. By action of the state legislatures a bank was held to be not a corporation, which then and for many more years required a special charter from the state, but a voluntary association of individuals and thus, like blacksmithing or rope-making, open to anyone. There were rules, notably as to the hard-money reserves to be held against notes and deposits. In some states these were enforced with considerable firmness, usually after a saddening experience with no enforcement at all. But frequently failure to abide by regulations was discovered only after the failure of the Bank had made the question academic. In these years in the by then conservative Commonwealth of Massachusetts, a bank with a note circulation of $500,000 was discovered after its demise to be holding a specie reserve of only $86.48. A modest backing. Perhaps because the history was better preserved there than elsewhere, the annals of Michigan banking in the 1830s are especially engaging. The law required a 30 percent reserve of gold and silver against note circulation—a very solid foundation. And commissioners were put in circulation to inspect the banks and enforce the requirement. Also put in circulation, just in advance of the commissioners, was the gold and silver that served as the reserve. This was moved in boxes from bank to bank; when required, the amount was extended by putting a ballast of lead, broken glass and (appropriately) ten-penny nails in the box under a thinner covering of gold coins. One of the enforcing commissioners, with the ever-present gift for metaphor of the age, complained that "gold and silver flew about the country with the celerity of magic; its sound was heard in the depths of the forest, yet like the wind, one knew not whence it came or whither it was going."[4]

On occasion, the depth of the forest, the middle of the swamp or, more plausibly, a desolate country trading post was considered an especially excellent site for a bank. For from there the bank could issue notes to a borrower (who in turn would pass them on) and hope that no eventual recipient would know where to send them for redemption. However, again it must be emphasized that it is the worst in history that has survived. Spiro Agnew's place among Vice-Presidents is secure. So with the banks. Many banks of the period, including several of the publicly owned state banks, were carefully and responsibly managed. And even among those that failed, there were many that did so after honest and useful effort that left worthy men established on farms or in business and making a living.

In 1836, the Federal government decreed that, henceforth, public lands must be paid for in hard money or the notes of banks that redeemed their notes in specie. This inconvenient and widely criticized requirement tested the quality of the note issues of the state banks somewhat as did the insistence of the two Banks of the United States on returning the notes for redemption. It was long believed to have put a modest crimp on both bank lending and bank creation. Then in the following year, though not necessarily as a consequence, came panic.[5] There ensued the remorse that so reliably follows speculative euphoria and which

---

[4] Angell, p. 290.
[5] Historians once attributed much importance to the so-called Specie Circular. This is now doubted. On this (as on other matters) I am indebted to Peter Temin's *The Jacksonian Economy* (New York: W. W. Norton & Co., 1969). Cf. p. 120 et seq.

would be useful if it came earlier. State banking laws and their enforcement were much tightened. Between 1840 and 1847, the number of banks actually declined and the note circulation much more. Thereafter both again increased but in a more sedate fashion.

Still, by the time of the Civil War, the American monetary system was, without rival, the most confusing in the long history of commerce and associated cupidity. The coins coming to Amsterdam before 1609 were simplicity itself by comparison. An estimated 7000 different bank notes were in greater or less degree of circulation, the issue of some 1600 different or defunct state banks. Also, since paper and printing were cheap and the right of note issue was defended as a human right, individuals had gone into the business on their own behalf. An estimated 5000 counterfeit issues were currently in circulation. No one could do any considerable business without an up-to-date guide that distinguished the wholesome notes from the less good, the orphaned and the bad. A "Bank Note Reporter" or "Counterfeit Detector" was essential literature in any significant business enterprise.

With the Civil War the sound-money forces made an appreciable gain against their opponents in the compromise—or at least what at first so seemed. The congressmen and senators from the South and Mississippi Valley were gone. The exigencies of war could be urged against the disorder and confusion of the state banks and their notes. A new central bank could not be contemplated but a new system of banks, chartered and regulated by the Federal government, was a possibility. In 1863, at the strong behest of Secretary of the Treasury Chase and the Congress, the National Bank Act was passed establishing a new system of national banks. First attention, as might be expected, was given to the regulation of their note issue. Notes could be issued but only to the extent of 90 percent of the value of Federal bonds purchased by the issuing bank and deposited in the Treasury. The safety of the arrangement will be evident; if a bank capsized, the bonds could be sold and the notes redeemed with, under all ordinary circumstances, a comfortable margin to spare. It was also a useful way of ensuring a wartime market for government bonds.

This arrangement did have an obvious flaw—one against which the Congress sought to protect. The size of the note issue would depend on the volume of government securities available for deposit against the notes. Were the government profligate, so would be the volume of securities and therewith, possibly, the volume of notes. To protect against the contingency Congress limited the national bank note issue to $300 million. Rarely has economic circumstance managed more successfully to confound the most prudent in economic foresight. In numerous years following the war the Federal government ran a heavy surplus. It could not pay off its debt, retire its securities, because to do so meant there would be no bonds to back the national bank notes. To pay off the debt was to destroy the money supply.

Though predictably the state banks opposed the National Bank Act, initially they did not suffer. The suspension of specie payments in 1861 relieved them of the always unwelcome need to redeem their notes in hard cash. The greenbacks (soon to be discussed) were made legal tender and served instead. But on March 3, 1865, a mere month before Appomattox, the financial power again asserted itself. Congress was persuaded to pass additional legislation sweeping all the state notes away. A tax of 10 percent per annum was levied on all state bank issues with effect from July 1, 1866. It was perhaps the most directly impressive evidence in the nation's history that the power to tax is, indeed, the power to destroy.[6]

Yet again less was destroyed than might be supposed. It was the moment in history when American borrowers were beginning to take their credit not in the form of notes but in the form of deposits against which they then wrote checks. In the next decade the use of deposits and checks expanded phenomenally. Meanwhile it was still possible for a new community to create a bank. The bank, in obliging a lender, put a deposit instead of a bank note at his command. The purpose served was the same.

Deposit creation, by its nature, was more cautious than note creation, a point already urged. Notes went out, passed on from hand to hand, and many might never come back for redemption. Checks on deposits always came in to be redeemed, and if the man who received the check had his account in another bank, the cash was promptly lost thereto. However, the bank's depositors would, at the same time, be receiving for deposit the proceeds of loans made to borrowers from other banks and paid by check to them. Only if the first bank was expanding its loans more rapidly than its neighbors would there be a net outflow of cash. The penalties of recklessness were more prompt with deposit banking but the difference was one of degree.

And it was not so great that it enforced any very ostentatious caution. Bank failures continued after the banning of the notes and in some years were epidemic —140 suspensions in 1878; 496 in 1893; 155 in 1908.[7] (To the consequences of these failures we will return in the next chapter.) Most of the casualties were small state banks. For another sixty-five years these continued to be created. And the resulting loans and deposits continued to put or sustain marginal but as-

---

[6]Cf. Hammond.

[7]U.S. Bureau of the Census, *Historical Statistics of the United States, Colonial Times to 1957* (Washington, D.C., 1960), p. 636.

piring farmers and deserving and undeserving entrepreneurs in business.

Although the Civil War played into the hands of the
hard-money adherents to the compromise and helped
them get rid of the state bank notes, it weakened their
position on the hard money itself. In the years before
the war the accepted currency was either silver or
gold coin, and increasingly it was gold. Legislation in
1834 and 1837 reduced the weight of gold in the dollar in relation to that of silver. (The silver dollar remained at 371.25 grains pure; the gold dollar was
reduced from 24.75 grains of pure metal to 23.22.)
Now for those with an eye for such gain the best bargain was to sell silver in the open market, buy gold
and take that to the mint. After the California discoveries gold came to the mint in volume. For a while
it was even profitable to melt down the subsidiary
coins—half-dollars, quarters and dimes—and exchange
the resulting silver for gold to be coined. This tendency
Congress remedied in 1853 by diluting the silver in
the subsidiary coins so that, after melting, no profit
could be gained from taking the resulting amalgam to
the mint. So, after 1837, the money of the United
States was precious metal, and the metal was gold. The
only paper currency was the notes of the banks. Those
that were good enough to be exchangeable into anything were exchangeable into gold. Silver, having
dropped from sight, now dropped from mind. The
country, *de facto* if not *de jure,* was now on the full
gold standard.

Truth has anciently been called the first casualty of
war. Money may, in fact, have priority. In the fiscal
year ending June 30, 1861, the expenditures of the
United States government were $67 million. The fol-

lowing year they were $475 million. They rose steeply in the next years, reaching $1.3 billion in 1865, a level not again matched until 1917.[8] Faced with outlays of such magnitude, Salmon Portland Chase rose to the occasion with historic uncertainty of purpose. He warned solemnly against resort to paper money: ". . . no more certainly fatal expedient for impoverishing the masses and discrediting the government of any country can well be devised."[9] But he revealed also a remarkable, if predictable, reluctance to recommend taxes, and Congress did not outdo him in this regard. For the fiscal year ending June 30, 1862, the government had revenues of $52 million. Given the aforementioned expenditures of $475 million, this meant a truly notable deficit of $423 million. Revenues were a mere 11 percent of outlays. In the next three years taxes were increased, and they included the notable, though short-lived, innovation of the income tax. But, under the intransigent pressures of the war, expenditures increased much more. Although by 1865 revenues were $334 million, the deficit was approaching a billion.[10] It was by the paper money and borrowing that this deficit was covered. From 1862 on, the selling of government securities became a major enterprise. Jay Cooke organized a sales staff of 2500 to persuade people to buy bonds and so support the Union. So successful was the effort that initial sales exceeded the amount that Congress had authorized. Congress then moved promptly and cooperatively to increase the authorization. But more funds were needed. In 1862, Congress, with Chase acquiescing, authorized the issue of $150 million in notes, legal tender for all purposes except the payment of customs duties. (The customs were

---

[8]U.S. Bureau of the Census, *Historical Statistics,* p. 711. Expenditures do not include debt repayment.

[9]Albert S. Bolles, *Financial History of the United States* (New York: Augustus M. Kelley, 1969), Vol. III, p.14.

[10]U.S. Bureau of the Census, *Historical Statistics,* p. 711.

counted on to bring in the gold that would pay the interest on the debt.) The notes were printed in green ink. Thus their historic name—the greenbacks. In ensuing months more were authorized. Soon Chase, his misgivings now under full if temporary control, was asking that notes be authorized in denominations of less than five dollars so they would serve more adequately as a circulating medium. Before the end, $450 million was authorized.

Historians have been very hard on the greenbacks. To this day the term symbolizes fiscal and monetary laxity—"it would be like issuing greenbacks." The inevitable Professor Wright concludes that ". . . the outstanding mistakes in financing the war were the failure to tax promptly and vigorously, the use of paper money with all its attendant evils . . ."[11] Even more tolerant students have taxed Chase with "the over-issue of paper currency of legal-tender quality, thereby providing fuel for inflation."[12]

By now the reader can safely be left to form the only available conclusion. Not a great deal more could have been done with bonds. The sales effort was exceedingly vigorous and imaginative. And money from deposits or hoards, when put into bonds and spent by the government, added, as any other new expenditure, to demand and therewith to inflation. Taxation could have been sooner and more. But, after the best had been done, the greenbacks would still have been necessary.[13]

---

[11]Wright, p. 443.

[12]Paul Studenski and Herman E. Krooss, *Financial History of the United States* (New York: McGraw-Hill Book Co., 1952), p. 146. These authors add sensibly: "Yet somehow he did secure all the funds that were necessary to conduct the war, and this, after all, was most important."

[13]Cf. Irwin Unger, *The Greenback Era* (Princeton: Princeton University Press, 1964). One is compelled also to mention Wesley C. Mitchell's *A History of the Greenbacks* (Chicago: University of

Nor were the results so deplorable. In 1861, as noted, the Treasury and the banks suspended specie payments—the giving of gold for notes. In New York an uncouth speculative market developed in gold, a rather disenchanting spectacle in wartime and one that greatly troubled the authorities, although it seems to have accomplished no great damage. As a much more practical matter, prices in paper money rose until they were, at their peak in 1864, a little more than double what they were in 1860. (On a 1910–1914 base, the wholesale index was 93 in 1860, 193 in 1864.)[14] This gave workers a hard time; wages during the war went up but by less than half as much as prices.[15] But farmers rejoiced in two-dollar wheat (and even more after the war ended), and, stimulated by the rising prices and wartime needs, industrial capacity and output increased wonderfully. For a country torn in two, supporting an army that at its peak numbered a million men and engaged in one of the bloodiest passages until then arranged by men for their own extinction, this cannot be considered a bad performance. The evil financial reputation of the Civil War arises from the determination of later and notably conservative historians to prove that whatever was accomplished with anything so inimical to the hard-money morality as the greenbacks must be comprehensively unwise.

Chicago Press, 1903), a classic in its time, though with conclusions that are now open to challenge.

[14]U.S. Bureau of the Census, *Historical Statistics*, p. 115. This is the historic Warren and Pearson index named for George F. Warren and Frank A. Pearson of Cornell University. It proved to the authors—and perhaps to Franklin D. Roosevelt—that wholesale prices moved up and down with the price of gold and would be raised by raising the gold prices—which is to say lowering the gold content of the dollar. (See Chapter XV.)

[15]The index of weighted average daily wages, January 1, 1860 = 100, was 134 in 1864, 149 in 1865. U.S. Bureau of the Census, *Historical Statistics*, p. 90. These calculations are based on limited information. Unlike prices, wages did not fall much after the war.

The above is so at least as far as the Union is concerned. A better case can be made against the monetary management of the Confederacy. In the South the feeling that the horrors of war were bad enough without the horrors of taxation was decisive. Taxes by the Confederate government—a property tax on land and slaves, an export tax on cotton that was soon nullified by the Union blockade—had insignificant yields. Revenue requisitions were made upon the states. These were returned in currency issued by the Confederacy in volume to pay its bills or even, more thriftily, in currency issued for this and like purposes by the states themselves. Such currency issues, along with domestic borrowing, paid for the war. All the Confederate note issues totaled by the end about a billion dollars; borrowing came to about a third that amount. Prices rose throughout the war—until March 1864, at a rate of about 10 percent per month. An index of prices for the eastern states of the Confederacy, with the early months of 1861 equaling 100, was at 4285 by December 1864, 9211 the following April when the end came. Wages lagged far behind. While prices were 90 times higher in 1865 than in 1861, wages by one calculation were up only about ten times.[16] Price commissioners sought to arrest the price increases by setting ceiling prices for staples. On occasion, the newspapers printed these prices side by side with those actually being charged. Confederate notes and bonds alike were worthless after Appomattox.

No serious scholar has defended this method of war finance. But neither have they stopped there. "Northern writers of an economic turn of mind have oftentimes attributed the collapse of the Confederacy to its paper money . . ."[17]

---

[16]Price and wage data are from Eugene M. Lerner, "Money, Prices and Wages in the Confederacy, 1861–65," *The Journal of Political Economy,* Vol. LXIII, No. 1 (February 1955), p. 20 et seq.

[17]Edward Channing, *History of the United States* (New York: Macmillan Co., 1925), Vol. VI, p. 411.

Without question, more and heavier taxes could have been levied. These would have equalized somewhat the burdens of war. The chaos attendant on the gross price increases would have been lessened; the reputation of the Confederacy for stability and good sense would have been enhanced and conceivably also the morale of the troops, not to mention that of the workers. But it also remains that a small new country, under blockade, severed from its sources of industrial products as well as its markets, fighting mostly on its own territory, sustained a large army—estimates range from 600,000 to an improbable million—in the field for four years. This was a most formidable enterprise. That it did so on aggregate hard-cash resources of around $37 million was, at a minimum, a major feat in financial legerdemain. The miracle of the Confederacy, like the miracle of Rome, was not that it fell but that it survived so long. The tale is told of an archaeologist who, ten thousand years hence, in the diggings that were New York, finds the remnants of a pay toilet and identifies its purpose. He concludes that the civilization failed because something went wrong with the coinage. Those who attribute the collapse of the Confederacy to its paper money are of the same school.

In the thirty-five years remaining in the century the hard-money party in the compromise grew greatly in power.[18] Their retreat on the greenback issue was over and a counterattack repelled. Repelled also was a new attack in support of silver. And, of course, the gain that had resulted from the elimination of the state bank notes was maintained.

Retirement of the greenbacks was started in 1866 at

---

[18]In the controversies of these years I am engaged in an especially ruthless exercise in condensation. For a richly detailed history, the reader should go to Unger.

a regular rate of ten million in the first six months, thereafter at the rate of four million a month. It was not a popular policy. Government expenditures, including the costs of supporting the Reconstruction regimes in the South, were still high. And prices were falling. Wheat had continued to rise after the war and reached $2.94 in 1866. In 1868, it was down to $2.54, and it fell by nearly a dollar more the following year. The index of all farm prices, which was 162 in 1864, was down to 138 in 1868 and 128 the year following. (Ten years later it was 72.)[19] Farm-mortgage debt had increased during the war; soldiers, out of the army and resuming farm life at home or on the frontier, were among the many who reacted adversely to the lower prices.

Those so affected held the withdrawal of the greenbacks responsible. In 1868, by large majorities in both houses, Congress stopped the retirement, and, in 1871 and 1872, the Treasury, over the opposition of the hard-money men, authorized a few million of increase. The following year was one of classical panic when people came in numbers to the banks for their money. To meet this demand there was a further and larger reissue. In 1874, Congress passed legislation calling for expansion of the greenback circulation to a permanent total of $400 million.

This Grant vetoed—"I am not a believer in any artificial method of making paper money equal to coin, when the coin is not owned or held ready to redeem the promises to pay."[20] The question was then carried to the electorate. In 1876, the Greenback Party appeared to fight the case for paper money (and some other financial novelties, including the suppression of the new national bank notes which were held to violate the sole and sacred right of the government to issue

[19]U.S. Bureau of the Census, *Historical Statistics*, p. 115.
[20]Davis Rich Dewey, *Financial History of the United States* (New York: Longmans, Green and Co., 1903), p. 361.

money), and in the congressional election of 1878 it polled more than a million votes and elected fourteen congressmen. (It was this election that also brought durably into the language the distinction between soft money and hard.) Meantime, although new issues of the greenbacks had been refused, withdrawal was also halted. The issue was settled simply by leaving things as they were. The total circulation of greenbacks was fixed at the remarkably precise figure of $346,681,016. There, so far as anyone could tell, it remained for many decades to come. The year 1878 was the high tide of the greenback cause. Attention now shifted to silver.

Silver, from ancient times the hardest of hard money, now became a soft money. In 1867, it will be recalled, the leading European states, meeting in Paris, had resolved to make gold the basic and sole reserve against their several currencies and the medium of payment between themselves. What seemed right for Europe was taken to be right also for the United States. Accordingly, in 1873, in what then seemed to all a routine action, the ordinary silver dollar was dropped from the coinage.[21] (A heavier trade dollar was still minted for a few years for use by merchants doing business with the Orient where silver was still demanded by those taking payment.) And six years later, in keeping with earlier legislation, the surviving greenbacks were made convertible into gold and gold alone. And the national bank notes, since they were interchangeable with greenbacks, were now also fully exchangeable into gold. Resumption—the return to a gold

---

[21]Though the motives are still disputed. There is an influential view that, while the westerners did not notice, the proponents of gold knew well what they were about. Cf. the interesting observations of Paul M. O'Leary, "The Scene of the Crime of 1873 Revisited: A Note," *The Journal of Political Economy*, Vol. LXVIII, No. 4 (August 1960), p. 388 et seq.

standard—was accomplished with ease. Prices were now back to prewar levels.[22] The rapid expansion of industry and agriculture had made the paper circulation, once large in relation to the volume of transactions, now small. So when gold could be had, no one came for it; the development attracted little comment.

This was not to last. The low prices that had made it so easy were a source of no pleasure to farmers. Meanwhile the adoption of the gold standard in Europe caused governments (notably that of Prussia) and banks to sell their silver for gold. In consequence, silver fell in price in relation to gold. During the '70s, it fell yet more in consequence of big silver discoveries in Nevada. For half a century, silver being above the mint price, Gresham's Law had kept it from being coined and brought gold there instead. Now silver was cheap; it was the turn of this metal at the mint; and, lo, the legislation of 1873 was now found to exclude it. The silver dollar was no longer coined. The legislation of 1873, so unremarkable at the time, now became the crime of '73. An English financier, one Ernest Seyd, had bribed Congress to the act. Later the conspiracy was improved to make it the work of a cabal of Jewish bankers.[23] So, as the greenback agitation receded in the '80s, the silver counterattack took its place.

Politically it was much stronger. The greenbackers launched a party. The free-silver men did likewise— the Populists. But far more important, they captured one—the Democrats. The reference to "free" meant the free or unlimited coinage of silver at the old rate of 371.25 grains to the dollar—a rate, needless to say, which involved a return in dollars for the silver well

[22]"The generally lower price level . . . was the factor which permitted resumption in 1879." James K. Kindahl, "Economic Factors in Specie Resumption, The United States, 1865–79," *The Journal of Political Economy,* Vol. LXIX, No. 1 (February 1961), p. 30 et seq.
[23]Unger, pp. 339–340.

above that which could now be obtained on the market. With 371.25 grains of silver in the dollar and 23.22 grains of gold, the relative value of the two metals was the earlier (though not historic) 16 to 1.

The free-silver supporters made their first gain in 1878. Following the war the soft-money men, sent now by yet newer states to the west, had the Congress; the hard-money men invariably had the President. In February 1878, overriding a veto by President Hayes, Congress ordered the purchase of two to four million dollars' worth of silver a month at its market price. This was to be coined into dollars at the old weight. More dollars would emerge from the mint than would be required to buy the low-priced silver in the market. This profit would belong to the government.

It was hoped by hard-money men that this step, unwise though they regarded it, would at least satisfy the proponents of silver. Alas, the latter remained unappeased. Agitation continued not for the coinage of a limited amount of silver but of all that was offered. To the feeling that this would raise the prices not only of silver but of farm products in general was added, the proponents of silver being good and religious men, the deep conviction that the case for silver was the case for God. In ensuing years God, whatever His wishes, became deeply involved in American monetary policy.

In 1890, in consequence of devious horse-trading between advocates of higher tariffs and advocates of silver, purchases of silver were further liberalized. The Treasury notes issued for the silver so bought were redeemable in gold or silver as the holder might prefer. Now, predictably, Gresham's Law began to operate against gold. Silver was passed on in transactions. Holders of Treasury notes redeemed them in gold which they then held or sent or used abroad. The Treasury gold reserve dwindled, and in 1893 there was a powerful run on gold stocks. To replenish them, gov-

ernment bonds were sold for gold but the gold so received then went out to redeem notes that had been
issued to buy silver.

Misfortune can often be turned to good account if
men are sufficiently alert in assigning cause. Eighteen
ninety-three provides a good example. The rush for
gold assumed the proportions of a panic. The panic
had other causes, including as ever the previous speculation. However, the hard-money men and their
spokesmen attributed all the blame to silver as did the
President, Grover Cleveland. During the summer of
1893, Cleveland called the Congress into special session to lower the lid on silver. Over the eloquent opposition of William Jennings Bryan, who was then in
the House, and after a long debate in the Senate, the
subdued and frightened Congress did so.

The silver men were not yet quite defeated. In 1896,
they carried the struggle to the electorate. Bryan, in the
view of the hard-money men, "fatuously insisted upon
making the silver question the main issue."[24] Before
the Democratic Convention he issued his immortal
challenge, ". . . we will answer their demand for a gold
standard by saying to them: You shall not press down
upon the brow of labor this crown of thorns, you shall
not crucify mankind upon a cross of gold."[25] Having
previously been advised of the righteousness of silver,
God now learned that gold was implicated, at least
symbolically, in the death of His son.

In the election Bryan was decisively beaten. Time
had worked its usual result. Now the Midwest was for
hard money. McKinley won 271 electoral votes to 176.
The New York *World* said: "Not since the fall of Rich-

---

[24]A. Barton Hepburn, *A History of Currency in the United States*
(New York: Macmillan Co., 1915), p. 378. Dr. Hepburn, a former
Comptroller of the Currency, was Chairman of the Board of the
Chase National Bank.
[25]Studenski and Krooss, p. 233.

mond have patriotic Americans had such cause for rejoicing . . . honor is preserved."[26]

In 1900, cosmetic legislation affecting coinage and notes further affirmed the commitment to gold. In consequence, some purists date the American adoption of the gold standard to this year. In fact, its victory had already been won.

There was, however, a revealing humor in the 1900 law. It allowed the national banks, the good banks of the Establishment, to issue notes up to a full 100 percent of the value of government bonds deposited with the Treasury. It also cut in half a small tax that had been levied on this circulation. The result was prompt increase in the note circulation of the national banks —in the next eight years it more than doubled. All good financial men praised the step as necessary for the growing commerce of the country—a sound and beneficial action. In the form of greenbacks, silver certificates or Treasury notes paid out for silver, all indistinguishable in effect, such currency expansion was unsound, unwise and reckless—or, as seen by the New York *World,* deeply dishonorable and unpatriotic. No principle distinguishes the two cases, only the engaging association of truth with reputable financial interest.

[26]Studenski and Krooss, p. 234.

CHAPTER IX

The Price

THERE CAN NEVER have been a time when it was as good to be rich as in the late years of the last century, the first decade of the present one. There was no income tax, the Civil War impost having been obliterated soon after the war. There was the rewarding contrast with the vast majority which was still very poor. Writing in 1899, Thorstein Veblen observed that property was then "the most easily recognized evidence of a reputable degree of success as distinguished from heroic or signal achievement. It therefore becomes the conventional basis of esteem."[1] With sound instinct, historians refer to these years as the Gilded Age.

They might as accurately be called the age of gold. For some, and perhaps much, of the esteem ascribed by Veblen to wealth was given by the nature of the money. If money is weak and wasting in value, even the rich lack something in certainty as to their worth. Their minds, like those of others, leap forward to the day when their money will have disintegrated, as did the Continental notes or the reichsmark. They have a strategy for protecting themselves but maybe it will not work, and for what then does money count? No such question arises either in the mind of its possessor or of those who would denigrate him if money is hard and eternal.

[1]Thorstein Veblen, *The Theory of the Leisure Class* (New York: Macmillan Co., 1899; Boston: Houghton Mifflin Co., 1973), p. 37.

In 1900, prices had been generally falling since the end of the Civil War. The prices of wheat, cotton and other staples were lower by a half as compared with a hundred years earlier. Men of substance could reasonably expect to gain in wealth not only from accumulation of money but from a continuing increase in the purchasing power of what they had.

There were, for the affluent, other agreeable features of the time. Many enjoyments were exclusively the prerogative of the rich, and others did not aspire to them—an important point to which we will return in the final chapter. One such enjoyment was travel. Only the rich went to Europe; the proletariat essayed one westward passage across the Atlantic to America, and that, given the grim amenities of such movement, was more than enough. As no passport was needed unless one ventured into the dubious precincts of the Sultan or the Czar, so no one needed to worry about rates of exchange. The number of pounds, shillings and pence that could be had with a hundred dollars was as invariant as the rate at which both currencies could be exchanged into gold. Tariffs apart, there was a similar uniformity in the prices of staple products when converted into sterling, francs or dollars. In the days before wireless, signal flags at Land's End or other first landfalls told grain ships from the St. Lawrence to proceed to the Thames, Rotterdam, Antwerp or Hamburg in accordance with fractional advantages in the price in one port or another. Nothing now envisaged or even imagined for the Common Market comes close to approaching the single and universal monetary system that then existed.

The ability of the rich and their acolytes to see social virtue in what serves their interest and convenience and to depict as ridiculous or foolish what does not was never better manifested than in their support of gold and their condemnation of paper money. The parallel tendency of economists to find virtue in what the reputable and affluent applaud was similarly evident. But there were also a precision and harmony and a unifying tendency in the operation of the gold standard that commended themselves even to those who were neither consciously nor wittingly the servants of the rich. It did make simple and certain the relations between the currencies of different countries and gave the industrial countries and their empires a single money. It was sad that it also had serious, even fatal flaws, that it could inflict heavy punishment on the ordinary person and, as time passed, also on the affluent themselves. These flaws were especially serious in the context of the compromise that ruled in American monetary affairs.

Where economic misfortune is concerned, a word on nomenclature is necessary. In the course of his disastrous odyssey Pal Joey, the most inspired of John O'Hara's creations, finds himself singing in a Chicago crib strictly for cakes and coffee. He explains this misfortune by saying that the *panic* is still on. His term —archaic and thus slightly pretentious—reflects the unfailing O'Hara ear. During the last century and until 1907, the United States had panics, and that, unabashedly, is what they were called. But, by 1907, language was becoming, like so much else, the servant of economic interest. To minimize the shock to confidence, businessmen and bankers had started to explain that any current economic setback was not really a panic, only a crisis. They were undeterred by the use of this term in a much more ominous context—that of the ultimate capitalist crisis—by Marx. By the 1920s, however, the word crisis had also acquired the fearsome connotation of the event it described. Accordingly, men offered reassurance by explaining that it was not a crisis, only a depression. A very soft word. Then the Great Depression associated the most frightful of economic misfortunes with that term, and economic semanticists now explained that no depression was in prospect, at most only a recession. In the 1950s, when there was a modest setback, economists and public officials were united in denying that it was a recession—only a sidewise movement or a rolling readjustment. Mr. Herbert Stein, the amiable man whose difficult honor it was to serve as the economic voice of Richard Nixon, would have referred to the panic of 1893 as a growth correction.

The disenchanting character of the events described in the last century as panics and in the early years of the present one as depressions is not in doubt. They occurred in and after 1819, 1837, 1857, 1873, in a minor way in 1884, with great severity in 1893 and again in 1907. There was a brief but harsh one in 1921 and then the most drastic and enduring of all in—and after—October 1929. So regular had been their recurrence that by the early years of the present century a systematic, wavelike movement was thought to be characteristic of economic life and development. One could gain an advanced degree in economics by specializing in business cycles, called by the informed just "cycles." It was one of the more arcane, uncertain, disputatious and hence distinguished branches of the subject.

There was also, as noted, the interpretation of Marx. This too saw the crisis as normal, at least to a capitalist society. A progressively increasing productive power returned but a fraction—and a diminishing fraction —of the value of the goods so produced to labor. From the inability of workers to buy what they produced and the tendency of the capitalists' savings to go into even greater expansion of plant and product came cumulative overstocking, diminishing profits and crises of ever-increasing severity. In the ultimate crisis capitalism, now attenuated by concentration in the hands of the few, would be destroyed. Marx was not a household word in the United States or even in Britain where he lived and toiled. But in Europe, and at second- or third-hand in the English-speaking countries, or in the comment of scholars, there lurked the thought that the succession of panics or crises foretold the end of capitalism.[2]

The usual image of the business cycle was of a wave-like movement, and the waves of the sea were the accepted metaphor. Prices and production rose gradually, then more rapidly, reached an apex and then subsided. One measured the length of the cycle from crest to crest or trough to trough; thus again the wave. The reality in the nineteenth and early twentieth centuries was, in fact, much closer to the teeth of a ripsaw which go up on a gradual plane on one side and drop precipitately on the other. Or, if a wave, it was the long mounting roll and then the sharply breaking surf.

In all of the panics there were recognizable constants. First came an expansion in business activity. This usually centered on some dominant form of investment, one that reworked the economic geography of the country. The first such object of investment was the canals; then, and much more important, came the railroads. With canal and railroad building went expansion into new lands. Often, although not invariably, prices rose.

Then, as time passed, expansion gave way to speculation, a term that needs to be understood with some precision. (A thoughtful Boston observer in 1840

---

[2]For example, in the classic work of Wesley C. Mitchell, *Business Cycles* (New York: National Bureau of Economic Research, 1928), pp. 8–9.

noted that speculation was what, when it succeeds, is called enterprise, an evil thing only when it fails.)[3] Speculation centers on one or more of those assets, real or fiduciary, that are central to the expansion currently under way. In 1819, and again in 1837, it was, not surprisingly, land. In 1829, the government sold 1.2 million acres of public land for $1.5 million. In 1836, before the crash, it sold 20 million for $25 million, much of it to operators who promptly resold it at a profit to others who resold it for yet more. These too were the great years of canal building. There was also a boom in public improvements—turnpikes, statehouses, schools and some jails—and in the securities that financed these rewarding enterprises.

By 1857, speculative interest had shifted to railroads. There it remained for the rest of the century. In the years preceding the panic of 1873 and again before that of 1893, there was a great boom in railroad construction. With it went speculation in the facilitating railroad securities. Nothing in the nineteenth century is more remarkable than the way men forgot the last railroad debacle and proceeded to lose money in the next. Other and lesser objects of speculation also attracted attention. Prior to the 1873 panic there was still an open market for gold as quoted in greenbacks. In 1869, Jay Gould, with Jim Fiske as his agent, sought to corner the gold market—to control the gold from which dealers had to fill their contracts to supply the metal. Success for these notable scoundrels depended on the government's not selling gold, which Gould thought he had ensured by buying Grant's brother-in-law (and thus the President) and also a minor official or two. His men couldn't, as it happened, deliver Grant. The effort collapsed. In the period before the 1907

---

[3] R. Hildreth, *Banks, Banking, and Paper Currencies* (Boston: Whipple and Damrell, 1840). Cited by Samuel Rezneck, *Business Depressions and Financial Panics* (New York: Greenwood Publishing Corp., 1968), p. 85.

panic there was an amateurish effort to corner the copper market.

By 1907, though railroads were still important, the speculative interest was shifting to common stocks in general. The 1921 depression was preceded, somewhat atypically for the time, by speculation in land and in the commodity markets. The great bull market of the twenties was again in common stocks. By 1929, the infinite horizons of technology had captured the sanguine mind. So had the notion that there was a peculiarly omniscient form of financial genius to whom the task of winning speculative wealth could be delegated. In consequence of the first belief, RCA, a pioneer in what would now be called electronics, was a major speculative favorite, although it had never paid a dividend. Seaboard Air Line, which was thought by numerous innocents to provide a foothold in aviation, was another favorite, although, in fact, it was a railroad. And the closed-end investment trust, precursor of the mutual fund, was the device by which financial genius took over the speculative task from individuals of uninspired cupidity. In the late twenties there was a vast multiplication of investment trusts.

Speculation occurs when people buy assets, always with the support of some rationalizing doctrine, because they expect their prices to rise. That expectation and the resulting action then serve to confirm expectation. Presently the reality is not what the asset in question—the land or commodity or stock or investment company—will earn in the future. Rather it is only that enough people are expecting the speculative object to advance in price to make it advance in price and thus attract yet more people to yet further fulfill expectations of yet further increases.

This process has a pristine simplicity; it can last only so long as prices are rising reliably. If anything seriously interrupts the price advance, the expectations by which the advance is sustained are lost or anyhow endangered. All who are holding for a further rise—all but the gullible and egregiously optimistic, of which there is invariably a considerable supply—then seek to get out. Whatever the pace of the preceding buildup, whether slow or rapid, the resulting fall is always abrupt. Thus the likeness to the ripsaw blade or the breaking surf. So did speculation and therewith economic expansion come to an end in all of the panic years from 1819 to 1929.

There were other constants in this experience. Although prices in general did not always rise greatly during the booms, they always fell markedly during and after the panics. This asymmetry came partly from the fact that the trend of prices was generally down during the last century. The boom arrested the decline. Then, in the ensuing collapse, the downward trend was sharply accentuated. These reductions, especially in farm prices, were in an amplitude that, in a later age of farm lobbies, sensitive legislators and price supports, it is difficult to imagine. In 1818, the index of farm prices was 117; by 1821, it was down to 64. Wheat in Cincinnati was then twenty-five cents a bushel, corn a dime and whiskey a literal drug on the market at fifteen cents a gallon. Between 1836 and 1840, the farm price index fell from 89 to 65 and then went on down to 48 in 1843.[4] Nor were such movements a distant, archaeological phenomenon. In the single year from 1920 to 1921, farm prices fell by nearly one-half. Between 1929 and 1932, they fell by rather more.

The effect of the panics on urban employment and output is much less certain than on prices. Price quo-

---

[4] U.S. Bureau of the Census, *Historical Statistics of the United States, Colonial Times to 1957* (Washington, D.C., 1960), p. 115 et seq. The index, as earlier noted, is that of Warren and Pearson and on a base of 1910–1914 = 100. The Cincinnati quotations are from Rezneck, p. 58.

tations can be found; the unemployed had to be counted, and that was not done with any precision until the Great Depression. The years before 1840 in particular, are, as Professor Paul David has said,[5] a statistical dark age. In the years of panic and ensuing depression economic growth certainly slowed and perhaps, on occasion, came to a halt. Not much more can be said with certainty.[6]

However, there is ample if subjective evidence of suffering. In the summer of 1819, 50,000 workers were thought to be unemployed in New York, Philadelphia and Baltimore. In Poughkeepsie an ingenious and self-reliant toiler named John Daley pleaded guilty to stealing a horse, explaining that "he could get no work, and could hit upon no other plan so ready and certain to provide him with a home and steady employment."[7] His plan succeeded; he was given eight years. A newspaper, surveying the situation, thought that "A deeper gloom hangs over us than was ever witnessed by the oldest man. The last war was sunshine compared with these times."[8] Eighteen years later, after the panic of 1837, the New York *Herald* concluded that "The United States were never in such a perilous condition as they are at this moment."[9] In a burst of chivalrous compassion it said that especially "We weep and mourn for the poor, blushing, weeping, defenceless, innocent, beauteous females who are involved in the general crash."[9] Every later panic

---

[5]P. A. David, "New Light on a Statistical Dark Age: U.S. Real Product Growth before 1840," in *New Economic History*, Peter Temin, ed. (Baltimore: Penguin Books 1973), p. 44 et seq.

[6]Moses Abramovitz, "Resource and Output Trends in the U.S. Since 1870." Occasional Paper 52 (New York: National Bureau of Economic Research, 1956), pp. 6–7.

[7]Rezneck, p. 56, whence also the guesses on unemployment.

[8]Rezneck, p. 56.

[9]Both quotations are from Wilfred J. Funk, *When the Merry-Go-Round Breaks Down* (New York: Funk & Wagnalls Co., 1938), pp. 10–11.

brought similar expressions of despair and almost equally alarming prose.

The panics also brought recourse to two lines of remedial action which have always been much favored, although with no proof that they have ever been greatly effective. One is to seek to exorcise economic misfortune by affirming that it does not exist. In November 1820, a very dark month following the crash of the year before, President Monroe advised the Congress of the "prosperous and happy" condition of the country, adding that "it is impossible to behold so gratifying, so glorious a spectacle, without being penetrated with the most profound and grateful acknowledgements to the Supreme Author of All Good for such manifold and inestimable blessings."[10] The government at the time was known to be deeply concerned over the economic crisis. In March 1837, as the trials of that terrible year were becoming felt, Andrew Jackson said in his farewell address: "I leave this great people prosperous and happy."[11] In June of 1930, Herbert Hoover was visited by a delegation of public-spirited men who urged an expansion of public works to ease the plight of the unemployed, who were then rising into the millions. " 'Gentlemen,' the President said, 'you have come sixty days too late. The depression is over.' "[12] In the sincerity of manner with which they endlessly proclaimed the end of inflation, Mr. Nixon and his economists were acting in a tradition that was older than they knew.

The other favored response is to urge resort to religious solace as a substitute for more expensive action. In 1837, a thoughtful divine urged sufferers to use

---

[10]J. D. Richardson, *A Compilation of the Messages and Papers of the Presidents 1789–1908,* Vol. II (Washington: Bureau of National Literature and Art, 1908), pp. 74–75.

[11]*The Statesmanship of Andrew Jackson,* Francis N. Thorpe, ed. (New York: The Tandy-Thomas Co., 1909), p. 493.

[12]Arthur M. Schlesinger, Jr., *The Crisis of the Old Order* (Boston: Houghton Mifflin Co., 1957), p. 231.

the bad times to "Lay up treasure in Heaven," adding helpfully that, "All this may be done on a small income."[13] In 1857, another bad year, the *Journal of Commerce* offered similar counsel in an approximation to verse:

> Steal awhile away from Wall Street
> and every worldly care,
> And spend an hour about mid-day
> in humble, hopeful prayer.[14]

In 1878, Archbishop Williams of Boston took the more practical step of circulating an address to his churches asking his people not to react to their fears by going to the banks for their money. That caused runs. In October 1907, as the culminating step in his effort to arrest the panic of that year—manifested in heavy runs on the New York trust companies and banks—J. P. Morgan, himself high in Episcopalian councils, called the leading divines of the city to his office and asked them to give encouraging sermons the following Sunday. "Religious leaders of all denominations agreed to paint cheerful pictures that weekend."[15] A long history thus introduces the Reverend Dr. Peale and the Reverend Dr. Graham, the latter-day exponents of the economically useful and socially tranquilizing gospel.

There were, however, factors which sharply distinguished the booms and panics of earlier times from later misfortunes. In the last century the urban working force was relatively small, that in agriculture huge. In the post-panic year of 1820, of an estimated 2.9 million gainful workers in the United States, 2.1 million were in agriculture. Fifty years later, in 1870, the

---

[13]Rezneck, p. 84.
[14]Robert Sobel, *Panic on Wall Street* (New York: Macmillan Co., 1968), p. 108.
[15]Sobel, p. 315.

agricultural working force was still half of the total. By the time of the Great Depression it was less than a quarter.[16] In agriculture in times of economic distress, prices fall, men may lose their farms to creditors but few or none become unemployed. (In the depression of the 1930s, agricultural employment of a sort increased as people retreated from the cities.) And in the last century urban enterprises were more like farms than they are now. The large bureaucratic corporation had not yet gathered to itself the power to maintain its prices. Unions did not yet exist with power to defend wage rates. So in the cities, too, prices fell, and so did wages, and in some industries wages fell more than prices. It was this reduction in money income for the enterprise and in real income for the wage-earner which, more than mass unemployment, caused distress. It made the depression of the last century a very different thing from what depression later became. We now return to the role of money in these misfortunes.

The banks, needless to say, provided the money that financed the speculation that in each case preceded the crash. Those buying land, commodities or railroad stocks and bonds came to the banks for loans. As the resulting notes and deposits went into circulation, they paid for the speculative purchases of yet others. It helped that the banks were small and local and thus could believe what the speculators believed, be caught up in the same euphoric conviction that values would go up forever. The banking system, as it operated in the last century and after, was well designed to expand the supply of money as speculation required.

Banks and money also contributed to the ensuing crash. A further constant of all the panics was that

---

[16] U.S. Bureau of the Census, *Historical Statistics*, p. 74. Once again the reader is reminded that the earlier figures, although valid enough as orders of magnitude, antedate the era of statistical precision.

banks failed. In the earlier panics the will-of-the-wisp enterprises of the swamps and crossroads disappeared as, in some cases, their creators knew they would. Later in the century the casualties continued, and still most heavily among the smaller state banks. In the panic year of 1873 and in 1874, 98 banks suspended, as compared with 29 in the two preceding years. In 1892, there were 83 suspensions and 496 in the panic year following. In 1907 and 1908, 246 banks fell. After 1920, the real slaughter began, and, after 1929, it approached euthanasia. In the four years beginning in 1930, more than nine thousand banks and bankers bit the dust.[17]

A bank failure is not an ordinary business misadventure. As Professor Friedman has pointed out,[18] it has not one but two adverse effects on economic activity: Owners lose their capital and depositors their deposits, and both therewith lose their ability to purchase things. But failure (or for that matter the fear of failure) also means a shrinkage in the money supply. No mystery attaches to this. A healthy bank is making loans and, in consequence, creating deposits that, in turn, are money. A bank that fears failure is contracting its loans and therewith its deposits. And one that has failed is liquidating its loans, and its frozen deposits are no longer money. The liquidation also draws on the reserves, loans, deposits, and thus the money supply of other banks.

As noted, when panic came in the last century, it was mostly the small state banks that went under. This was in keeping with the great compromise. Those who

---

[17] U.S. Bureau of the Census, *Historical Statistics*, p. 636 et seq.
[18] Milton Friedman and Anna Jacobson Schwartz, *A Monetary History of the United States, 1867–1960*. Study by the National Bureau of Economic Research (Princeton: Princeton University Press, 1963), p. 353. While this study has led Professor Friedman to conclusions rather different from those reached here, it is a model of scholarly precision to which, as with everyone concerned with these matters, I am indebted.

wanted hard money had hard money, and they had large and reliable banks. The new country and the frontier had the far more relaxed enterprises that served their needs by accepting their much more dubious loans and collateral. The bank failures inherent in this system were not the concern of the sound-money establishment. Recalling later a meeting of bankers in 1931 to discuss the rising tide of bank failures, George L. Harrison, then the Governor of the New York Federal Reserve Bank, noted that "at one time it was the feeling of many of us down town [i.e., on Wall Street] that the effects of the failure of . . . small banks in the community could be isolated."[19] Things became serious, he went on to say, when it became evident that the big New York banks might also be affected by the spreading panic.

However, well before 1931, the separation of the central financial interest from that of the country banks that underlay the great compromise had been disappearing. Better communications and the growing density of commercial intercourse between different parts of the country were factors. In consequence, and immediately more important, country banks increasingly kept deposits in the New York and other big-city banks. When depositors descended on the small banks for their money, the small banks came to the large. The latter thus felt the strain.

Also, as the nineteenth century passed and gave way to the twentieth, speculation became less of a local, more of a national phenomenon. Land speculation occurred in the farm country and on the frontier. So did that which anticipated or followed the arrival of the railroads. The collapse of such speculation affected primarily the country banks. Securities speculation, in contrast, was the business of the financial centers. Loans to buy securities were made by the big-city

---

[19]Friedman and Schwartz, p. 359.

banks. These banks also underwrote and bought stocks and bonds. When these collapsed in price, it was the banks of the cities that were affected, and it was their depositors who took alarm and came for their money.

Additionally, by the end of the last century, New York was developing a new kind of bank, one that reflected some of the tendencies of the gamier West. These were the state trust companies. They could be chartered to engage in a wider range of activities—handling assets for the affluent, registering and transferring corporate securities, acting as trustee for bond issues and as trustee for estates—than state or national banks. And they were much less closely regulated. So, not surprisingly, they had a phenomenal growth. The head of a large trust company, the Knickerbocker Trust, was deeply involved in the copper speculation in 1907. When this bubble collapsed, the word spread that Knickerbocker was in trouble. Depositors swarmed in for their money, thus, as ever, making the trouble real. Soon other trust companies, including the Trust Company of America, which was also deep in the copper mess, were running short of cash. The 1907 panic, unlike earlier ones, did not come in from the country; it was a New York product.

It was, for that reason, far more serious. This was not so much that its impact on the country was greater than that of earlier panics. It was rather that the impact was on much more important people. From the sense of urgency thus induced came the pressure for the next great step in monetary change and reform, the Federal Reserve System.

Well before 1907, trouble in the big-city banks was an occasion for public action. In the panic year of 1873, the withdrawal of the hitherto wicked greenbacks was halted, and $26 million was reissued to provide reserves and ease tension in New York. In subsequent panics the Treasury deposited government funds to help the big banks withstand runs. In 1907, J. P. Morgan, who is celebrated by all historians for saving the Trust Company of America after declaring that the panic might as well be stopped right there, appealed to Secretary of the Treasury George B. Cortelyou for deposits to save the Trust Company. Resources subscribed for the rescue by other New York bankers, including Morgan's, were insufficient. Cortelyou was not authorized to deposit public funds with a trust company. This was a detail; $35 million was promptly deposited in the national banks and just as promptly reloaned to the Trust Company of America. It was thus provided with the funds that persuaded its depositors that it was safe. These arrangements were *ad hoc* and unreliable.[20] They also lacked compassion. In 1907, when Charles Barney, head of the desperately beset Knickerbocker Trust, went to J. P. Morgan to seek help, he couldn't get in to see him. Barney thereupon shot himself. A central bank would at least have let Barney in. Partly to help beleaguered men like Barney, but more to serve the interests of more important men, the United States in ensuing years revived the idea of a central bank.

In any retrospect on the panics or crises of the last century the question that concerned the Bullion Committee recurs. Obviously money had a role. Was it a primary cause? Or were money and the associated

---

[20]Not that it was considered a wholly *ad hoc* or accidental function by the Treasury at the time. Leslie M. Shaw, who was Secretary from 1902 to 1907, explicitly envisaged the Treasury in the role of a central bank. He thought that "No central or Government bank in the world can so readily influence financial conditions throughout the world as can the Secretary under the authority with which he is now clothed." Friedman and Schwartz, p. 150.

banking more the response to the uniquely unstable tendencies of growth in the new country?

There is no easy answer, although this has not kept historians from offering one. The banking and monetary arrangements of the last century, as just seen, were admirably designed to respond to euphoria, finance it, enhance it and then add force to the ensuing collapse. Banks and money could be created, without effective constraint, to finance the expansion and speculation. Failure or fear of failure, the contraction of loans and deposits then made the day of contrition worse.

But also essential was the impulse to borrow, invest, risk, speculate. Had this not existed, no bank could have created it. In the United States in the nineteenth century this instinct was highly developed, and for good reason. A new continent rich in land and raw materials was suddenly available for use. Possession of its resources provided the revenues from their use. It also accorded to the owner the increase in value of the property that went with such use. And these opportunities existed on a vast scale.

The decisive thing was to have possession of property. And this the banks provided. So, while the banking system was manifestly designed to accommodate expansion and speculation, there was also a powerful incentive sending people to the banks. No one can say which was the more important. In Britain and France during the last century, as earlier, there were also panics or crises. They were much milder than in the United States, and this has commonly been attributed to the greater maturity and conservatism of their banking and monetary arrangements. This explanation may well be valid. But something must also be attributed to the absence of similar inducement to expansion and euphoria. And the point gains force when it is recalled that in both Britain and France the greatest episodes of speculative euphoria and collapse were based on optimism engendered by the limitless opportunities that were thought to exist in the Americas. The Mississippi Company, the South Sea Bubble, the Darien disaster, the rush of British capital into construction of American canals in the 1830s, the recurrent fascination of British investors with South America are all cases in point.

The most that can be said is that the easy provision of money by the banks and the urge to get it for speculative or productive purposes were intimately intertwined. In later years when there was no longer the same prospect for gain from participation in the use of new resources or the possession of property, things would, on occasion, be very different. Banks could then be ready and anxious to make loans, create deposits and thus enhance the money supply, and no one would come to them for the loans.

CHAPTER X

The Impeccable System

THE FEDERAL RESERVE SYSTEM is treated by nearly all economists with reverence. On no matter is their instruction of the young in the subtlety and benignity of established institutions more admiring—or, in broad effect, more successful. Corporations are flawed by an instinct for monopoly. Trade unions interfere with the market, urge trade restrictions, resist new technology and thus obstruct progress, and they can fall victim to extortionists and racketeers. The regulatory agencies of the government are notably imperfect instruments of economic guidance. The Federal Reserve System is not totally above criticism. It makes many mistakes but these are always interesting errors of judgment. They are examined not critically but respectfully to discover why men of insight went wrong. That for such error anyone should be sacked or even seriously rebuked is, for economists, nearly unthinkable.[1] This approval goes back to the origins and can be highly negligent of circumstance. The most widely read ac-

---

[1] A recent writer, Edward J. Kane, holds that this immunity is weakening—that economists in recent times have reacted much more strongly to the "inevitable ineptness of its [the Federal Reserve's] interventions into specific markets and its extraordinary penchant for humbug." See his "All for the Best: The Federal Reserve Board's 60th Annual Report," *The American Economic Review*, Vol. LXIV, No. 6 (December 1974), p. 835 et seq. Judging, possibly, from a smaller sample of such comment, I believe that Professor Kane overstates his case.

count of the genesis of the System tells glowingly of its birth in the closing weeks of 1913 when the Federal Reserve Act was passed by Congress and signed by President Wilson. "It sprang from the panic of 1907, with its alarming epidemic of bank failures: the country was fed up once and for all with the anarchy of unstable private banking."[2] Professor Samuelson, the author of the foregoing summary, adds that the System is referred to by economists as "The Fed" and that this affectionate, if repellent, contraction carries no connotation of disrespect. He observes that the effect of the decisions of the principal policy-making authority of the System, the Open Market Committee, makes its members, with "pardonable exaggeration," perhaps "the most powerful group of private citizens in America."[3]

That there is conflict here with circumstance, even the minimally alert will have sensed. As an answer to the great panics, the System was notably defective. In 1920–1921, seven years after the System was established, there was a severe one, and this was followed ten years later by the worst depression of all time. There is much evidence, which orthodox professional opinion does not reject, that Federal Reserve policy made all worse—that it helped finance the antecedent speculation and helped intensify the ensuing contraction in both 1920–1921 and 1929. Nor was it better as an antidote for an alarming epidemic of bank failures. In the twenty years before the founding of the System there were 1748 bank suspensions; in the twenty years after it ended the anarchy of unstable private banking, there were 15,502.[4]

As restraint on bank lending during the boom is a basic central-bank function, so serving as a lender of

[2]Paul A. Samuelson, *Economics,* 8th ed. (New York: McGraw-Hill Book Co., 1970), p. 272.

[3]Samuelson, pp. 272–273.

[4]U.S. Bureau of the Census, *Historical Statistics of the United States, Colonial Times to 1957* (Washington, D.C., 1960), p. 636.

last resort is its main task in the ensuing depression. However, during the Great Depression not the Federal Reserve but the Reconstruction Finance Corporation, newly created for the purpose, served this function. And when unstable banking was finally brought to an end in 1933—when all banks were made subject to effective supervision and depositors were assured, in consequence, that when they came for their money they could have it—it was not the Federal Reserve System but the Federal Deposit Insurance Corporation, a relatively anonymous and wholly unprestigious institution, which did the job. In the 1930s, it was learned that an abundant supply of funds for lending by the banks did not ensure their use. In consequence, it became necessary for the government to make spending not permissive but assured. This it did by borrowing and spending itself—by fiscal as opposed to monetary policy. A depression, when bad, was shown to be beyond the reach of the Federal Reserve.

Finally there is inflation. In 1963, to celebrate the fiftieth anniversary of the founding of the System, the Board of Governors (as it is now styled) published (more precisely, republished) a small volume on its purposes. "Today," it said, "it is generally understood that the primary purpose of the System is to foster growth at high levels of employment, with a stable dollar . . ."[5] In the next decade there occurred the most severe inflation ever in peacetime. The Open Market Committee, still presumably the most powerful group of private citizens in America, met repeatedly on the problem. The inflation continued. When it slowed, unemployment grew grievously instead. Power is as power does.

In the United States one important tradition in economics runs less to conservatism than to a com-

---

[5]Board of Governors of the Federal Reserve System, *The Federal Reserve System: Purposes and Functions* (Washington, D.C., 1963), p. 2.

fortable conformity. At Harvard University it has sometimes been called the Belmont Syndrome—the desire of numerous Harvard faculty members of much professional distinction to commute from home, wife and issue in an amiable suburb to office, computer and classroom with no disturbance or dismay resulting from controversy, criticism or even unsettling thought. This preference for comfort excludes evidence where it is in conflict with convenience. The Belmont Syndrome is a natural and, no doubt, a harmless thing. Academic life would not, for certain, be improved if all its participants shared a compulsion to shake or change the world. Someone must teach what is commonly believed. But it is also essential, as we come now to the Federal Reserve System, to recognize that for some sixty years it has been a major institutional beneficiary of the Belmont Syndrome or its equivalent in other academic precincts. Almost every aspect of its history must be approached with a discriminating disregard for what is commonly taught or believed.

Not that the accomplishments of the System have been minimal. Some have been insufficiently praised. In the early years of the Federal Reserve, in the better downtown sections of major American cities, real estate of superior quality was acquired, and buildings of somber fiduciary classic were erected. Ever since, they have contributed an impression of solid substance to such otherwise secondary financial centers as Cleveland or St. Louis. In England or France only the capital has such a center of financial gravity; in the United States a dozen big cities are so blessed. These symbols, though not of great importance, are not without significance. Nor is the sobriety of the architecture to be deplored. Money is, to most people, a serious thing. They expect financial architecture to reflect this quality —to be somber and serious, never light or frivolous.

The same, it may be added, is true of bankers. Doctors, though life itself is in their hands, may be amusing. In *Decline and Fall,* Evelyn Waugh even has one who is deeply inebriated. A funny banker is inconceivable. Not even Waugh could make plausible a drunken banker.

The Federal Reserve System also brought into operation a highly efficient method of clearing and cashing checks. Previously when the check of one bank was brought to another, a charge was automatically levied —a small tax, in effect, on every expenditure of money. Now paying by check was, in effect, free. A small but manifestly useful step.

Finally, from its earliest days, the Federal Reserve established an unexampled reputation for probity. No officer has ever been apprehended for theft or embezzlement, although something must be attributed to the fact that so few handle or ever see actual portable money. And officers have rarely, if ever, been suspected of using their knowledge of the intentions of the System for their personal enrichment. Again something must be attributed to the limited number of people who have access to such information and the fact that profitable knowledge is in more limited supply than is commonly imagined. In recent times, subordinate employees of the Boston and Philadelphia Federal Reserve Banks have been taken into custody for making away with old notes that they had been directed to destroy. It had occurred to them, not illogically, that these could still be used. It remains that the standards of honesty in the System are admirably severe.[6]

For the rest, in its early years, the System was a victim of its legislative parthenogenesis. The planning for the System activated both parties to the old compromise. Those who wanted a central bank surrendered

---

[6]For confirming my impression as to the probity of the System I am indebted to my colleague, Andrew Brimmer, until recently a member of the Board of Governors of the Federal Reserve System.

enough to the old opponents of centralized financial power to render the new structure diffuse as to power, uncertain as to method and purpose. So the Federal Reserve System remained until the decade of the '30s, by which time the opportunities inherent in the management of money and therewith the institution of central banking were in decline.

In 1908, in the aftermath of the panic, Congress passed the Aldrich-Vreeland Act. In previous years, when frightened people had descended on the banks, the latter had, on occasion, issued scrip—literally I.O.U.'s to bearer—to settle their balances one with another or with their more trusting creditors. In this way the banks had been able to keep their more acceptable cash for their more demanding depositors. The new legislation regularized these arrangements. Banks were allowed to unite to issue an emergency currency. This could be done against the security of sundry bonds and commercial loans—these could, in effect, be turned into cash without being sold. A tax ensured the withdrawal of this surrogate currency once the emergency had passed. The law was invoked but once—at the outbreak of war in 1914. A more important provision of the law created a National Monetary Commission to devise a permanent procedure for minimizing, or countering, the effect of panic and otherwise providing a stable monetary system.

There now, appropriately, appeared two bodies to study the management of money in the United States, one for each of the parties to the old compromise. The first, the National Monetary Commission just mentioned, was under the chairmanship of Senator Nelson W. Aldrich of Rhode Island. A gentle, courtly man of profoundly senatorial aspect, Aldrich had an unabashed commitment to high tariffs, sound money, and untrammeled operations of big bankers and to all other measures which would, with reasonable certainty, enhance the wealth or power of the already rich, a community that very definitely included Aldrich himself. This identification had recently been further affirmed by the marriage of his daughter Abby Aldrich to John D. Rockefeller, Jr., a union commemorated in modern times by the name of Nelson Aldrich Rockefeller. Aldrich, in the early years of the century, was by common calculation the most influential man in the Senate. Lincoln Steffens, who preferred a strong phrase to precise statement, called him "the boss of the United States."[7] Under Aldrich's direction a score or more of studies of monetary institutions in the United States and, more particularly, in other countries were commissioned from the emergent economics profession. It is at least possible that the reverence in which the Federal Reserve System has since been held by economists owes something to the circumstance that so many who pioneered in the profession participated also in its birth.

The competing study, which got under way a little later, was headed by Representative Arsene Pujo of Louisiana. The active guidance was provided by Samuel Untermyer. Its purpose was to examine the operations of the money trust—the shadowy power in New York which Nelson Aldrich was rightly suspected of seeking to strengthen. The high noon of Pujo and Untermyer came on December 18, 1912, with the calling to the witness stand in Washington of the now ancient J. P. Morgan. Though old, Morgan knew the value of settling on a simple proposition, however improbable, and sticking to it. Money, he told the committee, was not the source of power. Character was. From this he could not be budged, although by the agrarian adherents to the old compromise he was not widely believed.

Pujo's hearings were to alert the troops; it was from the Aldrich study that came the concrete propo-

[7]Lincoln Steffens, *The Autobiography of Lincoln Steffens* (New York: Harcourt, Brace & Co., 1931), p. 507.

sals. In 1910, before the work of the National Monetary Commission was much advanced, Paul M. Warburg, a Wall Street investment banker of strong and original mind and great independence—two decades later he was to invite the wrath of the Street by warning, almost alone, of the insanity and ultimate danger of the great bull market—had come up with a design for a single central bank. He called it the United Reserve Bank. From this and his later service on the first Federal Reserve Board, Warburg has, with some justice, been called the father of the System. His design, however, was sadly impaired by Aldrich.

The latter, when the time came to introduce legislation, took steps to meet the long-standing opposition of the Democrats—iterated and reiterated for years in party platforms—to any and all proposals for a central bank. It was his thought to outflank the opposition by having not one central bank but many. And the word bank would itself be avoided. In 1912, he introduced legislation to establish a National Reserve Association along with fifteen regional associations. These would hold the reserves—the deposits—of the participating banks. To them the banks would turn for loans, including rescue in time of emergency. All would be solidly under the control of the bankers whom they comprised. It was a fateful concept. The opposition accepted the regional idea. It was then able to exclude the idea of a national or central reserve-holding authority. It was also able to water down the banker control of the regional institutions to which it agreed. It conceded that the resulting institutions could be called banks. Thus emerged the basic form of the Federal Reserve System.

However, the ultimate legislation was the work not of Aldrich and his fellow Republicans but of the Democrats. Perhaps it could not have been otherwise. No feature of American—to some extent of Anglo-Saxon —politics is so certain as the tendency of politicians to become first the captives, then the agents, of their opposition. In consequence, major initiatives are not taken by those who originally most favor them. Those so captured by an idea are too much in fear of their opponents. The action comes when the opposition accepts the need and wishes to disarm the original proponents. In the 1960s, liberal Democrats in the United States urged peace and international amity but continued the Cold War and plunged the country into Vietnam. They did so partly because they feared being called appeasers and crypto-Communists by the right. Richard Nixon, having impeccable credentials as a Cold Warrior, moved toward peace or accommodation with Moscow and Peking and withdrew, if very gradually, from Vietnam. Thus on foreign policy he outflanked his liberal opposition. When Professor Milton Friedman proposed a guaranteed income for the poor, it was considered (quite correctly) an act of creative imagination. When a Republican administration proposed it to Congress, it was a mark of conservative statesmanship. When George McGovern, running for President, advanced a close variant on slightly more generous terms, it was condemned by conservatives as the dream of a fiscal maniac. As known and stalwart defenders of the dollar, the Republicans were able, in the early 1970s, to devalue it not once but twice. For anyone suspected of a more flexible attitude toward the integrity of the dollar, such action would have been exceedingly perilous.

Thus it was in 1912. Woodrow Wilson, on becoming President, quickly accepted the opposition's view that a central bank was now necessary. The opposition having made the concession of not one but numerous central banks, this became the frame of reference. In 1913, the President called a special session of Congress to enact the legislation. It was still a long battle. Bryan's men came forward once more with a number of imaginative proposals, including one for a $200 million greenback issue for loans to cotton, wheat and corn producers and similar funds for general commerce and public works. They also wanted a dirt farmer on the Federal Reserve Board by statute. But William Jennings Bryan was now the Secretary of State, a most ingenious design for co-opting him for the Establishment. Some of the Bryanesque proposals—mostly those limiting the role of bankers in the new System—were accepted. More lost to the more conservative designs of the bill's principal sponsor, Representative Carter Glass of Virginia. Some of the proposals, including the special currency funds for farmers, were disavowed by the Secretary of State himself. A proposal for an elementary form of deposit insurance supported by the earnings of the System was abandoned in conference between the two houses at the insistence of Congressman Glass.

Two days before Christmas 1913, Woodrow Wilson signed the Federal Reserve Act into law. It provided not for a central bank but for as many as twelve—the number later chosen. Washington guidance was to be by a Federal Reserve Board of seven, of which the Secretary of the Treasury and the Comptroller of the Currency were to be *ex officio* members. The powers of the Board were slight. The regional idea had, in fact, triumphed, and the real authority lay with the twelve banks. These were each to be governed by a board of nine directors, six of whom were to be selected by the participating or member banks, although only three of these could be bankers. The remaining three were to be appointed by Washington. The American Bankers Association, contemplating the attainder of its members and the seemingly large role of the government in the System, said: "For those who do not believe in socialism it is very hard to accept . . ."[8]

On the tenth of the following August, at the offices

---

[8] Paul Studenski and Herman E. Krooss, *Financial History of the United States* (New York: McGraw-Hill Book Co., 1952), p. 258.

of Secretary of the Treasury William Gibbs McAdoo, the first Board was sworn in. Unlike those that were to follow, it was a group of considerable distinction. The first Governor was Charles S. Hamlin. Among the members were W. P. G. Harding of Birmingham, Alabama, Warburg, Frederick A. Delano of Chicago, later to acquire fame as Franklin D. Roosevelt's Uncle Fred, and A. C. Miller, a professor of economics at the University of California. Miller was destined to provide a substantial measure of continuity; he served for the next twenty-two years. Woodrow Wilson, in his view of the prospect, was more affirmative than the bankers. He wrote to McAdoo that "A new day has dawned for the beloved country whose lasting prosperity and happiness we so earnestly desire."[9]

The detailed provisions of the law, as they were finally passed, combined comparatively straightforward arrangements with some splendid intrusions of illogic reflecting concessions to the agrarian wing of the old compromise.

All national banks were required to belong to the System; state banks of minimal repute were allowed to join. (The national banks were encouraged to surrender the bonds by which their note issues were secured, although this operation was not finally completed until 1935.) The membership fee of the member banks, as henceforth they were called, was 6 percent of their capital, half of which remained on call. This investment, in turn, became the capital of the local Federal Reserve Bank. Return on this capital was limited; it was fully and wisely clear from the beginning that the System was not to be tested by its ability to make money. Member banks were required to main-

---

[9]Quoted in Benjamin Haggott Beckhart, *Federal Reserve System* (New York: American Institute of Banking, 1972), p. 134.

tain a specified minimum of reserves against their deposits, and at least a third of these reserves were to be kept on deposit at the Reserve Bank. Reserves could be of gold, the equivalent of gold in yellow-backed gold certificates that were issued by the Treasury in return for gold brought to the mint or otherwise to the government, or reserves could consist of the currency salad as it now was—greenbacks, silver certificates, the treasury notes of the 1890 experiment—all of which now carried the honorable cognomen, "lawful money." The nature of unlawful money, counterfeit notes apart, was never indicated. All lawful money was, of course, exchangeable into gold at any bank, at any time, on demand. The reserves of the member banks became the deposits of the Federal Reserve Banks.

The prime reward of membership was the ability to borrow, for need or profit, from the Reserve Bank. The security for such loans was short-term commercial or agricultural debt, called commercial paper or bills. These, in the early years of the System, acquired a great mystique as the proper basis of central-bank lending. As borrowing by a customer of the member bank appeared as a spendable deposit to the account of that customer, so borrowing by a member bank appeared as a transferable or withdrawal deposit of the member bank at the Reserve Bank. This borrowing by members, then as ever since, was called rediscounting; the interest rate charged was (and remains) the rediscount rate. Instead of a deposit, the member bank could take notes—Federal Reserve notes. As a concession to the old supporters of government paper and, perhaps also, the even older suspicion of banks, these were made full-scale obligations of the United States. In this spirit, as inspection will show, Federal Reserve notes are now signed not by an officer of a Federal Reserve Bank or the System but jointly by the Secretary of the Treasury and the otherwise deeply obscure politician who rejoices in the title of Treasurer of the United States. For some reason it has long been thought good that this redundant functionary should be a woman.

Against its deposits the Federal Reserve Bank was required to maintain a reserve of 35 percent in lawful money. Against the Federal Reserve notes it was required to have a reserve of 40 percent in gold or gold certificates representing gold on deposit at the Treasury. The System was henceforth to be the place of deposit for government funds. It was authorized to deal in government bonds. Unlike the Bank of England the Federal Reserve Banks could not do business directly with the public. There was much other detail in the legislation, nearly all unimportant.

The old compromise, we have seen, had given to the financial community the good banks and the sound currency that it wanted. To the frontier and the farms it allowed the casual banking that, not without reason, the agrarians saw as serving their interest. It was here, in the small country banks, that the anarchy existed; it was here that needy but aspiring borrowers were accommodated and deposits created on the basis of small or exiguous reserves. Here, were it to bring Professor Samuelson's anarchy of unstable private banking to an end, the new System would have to be most stern. In contrast, the big-city banks could be trusted to be responsible to a point, to maintain reasonably adequate reserves. Even in the panic of 1907, though its focus was New York, it was the *parvenu* trust companies that got themselves into trouble, not the larger commercial banks.

It was the small country banks that were dealt with by the Federal Reserve Act with the most impressive illogic. It differentiated the reserve of lawful money that banks were required to hold against deposits in accordance with the size of the cities—18 percent,

15 percent and 12 percent. But on those banks that had for a century been the most reckless—the country banks—it imposed the lowest requirement—12 percent. In the great, relatively conservative financial centers—New York, Chicago, Philadelphia and their near approximations—the requirement was stiffest—18 percent. Elsewhere, in the medium-sized cities, it was 15 percent. Almost no one mentioned the controlling reason for this arrangement which, in modified form, continues to the present time. It was that casual or even dangerous banking was much favored by the banks that engaged in it—and by those who, as for a hundred years before, greatly wanted the loans. Had the country banks been subject to the same reserve requirements as the city or the big metropolitan banks, they wouldn't have joined the System. So it was recognized that the old compromise required that they continue in their own way. The reserves were higher for the conservative big-city banks, for, being conservative, they kept higher reserves anyway.

But apt as was the strategy, it did not work. The country banks still had the alternative of not joining the System. And this was the course they mainly chose. The Federal Reserve System became, in practice, the banking system of the larger banks. In 1929, fifteen years after the founding of the System, almost two-thirds (65 percent) of all the banks were still outside. These two-thirds, however, had less than a third of all bank resources. The Federal Reserve was a club of the great and the strong.

In the discussions preceding the passage of the Federal Reserve Act, one magic reference recurred. That was to an *elastic* currency. Carter Glass declared during the debate on the legislation that "The currency based upon the Nation's debt [the National Bank Act] is absolutely unresponsive to the Nation's business needs."[10] The title of the legislation, when enacted, proclaimed the purpose—"to furnish an elastic currency." This phrase did much to allay the suspicions of the agrarians. Elastic suggested something flexible, soft. Something like that, in the money supply, was what they had long sought. If elastic, it could not be bad.

Unfortunately, elasticity was a word with varying interpretations.[11] Those who used it rarely paused to clarify their meaning. Thus elasticity could mean the ability to sustain a large increase in loans on the basis of a small increase in reserves. In this sense there was much elasticity. Were one of the district banks to acquire from a foreign central bank (as was authorized) a fresh deposit of $1000 in gold, it could, while abiding by the requirements as to reserves, sustain additional loans of $3000 to its member banks. The funds so borrowed would become deposits, which is to say reserves, of the member banks. For the big-city banks with their requirement of 18 percent reserve this addition to reserve would sustain a fivefold expansion in loans and resulting deposits.[12] The addition of $1000 back at the Reserve Bank from some outside source could, in principle, mean $15,000 more in deposits—in money to spend—at the member banks. This, indeed, was elasticity. It was yet greater, of course, for the smaller banks.

A number of things stood between the theory and

---

[10]Cited in "Economic Decision-Making Through the Political Process; The U.S. Federal Reserve Act: A Case Study," by William J. Raduchel (unpublished paper). I am grateful to my friend and former assistant for making this very good study available to me.
[11]A point emphasized by Professor Friedman. Cf. Milton Friedman and Anna Jacobson Schwartz, *A Monetary History of the United States, 1867–1960*. Study by the National Bureau of Economic Research (Princeton: Princeton University Press, 1963), p. 189 et seq.
[12]Including time and the requirement that member banks be participating generally in the expansion. If one alone is expanding, its deposits will be paid away to other banks without a reciprocal flow from the expansion of others.

the actual fifteen thousand. Since the Federal Reserve Banks were not operated for profit, they were under no compulsion to have loans outstanding and earning interest to the full extent allowed by their reserves. An inflow of gold would, in the practice of the time, go not to a Federal Reserve Bank but to a large member bank. Its ability to sustain new loans and deposits would have the simple expansion potential of any new addition to bank cash. It would not have the compound effect of an addition to the reserves of the Federal Reserve System. But even this elasticity was greater than that allowed under previous national bank legislation. Were there to be a large movement of gold from abroad such as might be occasioned by the need to pay for war or by the European rich seeking shelter for their funds, the ultimate expansion in loans and deposits could be large. Inflation could occur on a solid gold standard.

Such expansion could be prevented by the Federal Reserve Banks. They could, as just noted, keep their loans to banks below what their reserves allowed. And, by selling securities, they could transfer cash, e.g., the gold from abroad just mentioned, from the member banks and the member-bank reserves to their own vaults. Thus the potential for expansion would be reduced by discretionary action of the Federal Reserve authorities. The counterpart of an elastic currency was thus a greatly enhanced discretionary power for the central bank—the very thing that the proponents of elasticity most feared. In the next thirty years a huge inflow of gold would make this discretionary power anything but academic.

Elasticity had another meaning; that was the ability easily to exchange one kind of money, namely bank deposits, for another, namely hard or hand-to-hand currency. This, in turn, had two aspects. Prior to the passage of the Federal Reserve Act there was a seasonal need for more cash to pay for farm products when they moved to market. Numerous farmers, with others, then preferred to be paid not with a check on a deposit but in what seemed to them real money. This seasonal demand required that deposits be converted into cash; this depleted the cash reserves of the banks. To provide for the demand, the banks had sometimes to call some loans or, more probably, to loan less than they would have liked. There is no evidence that this seasonal strain was much more than an inconvenience; it was, however, the kind of problem that could be perceived by the most meager financial mind. With the new System the member banks could get Federal Reserve notes as required against the security of their commercial loans. These notes satisfied admirably the people who demanded to be paid in cash. When these notes were redeposited in a state bank, they served the same purpose there as well. As the farmers paid their debts or spent their notes, the latter came back into the hands of people who preferred deposits to currency. Being relatively unimportant, the problem of seasonal elasticity was, like most unimportant problems, rather readily solved.

But elasticity in the exchange of one kind of money for another had a more traditional and much more important aspect. That was in providing for such exchange during the tense and saddening occasions when people came to the banks for the cash that wasn't there. This problem, above all, the Federal Reserve Act was meant to solve. For some of the smaller member banks it could have made it worse. As borrowers in need of emergency help, they were not much welcomed at their friendly Federal Reserve Bank. Their paper was often regarded, sometimes rightly, with suspicion. And since the Act allowed them a greater volume of loans on the basis of a given cash reserve than was previously permitted—the first form of elasticity—it may well have made greater the need for such succor. More important, the small state banks were not members. They were also the banks which, for good reason, were most vulnerable to fear and the resulting descent by their depositors. When such descent occurred—when too many of their depositors tried to exchange their deposits for cash—the only recourse of these banks, as always before, was to close their doors and go out of business.

As the new System was getting under way, the United States was moving into war. It is part of the favoring cliché that this was the Federal Reserve's first crisis and that it met it well. This is nonsense. The Reserve Banks bought government bonds and helped sell them as the Treasury required at the interest rates the Treasury specified. Peacetime loans to private individuals can be refused. Government loans in wartime cannot. When its rates are set and its purchases of government securities specified, a central bank has no independent power. The System began its life as a routine adjunct of the Treasury, a role that required no thought.

Meanwhile it gradually became evident that the System had a basic structural defect. The regional design, however admirable for serving local pride and architectural ambition and for lulling the suspicions of the agrarians, was essentially unworkable.

In the earliest days the district banks took their autonomy seriously; this was especially true of the New York Federal Reserve Bank, which, under the leadership of an ambitious and prestigious governor, Benjamin Strong, assumed that its location adjacent to Wall Street itself made it the first among unequals. Meanwhile, as the coordinating authority, the Federal Reserve Board in Washington was handicapped by the slight power accorded it by the Federal Reserve Act. It also lacked prestige and, in time, simple competence as well.

The members of the Federal Reserve Board were government officials paid at government salaries. The heads of the Federal Reserve Banks, in contrast, were bankers and were paid bankers' salaries. (On two occasions in the early years chairmen of the Federal Reserve Board moved on at doubled salaries to become presidents of Reserve Banks.) In an age which measured men by what they earned, influence lay with the banker's pay and position.

Additionally, there was the belief, endemic in all American political attitudes, that an expert becomes such by appointment to the appropriate position. As the original members reached the end of their terms or otherwise moved on, the Federal Reserve Board fell increasingly prey to this doctrine. In the '20s, President Harding appointed as Chairman of the Federal Reserve Board one Daniel R. Crissinger, also of Marion, Ohio. Crissinger had trained for the post by serving as a neighbor and friend to Harding and as counsel to a steam-shovel corporation. He was in office until 1927. The other second-generation appointees who assisted Crissinger, Herbert Hoover described in his memoirs as "mediocrities."

Additionally, the Federal Reserve Board, in its early years, had a limited view of the instruments of control at its command. Often it could get the agreement of the district banks on an increase or decrease in the rediscount rate which it believed wise or on which Governor Strong had previously decided. It did not, for some years, grasp the nature of the companion step of open-market operations.

This was no detail. Open-market operations, to remind, involve the selling or buying of government securities.[13] A sale puts these bonds in the hands of

[13]Government bills, notes and bonds. Open-market operations also include the purchase of and sale of foreign currencies. An excellent modern account is in Sherman J. Maisel, *Managing the Dollar* (New York: W. W. Norton & Co., 1973), p. 35 et seq. Professor Maisel was, for a number of years, a member of the Federal Reserve Board. His book is the best interior view of its operations.

the member banks or their customers, puts the cash with which they are paid for in the vaults of the Federal Reserve Bank. The cash so transferred reduces the reserves of the member banks, and this requires them either to curtail their loans or borrow from the Federal Reserve Bank at the new and higher rediscount rate. Thus open-market operations are often what make the rediscount rate effective. In failing to appreciate the importance of open-market operations, the Federal Reserve Board denied to itself most of the power available to a central banker.

In 1935, as part of a general reform, the regional experiment was abandoned. The Roosevelt Administration, more vocally suspicious of financial power than that of Wilson, finally gave the country a single central bank. The functions of the district Federal Reserve Banks became, as Professor Friedman has observed, mechanical and advisory.[14]

Remarkably, this disestablishment has never been conceded. The twelve district banks and their buildings survive as branch operations. Their mechanical tasks, notably the clearing of checks, the routine movement of currency and the management of government financial transactions, are useful and vast. But the myth of autonomy and importance also survives. A pamphlet published in 1971 by the Federal Reserve Bank of Richmond, Virginia, the unit that sustains the dignity of the onetime capital of the Confederacy, shows the Board of Directors, all nine, deliberating around an adequately solid table in an appropriately paneled room. One man near the camera wears a sports jacket; otherwise all is in order. However, reluctantly and with indirection, the text concedes the truth. The directors, it is explained, do not establish dividends, control investment policy, supervise operations, as the term might imply. (Nor, though it is not explained, do they

---

[14]Friedman and Schwartz, p. 190.

appoint officers or fix salaries.) They do "establish, subject to the approval of the Board of Governors [of the System], the discount rates the Reserve Banks charge on loans to member banks." This is a difficult way of saying that the rediscount rate too is exclusively the domain of central authority. In the list of the functions of that somber deliberative body in Virginia, only one remains that is categorical. The Directors of the Federal Reserve Bank of Richmond "provide System officials with considerable 'grass roots' information on business conditions."[15] Richmond being only 109 miles from Washington, the roads good, the telephone service excellent and its newspapers readily available if wished, the volume of such information otherwise unavailable in Washington cannot be great. The textbooks, without exception, cooperate to sustain the regional myth. New York may be the financial center, Washington the capital. But important guidance is given by Kansas City. Perhaps there is something to be said for perpetuating legend, enhancing local pride, even at the expense of truth. But truth and reality have their claims, and these are that Aldrich's concession to the countryside was unworkable and has been undone these forty years.

[15]Robert P. Black, *The Federal Reserve Today* (Richmond: Federal Reserve Bank of Richmond, 1971), p. 7.

CHAPTER XI

The Fall

WITH THE CREATION of the Federal Reserve System the long struggle of the United States to perfect a sensible, conservative monetary system was over. Everywhere in the industrial countries money of whatever kind was now exchangeable, without pretense or delay, into gold. Silver was for silver-plating. It was especially important that the Americans, the most reckless and experiment-prone of people where money was concerned, the most suspicious whenever gold was mentioned, had now, however reluctantly, come abreast. In the Federal Reserve System they had an instrument for doing all that a modern state needed to do for its money—for monopolizing the note issue, regulating bank lending and the resulting deposit creation and for providing banks with the succoring loans of last resort. True, the Federal Reserve System had been crippled by the compromise that allowed it to be born. But this—including the uncertainty as to whether power lay with the Federal Reserve Board in Washington or the twelve Federal Reserve Banks—was as yet undiscovered. The idea of a decentralized central bank—twelve central banks, each operating in some measure of undefined independence of its fellows and of Washington—did not yet seem a contradiction in terms. Rather, it looked a spacious and democratic idea, somehow appropriate to the spacious democracy which the banks would serve. And, as already noted, the shortcomings of the

Federal Reserve System were not, like the failure of the mail to arrive, matters to be condemned. In the United States, as in other countries, ordinary bureaucrats are criticized for their mistakes. Diplomats and central bankers are, on the whole, cherished for them. If the errors are spectacularly disastrous, as for example those of the late John Foster Dulles at the State Department or the late Benjamin Strong at the New York Federal Reserve Bank (Strong is thought to have contributed effectively to the 1929 crash), their position in public esteem can be even more secure. They have made a mark on a peculiarly genteel current of history. In 1914, after 2500 years of trial and much error (and in the United States more than a century of bitter and confusing controversy), money could seem, in a sense, finished business.

All historians rejoice in the odd coincidence of great events. It is thought to relieve tedium for the reader, show how sensitive the writer is to paradox and suggest even to the most secular that either a benign, a malignant or an amused hand is ultimately in charge. No historian could be better pleased than by the events in the summer of 1914. On August 10, as the members of the new Federal Reserve Board assembled at the office of Secretary of the Treasury McAdoo to be sworn into their new posts, the August guns were sounding. They were sounding the end of the monetary system of which the new banks could be considered the culminating step.

This, not surprisingly, the members of the new Board did not see. And, in any case, the present had more pressing claims. The Board members were locked in a struggle with Secretary McAdoo over office space —they feared that their present offices in the Treasury Building would make them seem subservient to that Department. They were also deeply concerned by their position in the Washington system of social precedence. On this ladder they had been placed below both the Interstate Commerce Commission and the Civil Service Commission. This for central bankers was a shocking thing. The indignity was appealed eventually to President Wilson who was unsympathetic; he said only that "they might come right after the fire department."[1] The newspapers, however, referred helpfully to the Board as "the new Supreme Court of finance."

On the outbreak of the war the major industrial participants—Germany, France, Britain, Austria— suspended specie payments. That is to say, notes and deposits could no longer be redeemed in gold; these countries went off the gold standard. In the United States, though continuing noninvolvement was assumed, the same action was proposed and sharply debated. The case for going off gold seemed obvious: For a hundred years Europeans, most notably Englishmen, had been investing in the United States. In consequence, a vast portfolio of American securities—perhaps as much as $6 billion worth—was held abroad.[2] If any appreciable part of this was liquidated for cash, American gold reserves would soon be gone. (The Federal Reserve began business that autumn with only $203 million of gold in its vaults.) Better hold on to the gold that was in hand.

In response to fears of such liquidation and calculations of how quickly the American gold stock would be exhausted by sellers thus seeking cash, securities were dumped on the New York market in the first nervous days of the war. And the proceeds were converted, along with other balances, into sterling or gold.

[1] William Gibbs McAdoo, *Crowded Years* (Boston: Houghton Mifflin Co., 1931), pp. 287–288.
[2] Paul Studenski and Herman E. Krooss, *Financial History of the United States* (New York: McGraw-Hill Book Co., 1952), p. 281. Other estimates, such as that of Alexander D. Noyes (*The War Period of American Finance* [New York: G. P. Putnam's Sons, 1926], p. 60), are somewhat lower.

As a result, the dollar fell from its normal $4.87 to the pound to a phenomenal $7.00 to the pound. Dollars could be turned in for gold as before, and the gold could be sent to London where it would buy pounds at the old price, more or less. These pounds could then be used back in New York to buy $7.00, not $4.87, for further changing into gold. Here was a truly wonderful profit. Gold did start to flow out to buy pounds in this fashion, though the thought of loss from German U-boats and commerce raiders had a profoundly dampening effect on shipments. By largely immobilizing the gold, this fear was what kept the pound so high. Another course of action suggested itself, and that was to close down the New York Stock Exchange and thus prevent the liquidation of foreign-held securities. This was done.

The foresight of financial experts was, as so often, a poor guide to the future. When the New York Stock Exchange closed down, trading moved out into Wall Street to what reputable traders called the Outlaw Market. The Exchange indignantly forbade its members to have intercourse with the outlaws. The trading continued. By October the more enterprising of the outlaws were issuing typewritten sheets showing closing prices, and soon it was noticed that these were not very different from the prices at the time the Exchange was closed. European investors were obviously having second and more favorable thoughts about selling their investments in a country that was so safely remote from the fighting. And that fighting, it was now seen, was murderous beyond belief and with considerable likelihood of being prolonged. In December the Exchange reopened. Nothing happened. The calculation as regards gold was equally off. The Bank of England had meanwhile opened a branch in Canada to receive gold and thus obviate the risk of ocean shipment. But now gold started to flow in rather than out. Presently the flow was a flood. Soon the United States had

more gold than any country had ever possessed before
—the increase was from $1.5 billion at the end of
1914 to $2.0 billion at the end of 1915 to $2.9 billion
at the end of 1917.[3] It was a flood with a double
effect. It destroyed the gold standard in the countries
whence it came and also in the country where it went.

Some of the gold came for deposit and safekeeping;
some came to be invested in American securities; but
the fundamental force in the flow was the need of the
belligerent powers for American goods. In an age of
socialist agriculture and Soviet wheat purchases, it requires an effort of mind to remember that Russia was
once a major source of Europe's wheat. Now this market was cut off, and the United States became an important supplier of bread grain. Also needed were
ships, armor plate and, above all, ammunition. By
1915, it was evident that the participants, Britain in
particular, could never supply themselves with the in-
finity of shells which, according to the current con-
cepts of warfare, had to be flung across no-man's-land
before an offensive or even at random on a quiet day.
On assuming office as Minister of Munitions in May
1915, Lloyd George proceeded to place orders in
whatever amount his buyers thought could be filled.
Some of these supplies were paid for by conscript-
ing and selling in the United States the American securities which earlier it had been thought their frightened owners would dump on their own. The spending
of these proceeds involved no movement of gold. Some
of the payment was from loans raised from private investors in the United States, which also occasioned
no gold movement. In principle, it might be noted,
these loans were available to both sides. In practice,

---

[3]Valued at $20.67 an ounce. U.S. Bureau of the Census, *Historical
Statistics of the United States, Colonial Times to 1957* (Washington,
D. C., 1960), p. 649.

the British controlled the oceans. Thus they made it impossible for their enemies to move any appreciable quantity of the products the loans would buy, so the Germans and Austrians had no need for the loans that this even-handed policy allowed. In consequence, William Jennings Bryan was led to the last of his many acts of public inconvenience. He held that such loans to the British were inconsistent with any neutrality that was strict, as Wilson had demanded, as to both thought and deed. For this aberration he was severely rebuked by those who believed that obvious truth should be subordinate to the demands of patriotism or the prospects of pecuniary gain. To the intense relief of such citizens, Bryan left the Cabinet in June 1915 over Wilson's reaction to the sinking of the *Lusitania*. He remains one of the tiny handful of Cabinet officers in the American experience to register opposition to a policy of which they disapproved by resigning.

Gold was also used directly to purchase supplies. Some of this came from the reserves of the Bank of England, the Banque de France and the Imperial Bank of Russia. More was gold that previously had been in circulation or private possession. As gold coins came to the British or French banks in the ordinary course of business, notes were issued in their place. And Englishmen and Frenchmen were asked to turn in their gold for paper, a request that caused some to consider the superior rewards of hoarding. Thus, in 1914, private citizens in France were estimated to hold as much as $1.2 billion in gold. The appeal brought in some $240 million.[4]

For handling problems such as those facing the British or French treasuries during the war, there are no miracle men. Either current earnings from exports, salable assets, loans or credits of one kind or another or

---

[4]According to Noyes, p. 131. Needless to say, there is a major element of imagination in the estimates of such holdings.

gold exist for paying foreign suppliers, in which case the officials involved are a success. Or these assets do not exist, in which case those involved are a failure. However, nothing comes so easily to the press and public mind as the vision of financial genius. Both wish to believe that, where such important matters are involved, there are individuals of transcendental insight and power, men who can make something out of nothing. In Britain during the war (and after) the popular imagination thus stimulated settled on the thirty-one-year-old (in 1914) Treasury official, John Maynard Keynes. His papers of the period, recently published,[5] suggest that he was a hard-working, competent and resourceful man who matched resources to payments with attention and skill and who extended his mind to the similar problems of the French and the Russians. That was all.

The effect of removing the gold from Europe was to remove from the reserves of French and British banks, the Banque de France and the Bank of England the metal into which paper could be converted. And by removing gold from hand-to-hand circulation and replacing it with paper, it also increased greatly the proportion of the money supply that, given convertibility, would be subject to conversion into gold. The primary effect of this on the future of the gold standard will be evident. There was much more paper to convert, much less gold with which to do it.

There was, perhaps, a more serious effect. The calling in of the gold was a way of suggesting to the citizens that, as compared with paper or bank deposits, it had a superior significance. Before 1914, people passed on gold coins just as easily as they passed on subsidiary

---

[5]John Maynard Keynes, *The Collected Writings of John Maynard Keynes,* Vol. XVI, *Activities 1914–1919: The Treasury and Versailles* (London: Macmillan & Co., 1971).

silver or paper. Thereafter gold would always seem better—something that might prudently be held. So it came about that gold coins, which before 1914 were received and passed on without notice or thought, were ever after something to be scrutinized, shown, commented upon and retained. Partly for that reason—Gresham again—not many who were born after 1914 would ever receive a gold coin in the normal course of trade or compensation.

Such was the effect of the outflow. In the United States, meanwhile, the gold standard was being devastated no less by the flood. As noted, between the end of 1914 and the end of 1917, the gold stock of the United States almost doubled. Gold came to the banking agents of the British and French in the United States, was paid into the accounts of suppliers, remained in the vaults of their banks or was sent as deposits to the local Federal Reserve Bank. Had it all been used as reserves by the banks and the Federal Reserve Banks, it would have been capable of sustaining a truly phenomenal expansion in loans, deposits and note issue. This expansion being much in excess of any companion increase in the supply of goods and services, there would have been a very large increase in prices—one that would have appalled the followers of Bryan, for they wanted prices that did not fall or prices that recouped past reductions but not wildly increasing prices. And to their undoubted astonishment this increase in prices would have occurred with money that was fully convertible into gold. The United States faced an inflation caused by gold.

However, the fledgling central bankers of the United States as well as the commercial bankers allowed reserves to accumulate in excess of legal need. The limit on loans (and resulting expansion in notes and deposits) was set not by the reserves as so meticulously spelled out in the Federal Reserve Act. It was set by the needs and demands of borrowers and by what the commercial bankers and the Federal Reserve Banks severally and independently thought it wise to lend. Out of the plethora of gold came a money supply limited not, as in the case of the classical gold standard, by the supply of gold. It was limited by the decisions of commercial bankers and of the new central bankers, and by what borrowers sought to borrow. It was a primitive form of managed currency. It was not precise management. Rather it was the result of numerous uncoordinated actions, the kind of management that one finds in the Democratic Party or in a mental hospital run by the patients. It remains that, all but simultaneously with the appearance of the Federal Reserve, there also appeared the need for divorcing the supply of money from the supply of gold.

In 1917, when the United States entered the war, its loans to Britain and France replaced the conscripted gold (and securities) as the means by which these allies paid for their needs. Accordingly, gold ceased to flow to the United States, and instead a small outward flow began to Spain and the other remaining neutrals. This was stopped by law. The United States thus went off the gold standard where international transactions were concerned. It remained possible, although in the minds of many rather unpatriotic, for Americans to trade paper notes and bank deposits for gold so long as the gold was not taken out of the country. World War I was, domestically speaking, fought on the gold standard. It was—an exceptional thing—a hard-money war. More exactly, the inflow of gold provided a vast and elastic net within which almost anything could occur. The decisive question in this, as in other wars, was not what happened to the money; that, as always, was the servant of wartime need. What counted was how funds to pay for the war were raised.

As always for those not fighting, taxation cast a disagreeable pall over patriotism, one that in the United States in these years was made worse by the recently enacted income-tax amendment. (Things were more agreeable in France, where an income tax, though authorized, did not become fully effective until after the Armistice.) In consequence, conservatives were to be found arguing against an excessive commitment to a pay-as-you-go policy. Secretary McAdoo's initial instinct was for heavy taxation—he suggested, as a guiding rule, that 50 percent of the cost come from taxes. J. P. Morgan thought that the maximum should be 20 percent. In the event, by common estimate, about 30 percent of the cost of World War I was paid for from current tax revenues. The rest was covered by methods not appreciably different from those used during the Civil War.

For the first time since Sir William Phips returned from Quebec, a serious war did not bring a serious demand for forthright printing of paper currency by the government. That was only because a more subtle arrangement was now available. The Treasury could now borrow from the Federal Reserve System—whatever the latter's independence in principle, it could not refuse the government in practice or even dream of so doing. In consequence of this operation, the Federal Reserve had newly printed bonds, the Treasury had newly printed Federal Reserve notes or new and equally spendable deposits at the Federal Reserve Banks. In its ultimate nature as well as in the practical effect, this procedure differed only in superficial form from the printing of the greenbacks. Nor were matters much changed when the Treasury sold bonds, as it did, to the commercial banks. The government, in consequence of such sale, had cash or a deposit which it spent. The bank then took the government bond to the Federal Reserve Bank and borrowed on this good government security to replace the funds that the government had used. As with the direct sale to the Federal Reserve, more money was brought into existence to pay wartime expenses.

These transactions were conducted by men of grave and courteous manner, good tailoring and considered speech. There was none of the raucous advocacy that marked the issue of the greenbacks. The Civil War and the greenbacks remain the classic manifestation of irresponsible finance. World War I has no such reputation. Such are the services of style in economics and money management.

In fact, the World War I legerdemain involved an even more elaborate exercise in illusion. As under Jay Cooke during the Civil War, a legion of volunteer bond salesmen was recruited to sell government securities to the public. A commendable aspect of this effort was the three-minute speech—a recognition that exhortations on patriotism and public duty are effective in inverse proportion to their length. Such salesmanship has, in principle, some economic justification. Some people may be persuaded to buy bonds instead of spending money. By saving rather than spending, the individual diminishes the pressure on markets, reduces the severity of the inflation. The labor, materials and capital equipment so unbought or unused become available to the government for war purposes. In World War I, however, buyers of government bonds were encouraged to borrow from the banks for their purchases, using the bonds as collateral. Many did. Again the banks using the bonds so acquired replenished their reserves by borrowing from their Federal Reserve Bank. The immediate effect of this was again indistinguishable, except as it involved even greater indirection, from direct borrowing by the government from the Federal Reserve Banks. Later on there could be a difference. After the war people sought to keep their bonds and repay their bank loans. This had the effect of contracting expenditures for current consumption and thus, conceivably, made the postwar slump in consumer expenditure marginally worse. In the euphoria of war, not surprisingly, none gave attention to such possible effects. Nor, for that matter, did many wonder why people should be urged to borrow money from their banks to buy bonds which the government could as easily have sold to the same banks at less cost.

In the United States during all the war years, wholesale prices about doubled, with much of the increase occurring between mid-1916 and mid-1917, the months immediately before entry into the war. Britain and Germany, although far more deeply involved for a much longer time, had only a slightly greater increase. Taking wholesale prices in July 1914 as 100, they were 216 in Germany four years later. In Britain in 1918, they were 239. France, with her northern industrial territories torn away, the war on her own lands and an exceptionally strong aversion to taxation, had a much greater increase—by 1918, wholesale prices were about three-and-a-half times the prewar level. Italy, though physically less affected by the conflict but with an even greater aversion to taxation, had also a very large increase—by around four-and-a-half times.[6] In Britain and Germany serious efforts were made to arrest the price increases by price controls, and these, in turn, were combined with measures to ration scarce staples and materials. In France controls were used but not seriously enforced.

In the United States there were such informal restraints on consumption as the meatless and wheatless

---

[6]Comparative movements in wholesale prices are summarized in *Bulletin de la Statistique Générale de la France*, Paris, Librairie Felix Alcan, Vol. XII, No. IV (July 1923), pp. 347–348.

days, and, beginning in mid-1917, the United States
government, through the Grain Corporation headed
by Herbert Hoover, tendered for all wheat produced in
the United States at a price of $2.20 a bushel, raised
the following year to $2.26. This was a minimum price;
it remained open to farmers to get more if they could,
and many did. Maximum prices for fuel were formally
fixed by the Fuel Administration. Numerous other
products, principally although not exclusively those in
heavy military or other wartime demand, were made
subject to price agreements between the producers and
the Price-Fixing Committee of the War Industries
Board. Iron and steel, copper, lumber, wool, hides
and leather, cotton fabrics, nitric and sulphuric acid,
nickel, aluminum, mercury, zinc, brick, cement, hol-
low tiles as well as crushed stone, sand and gravel
were so controlled. Compliance was voluntary or, at
the most, subject to the sanction of seizure of the product by the government, the threat of withdrawal of
transportation priorities or the charge of being unpatriotic, which, at the time, meant pro-German. An exceptionally distinguished member of the Price-Fixing
Committee was F. W. Taussig of Harvard, perhaps the
most highly regarded economist of his time. Writing
soon after and at some length of the experience, he said
of the price-setting that "In the main it was opportunist,
feeling its way from case to case."[7] He was somewhat
impressed by one circumstance: the most successful
experience with price control was of nickel where
there was at the time a complete monopoly. That a
monopoly or an approach thereto greatly simplified the
trials of the price-fixer was to be one of the important
lessons of World War II.

While, as Professor Taussig strongly argued, the price
controls of World War I no doubt had a modifying

[7]F. W. Taussig, "Price-Fixing as Seen by a Price-Fixer," *The
Quarterly Journal of Economics,* Vol. XXXIII (February 1919),
p. 205 et seq. The quotation is on p. 238.

influence on the prices of products in exceptional demand, World War I, like the Civil War, was, in the main, fought under the aegis of the market, a circumstance that Bernard Baruch, the Chairman of the War Industries Board, never ceased to regret. (He believed that all prices and wages should have been frozen, a position which, though it was thought wildly eccentric, he was still urging at the outbreak of World War II.) The financing of World War I, the disguise apart, was about the same as that of the Civil War. So was the movement in prices. Everything considered, the management of the Civil War might be the easier to defend.

World War I marked the beginning of the end of the international gold standard—of the single world currency that, at whatever pain, gold had been. Not again was there a reasonably workable distribution of gold stocks between the industrial countries—mostly, and for many years, there was plethora in the United States and paucity almost everywhere else. Efforts at revival were made in the decade of the twenties in Britain, France and the other industrial countries. Except in the United States and briefly in France no major country again looked at its gold reserves and felt secure. None more than briefly allowed citizens to exchange their paper or bank deposits into gold. In its developed form the gold standard was a brief experiment, a matter of a few decades, a half-century at most. It was only the sense that it was the final step, the ultimate money, that made it seem so much older.

CHAPTER XII

The Ultimate Inflation

THE TENDENCY, indeed a principal purpose, of the gold standard was to unite the economic performance and policies of nations. This, during its brief rule, it did. Were business good in Britain and prices accordingly strong, goods flowed in for sale and gold flowed out to pay for them. This outflow observed and its effect accentuated by the Bank of England led to a reduction in the reserves of the commercial banks, an increase in interest rates, a consequent contraction of loans, a weakening of prices and cutbacks in output and employment. Meanwhile the gold arriving in Paris, Berlin or New York allowed an opposite—and rather more pleasant—expansion of loans and business activity there. In eventual consequence of this expansion and the associated increase in prices, the flow would be out of these countries and back once more to Britain. At all stages the movements would be anticipated and accelerated by men of means who would be moving their funds to take advantage of higher interest rates or prices. It was an arrangement that operated with more precision in the textbooks than in the real world, had a greater symmetry in the minds of those who adumbrated the theory of central banking than was revealed in the actions of those who handled these matters in practice. Nevertheless, that the gold standard (reinforced by the accepted fiscal morality of the balanced budget) was a notable arrangement for coordinating economic behavior in different countries cannot be denied.

It had also a notable flaw. That was in asking, in an age of growing nationalism with a growing tendency to hold governments responsible for economic performance, that both nationalist instinct and domestic economic management be subordinated to an impersonal, international mechanism, one capable of inflicting considerable hardship and distress. It was a flaw that supporters of gold did not accept. They saw any reluctance of governments as inhering in the lack of moral fiber of politicians—a lack that led them to try to ameliorate the strains that gold imposed. That the morality of politicians is difficult to alter in the short run was not recognized.

At the end of World War I, as just noted, all of the principal belligerents, the United States partly excepted, had abandoned the gold standard. No major country now allowed the free export of gold. It followed that none need now worry lest foreigners convert deposits or notes into gold to take out of the country. Nor was there danger that citizens, similarly motivated by caution or cupidity, would, other then surreptitiously, do likewise. Accordingly, domestic policy was no longer restrained by the fear that gold would be lost. And since gold could not leave, its loss could not reduce bank reserves, reduce bank deposits, reduce note circulation, all with further depressing effect on production, prices and employment. Each of the industrial nations, in other words, was now free to pursue internal economic policies that reflected its preference or necessity and with no immediate regard for what other countries were doing. The coordinating discipline imposed by gold no longer existed.

In the fifteen years following World War I, and especially in the immediate aftermath, the industrial nations exploited this new freedom in remarkably diverse fashion. The French followed the line of least resistance with, on the whole, the best results. The British followed the line of greatest resistance, causing great pain from the resulting self-inflicted wounds. The Germans so handled matters, or so yielded to circumstance, as to produce the greatest inflation of modern times. The United States, by a combination of mismanagement and nonmanagement, produced the greatest depression. In all the long history of money the decade of the 1920s—extended by a few years to the consequences—is perhaps the most instructive.

Of the major combatants, Russia apart, France was the only one to have suffered important physical devastation. A hideous scar, in width mostly about five miles though often more, lay across the whole country from the Straits of Dover to the Swiss frontier. Within was a moon landscape covered with the detritus of battle and in many places made mortal by a random seeding of unexploded shells. As in Britain and Germany, a whole generation of workers had been destroyed by the conflict—in France the losses were greater among the peasants of relevant age than in the industrial proletariat, for the mobilization and death of peasants was less harmful to the economy. There remained to be supported a heavy burden of crippled, mutilated or otherwise dependent men and women. The French had, however, one thing much in their favor. They could set about rebuilding without thought of the cost. It was their deepest conviction that the Germans both should and would be made to pay. Nor did this follow entirely from the congenital tendency of the French (as Anglo-Saxons believe) to misapprehend where economics are involved. Fifty years before, the Germans had levied the seemingly massive total of five billion francs on France following the Franco-Prussian War. The French had rallied and paid it off in twenty-four months.

Since the Germans would be paying, it seemed appropriate to French postwar governments that they borrow to get the work under way. When the German money came in, the loans could then be discharged. With this understanding French reconstruction proceeded with confidence and exemplary speed.

Under the stimulation of the borrowing and spending, prices went up and, subject to a considerable reduction in 1920 and 1921 when the postwar boom collapsed in the United States and Britain, continued to rise. In July 1920, French wholesale prices were five times the 1914 level; by July 1922, they had fallen to 3.3 times the prewar level. In 1923, the adverse world reaction to the Ruhr occupation, the evident difficulty in collecting reparations by armed action and the combination of these with the great German inflation of that year largely ended the hope that the Boches would pay. This prop to confidence having been knocked out, the rate of inflation much increased. In July 1924, prices were 4.9 times the 1914 level; by July 1926, they were 8.5 times as high.[1] Inevitably it occurred to Frenchmen that it would be sensible to hold currencies other than the franc, and during this particular era of inflation money of exemplary stability—dollars, Swiss francs, even pounds—was available. So while prices rose in France, the exchange value of the franc as people traded it for other currencies declined even more. In the months immediately following the war, when it still reflected the availability of American loans and supplies, the franc was around 5.45 to the dollar. In ensuing months it fell at an irregular rate, and, at the end of 1922, it was 13.84 to the dollar. At the end of 1923, it was 19.02.[2]

---

[1]Price data from *Bulletin de la Statistique Générale de la France*, Paris, Librairie Felix Alcan, Vol. XV, No. I (October 1925), p. 14 and Vol. XVII, No. II (January–March 1928), p. 132.
[2]Martin Wolfe, *The French Franc Between the Wars, 1919–1939* (New York: Columbia University Press, 1951), p. 213.

In consequence of the relatively greater decline of the franc as compared with the increase in prices, France in the first half of the twenties was a wonderfully inexpensive country in which to travel and buy things, and Frenchmen attributed some part of their price increases to the resulting influx of bargain-hunters. Suiting action to belief, Parisians, one day in 1926, successfully attacked and repulsed a busload of American sightseers on the streets of Paris in the belief that they were running up the cost of living.

In the years from 1919 to 1926, France was, in fact, exceedingly prosperous. The devastation, save for irretrievable land such as that around Verdun, was repaired. (The acreage on which the great battles were fought was often almost unbelievably small. The Battle of Verdun was fought on an area only slightly larger than that of the London parks.) Industry expanded, in many areas prodigiously. In 1929, steel production, enhanced by that of Alsace-Lorraine now redeemed from Germany, was twice as great as in 1913 and three times as great as immediately after the war in 1921. But it was prices that people noticed. Once again we see the great cycle that controls attitudes toward money. Given inflation, people yearn for stable prices. If there is stability, then high taxation, a sluggish economy, unemployment become the greater menace. The French experience in the twenties illuminated also a closely related principle. If there is prosperity, this is taken for granted. Attention then comes to focus upon the behavior of prices. If prices are stable, people then spare a thought for whether output and employment are all that they should be. What people do not have, seems most urgent.

Not having price stability in the twenties, Frenchmen wanted it greatly. This wish was enhanced by the belief, common in even the most sophisticated circles at the time, that inflation was without redeeming effect on the economy. It was bad and all bad. In these years two leading observers of the French economy reported, with genuine surprise, that "paradoxically as it may seem, the economic events of postwar France lend themselves to the interpretation that inflation has a stimulating effect on industrial development."[3] A radical thought.

But while Frenchmen yearned for stable prices, a reliable franc, they yearned very little for the measures, notably the taxes and restraints on borrowing, that would make these possible. An observer earlier in the decade might well have predicted that the franc would follow the mark; it remains something of a puzzle that it did not. However, in 1926, a new ministry of national consolidation headed by Raymond Poincaré came to office. It was pledged to save the franc and, in a general way, to the taxes and controls on business borrowing that would do so. Though it soon relented on taxes, people believed it was serious. From this belief and the general well-being of the country as much as from specific action came success. Prices began to level off; soon the franc was stabilized on the foreign exchanges. What had been called the battle of the franc, rather surprisingly, was won. A French historian with some justice called the French policy in these years an island of reason in a sea of errors.[4] The reason consisted in doing what seemed obvious at the moment—and recognizing, as ever, that the French economy is hard to damage.

At the time of stabilization, as before, the depreciation of the franc in relation to other currencies was

[3]W. F. Ogburn and W. Jaffe, *The Economic Development of Post-War France* (New York: Columbia University Press, 1929), Cited in T. Kemp, *The French Economy 1913–1939* (London: Longman Group, 1972), p. 67. This last is a most useful and succinct study.
[4]Alfred Sauvy, *Histoire Economique de la France entre les Deux Guerres*, Vol. I, *1918–31* (Paris: Fayard, 1965). Cited in Charles P. Kindleberger, *The World in Depression 1929–1939* (Berkeley and Los Angeles: University of California Press, 1973), p. 48. The latter is the best book in English on the Great Depression, and one to which I am much indebted.

greater than the companion rise in French prices. So France continued to be a good country in which to buy, a more difficult one in which to sell. In 1928, by now blessed with much gold, France returned to the gold standard. However, francs could only be exchanged for ingots, and the minimum number of francs required for a deal was 215,000. This was well beyond the reach of the average citizen. The gold in a 1914 20-franc piece was now worth almost 100 francs. The French family which had successfully resisted the wartime impulse to turn in its gold for patriotic use could not have thought itself misguided. As gold poured into the French banks and the Banque de France, the flow inspired the confidence that brought yet more with it for deposit. France now emerged as the most robust of defenders of gold and the gold standard.

France escaped the ultimate inflation. The demands for reparations that led her far along the road did have something to do—men at the time thought much—with the collapse that then occurred in Germany.

The Russian Revolution, in keeping with the tendency of revolutions, was floated in on a tide of paper. The succession regimes in eastern Europe after 1918, with heavy claims, little government and less revenue, had varying degrees of inflation, in most cases extreme. However, to the world at large the ultimate drama of postwar money was played out in Austria and Germany. The German inflation, in particular, ran the full and devastating course. Prices rose without limit. In the end, money would buy nothing. Every classic consequence of inflation—large debts paid off with a few pennies, scavengers and scalawags buying old masters for a few dollars, the rentier suddenly poor, the equally undeserving speculator suddenly rich—was present. If the case of the American Confederacy be excepted, there had been nothing like it since the

French and American Revolutions. China apart, there has been nothing like it since.

However, the Austrian inflation preceded the German, and a case could be made that its impact on economic thought was greater. It occurred under the aegis of the young Finance Minister of the new Republic, Joseph A. Schumpeter, who went on to a spectacular academic career in Germany and the United States. The inflation was experienced or remembered by the men who were to compose the world's most distinguished coterie of conservative (in the European sense, liberal) economists of the next generation—Friedrich von Hayek, Ludwig von Mises, Gottfried Haberler, Fritz Machlup and Oskar Morgenstern, all of whom also moved eventually to the United States. All shared with Schumpeter a profound mistrust of any action that seemed to risk inflation along with an even greater distaste for anything that seemed to suggest socialism. All were influential.

The Austrian inflation ran its course in 1922. When the League of Nations came to the assistance of the young republic at the end of that year—and fiscal and other financial reforms were put into effect—the crown was down to around 70,000 to the dollar. Before the war it had been 4.9 to the dollar. The German inflation flooded on through most of the following year. It is the one that calls for a closer look.

Other inflations are associated either with overriding circumstances—war or revolution—or with economic mismanagement. The great German inflation has the distinction of being attributed by historians not only to these causes but also to chicane. It was long believed to be the design by which the Germans, unscrupulous or desperate or both, showed to an impressionable world that the cost of collecting reparations under the Versailles Treaty would be greater than the cost of forgiving them. On examination the case for such guile largely disappears. The reparations claims played a part in the German inflation but in a thoroughly commonplace way. Save for the final absurdities, the forces contributing to the German inflation were not especially remarkable and show little trace of deliberate design.

In the months following the end of the war and the establishment of the Republic the German fiscal system was substantially strengthened. The old government, like that of France, lacked power to levy direct taxes, income taxes in particular. This (for the affluent) happy fault was now corrected, and revenues were increased. In consequence, in the early postwar years, the German domestic budget was nearly in balance. In 1921, excluding the railway deficit, revenues covered about 90 percent of domestic expenditure. In 1922, for a short time, the budget on domestic account was balanced. This was far better than the French performance at the time.

There remained, however, two grave problems. In all countries at any time there is a large volume of spendable assets which overhangs the market. Cash, bank deposits, savings deposits, government bonds, other securities can all be converted as necessary and spent if there is the impulse to do so. In Germany, as in other countries during the war, the volume of these spendable assets had increased greatly—government debt was up from a little over 5 billion marks in 1914 to more than 105 billion in March 1919. Currency holdings, which were a little under 6 billion marks at the end of 1914, were nearly 33 billion at the end of 1918.[5]

---

[5] Frank D. Graham, *Exchange, Prices and Production in Hyper-Inflation: Germany 1920–1923* (Princeton: Princeton University Press, 1930), p. 7. This study, by an admired friend and onetime Princeton colleague, is a basic source on the German inflation. It is a subject on which the literature is vast.

In modern times economists, looking at the effects of monetary and fiscal policy on the volume of demand in the economy, have spared little thought for the possibility that liquid assets might be tipped into markets, upsetting all the best macroeconomic calculations. The German experience of the early twenties is a useful reminder of this danger. And it reminds, also, that the danger is induced by inflation itself. It is inflation that causes thoughtful or worried people to wonder if money or money-denoted assets are good things to hold or if they hadn't better be exchanged for goods or tangible property before prices have gone up and up.

The second problem for the Germans was the reparations that had to be paid under the Versailles Treaty. These were in addition to the domestic budget and, in the early postwar years, about as great. Keynes's *The Economic Consequences of the Peace,*[6] perhaps the single most influential tract ever written on a subject of current economic importance, may well have left the world with an exaggerated impression of the unreasonableness of these demands. But the eventual bill, 132 billion gold or prewar marks (about $33 billion), was large. There is no particular mystery as to what payment would have required. Public expenditures in Germany would have had to be rigorously limited, as also investment in such consumer needs as housing. Taxes, especially on consumer goods, would have had to be ruthless. This combination would then have produced the surplus of public revenue over expenditure from which the reparations would have been paid. And both actions, but especially the heavy taxes, would have cut consumption and imports without much affecting exports. From this would have come an accumulation of dollars, pounds, francs and

---

[6] John Maynard Keynes, *The Collected Writings of John Maynard Keynes,* Vol. II: *The Economic Consequences of the Peace* (London: Macmillan & Co., 1971).

gold from a favorable balance of trade. When these were purchased by the government with the marks from the budget surplus and returned to the French, Belgians or British, the reparations would have been paid. The limiting factor on this ability to pay reparations was the willingness of the German people to raise and pay taxes, forgo public and private consumption.

This willingness is rarely high. It was not very high in Germany in the early twenties where already the reparations were seen more as an act of retribution than of justice. Additionally, the amount of the reparations bill was not fixed until April 1921, and thereafter the scheduling of the payments remained uncertain. This meant that the more paid in any one year, the greater in all likelihood would be the ensuing annual claim. This was not an arrangement conducive to a strong tax policy and to high tax-paying morale.

Prices in Germany increased approximately three-fold in 1919. It is perhaps remarkable that they did not go up more. A political revolution had occurred, and a social revolution was being suppressed. The Allied blockade did not end until well along in the year, and, in consequence of that and the general disorganization, food and raw materials were desperately scarce. The new taxes were not yet effective, and borrowing continued for domestic purposes as well as for obligations under the Armistice and later under the Treaty. The increase in prices continued in 1920 but then, remarkably, it came to an end, and there was a modest fall. The recession emanating from the United States, with the sudden abundance of farm and other products, had its effect even in Germany. From the spring of 1920 to the summer of 1921, German prices were, for all practical purposes, stable at about fourteen times the prewar level. J. M. Keynes was backing his by now widely advertised judgment that the Versailles requirements were far beyond the capacity of the German economy by speculating heavily on margin against the mark. He narrowly escaped financial ruin, was saved by loans from his publishers and a friendly financier. "It would indeed have been a disaster if the man who had so recently set world opinion agog by claiming to know better than the mighty of the land had himself become involved in bankruptcy."[7] Yes, indeed.

Keynes's error was only in timing. In the summer of 1921, prices began again to rise. In April in London the reparations bill was finally set at, as noted, 132 billion gold, i.e., prewar, marks. This sum may have caused some Germans to conclude that the prospect was hopeless and to begin turning in their spendable assets for goods. World commodity prices had also ceased to fall. And a growing budget deficit on combined foreign and domestic account was making itself felt. In any case, domestic prices went from 14 times the 1913 level at the middle of 1921 to 35 times that level at the end of the year. The increase continued in 1922; at the end of that year they were 1475 times higher than before the war. Then in 1923, things became serious. By November 27, 1923, domestic prices stood at 1,422,900,000,000 times the prewar level. Prices of imported items were up a bit more.[8]

The rise in prices was matched, in fact as in France somewhat outpaced, by the fall of the mark in relation to the pound and the dollar. At the time of momentary stability in 1921, the mark was around 81 to the dollar. By mid-1922, it had fallen to 670 to the

[7]R. F. Harrod, *The Life of John Maynard Keynes* (London: Macmillan & Co., 1963), p. 296. According to the legend current in Cambridge (England) during my time there, Keynes was bailed out by his father, John Neville Keynes, also of the University. This, according to Harrod, was not the case; Keynes, he says, did reveal his plight to his parents who, not surprisingly, counseled caution.
[8]Price levels are from Graham, pp. 156–159.

dollar. In the spring of 1923, a Reichstag committee was convened to examine into the reasons why the mark had fallen to 30,000 to the dollar. By the time the committee met on June 18, the mark was down to 152,000 to the dollar, and in July it went to a million to the dollar. Thereafter the decline was rapid. On July 22, the Berlin correspondent of the *London Daily Mail,* a usefully impressionable man, said in a dispatch that "I was amazed when I found today that one had to pay 24,000 marks for a ham sandwich whereas yesterday in the same cafe a ham sandwich cost only (sic) 14,000 marks." He added that fortunately wages were being increased and that "The salary of a Cabinet Minister has been raised from 23,000,000 ten days ago to 32,000,000 marks."[9]

In the ensuing weeks every trite comment ever made concerning inflation, and their number is legion, was made real. Men and women rushed to spend their wages, if possible within minutes of receiving them. Notes were trundled to the stores in wheelbarrows— or baby carriages. A reference to resort to the printing press has always had an especially prominent place in the monetary cliché. In Germany that autumn there was resort to virtually every press that was capable of printing money. Notes were in literal fact churned out. And, on occasion, trade stopped as the presses fell behind in producing new bills of large enough denomination so that the amount of paper required for the day's food was portable. Late in July the *Daily Mail* man told of this problem:

> It is difficult to get a check cashed. The 10,000-mark note is the highest denomination printed and the banks are denuded of them. This morning motor-lorries loaded with paper money kept on arriving at the Reichsbank but messengers with handcarts were also there to

---

[9]Norman Angell, *The Story of Money* (New York: Frederick A. Stokes Co., 1929), pp. 334–335.

take away the bundles of notes passed out by the Bank
. . . The cashier of my bank handed me 4,000,000
marks in 1,000-mark notes, each worth less than half
a farthing . . . He obligingly did them up for me in a
neat paper parcel which I afterwards put on the table
of the restaurant where I lunched and unpacked when
the waiter brought the bill. But this difficulty will soon
disappear for we expect to have 4,000,000-mark notes
by the end of next week.[10]

In the next weeks there were many such tales. At
the end of October the *New York Times* told of a
stranger in one of "the lesser restaurants" in Berlin
who flourished a dollar bill and asked for all the dinner
it would buy. He was amply provided, and, as he was
about to leave, the waiter arrived with another plate
of soup and another entrée and bowed politely: "The
dollar has gone up again."[11] An Associated Press dispatch told solemnly of a new affliction spreading over
the Reich. " 'Zero stroke,' or 'cipher stroke' is the
name created by German physicians for a prevalent
nervous malady brought about by the present fan-
tastic currency figures. Scores of cases of the 'stroke'
are reported among men and women of all classes, who
have been prostrated by their efforts to figure in thousands of billions. Many of these persons apparently are
normal, except for a desire to write endless rows of
ciphers."[12] The *New York Times* noted that the Poles,
whose currency could still be counted in thousands to
the dollar, were doing much better. Even the Bol-
shevik government, which earlier that year had announced the stabilization of the ruble and whose
undertakings were "naturally open to suspicion," recognized the need for a currency that inspired confi-

---

[10]Angell, pp. 335–336.
[11]The *New York Times,* October 30, 1923.
[12]The *New York Times,* December 7, 1923.

dence. And being cognizant of "the incredulity of outside financiers" where Communism was involved, the Soviet authorities had taken the admirable step of inviting a representative group of magnates into the vaults of their central bank to see the gold reserve for themselves.

The legend relating the great German inflation to reparations firmly holds that it got out of hand when the French occupied the Ruhr in 1923 to enforce reparations claims under the Treaty. The resulting disruption of production, combined with the heavy costs to the German budget of the passive resistance policy of the German government, put inflation out of control and destroyed the mark. The explanation is tendentious. The French were heavily criticized for the occupation. The explanation awards them the blame for the economic debacle as well. The flaw in the case is obvious. During 1922, before the French moved in, prices went from 3700 (1913=100) to 147,500. By the time the French arrived, the mark was down to around 10,000 to the dollar and falling fast. What was this if not inflation? At most, the French occupation of the Ruhr added a little oil to what was already a fire storm.

In the last months of 1923, inflation both built upon itself and also destroyed all of the accepted methods for controlling it. It was, of course, an exercise in incredible foolishness to hold money. So all current income, together with all past savings, were rushed to market. Taxation, as a restraining influence, became worthless. Payments to public servants, soldiers and for supplies had to be made currently. These, in the manner of the pay of the cabinet ministers mentioned by the man from the *Daily Mail,* were increasing by the day. The return from any compensating increase in taxes did not come in for weeks or months. By then, current payments would have gone up again and again. A vast government deficit thus became the consequence of the inflation itself.

Business had a similar need to bridge the gap between current requirements and the later arrival of receipts. And this gap too widened with inflation. Neither this nor any other credit needs could be had from the banks; no banker, sane or insane, would make a loan which a few weeks later· could be repaid with money having only a fraction of the value, i.e., purchasing power, of the original loan. So the Reichsbank had to provide loans directly to business. In December 1921, commercial discounts of the Reichsbank totalled 1.1 billion marks. In November 1923, they reached a peak of 347,301,037,776 billion marks. Government loans reached a total of 497 billion billion marks in December.[13]

As no one would wish to hold cash, neither would anyone want a bank deposit. And there was now difficulty, in any case, in making payment by check, for the recipient took thoughtful note of the likelihood that the payment would lose value before he could cash the check, and the bank had similar thoughts as to what would happen while the check was being cleared. So both business firms and the government, when they borrowed, took the proceeds, or much of them, in currency. Thus the vast demand for· paper money. Some German jurisdictions in need of loans promised their creditors repayment in money with an equivalent purchasing power in commodities—rye in the case of Oldenburg state; oats in the case of Berlin; Westphalian bituminous flaming coal No. IV in the case of Baden Electricity Supply Company.

The tendency of the exchange depreciation to anticipate and outstrip the domestic price increases, astro-

---

[13]Graham, p. 63.

nomic though these might be, attracted, again as in France, an international army of bargain-hunters. This was augmented by domestic entrepreneurs who acquired the property of those who, their savings now worthless, had to sell household goods, paintings, other family artifacts or real estate in order to eat. As the inflation proceeded, the export of personal treasure was prohibited, and people leaving Germany were made to open their baggage and surrender their loot. In France the bargain-hunters were assumed to be Americans. In Germany, much more ominously, word was passed that they were Jews.

On November 20, 1923, the curtain was rolled down. As in Austria a year earlier, the end came suddenly. And as with the milder French inflation, the end came with astonishing ease. Perhaps it ended simply because it could not go on. On November 20, the old reichsmark was declared to be no longer money. A new currency, the rentenmark, was introduced, and one of these was given for each thousand billion, i.e., trillion, of the old. The new rentenmark was declared to be backed by a first mortgage on all the land and other physical assets of the Reich. This idea had its ancestry in the assignats; it was, however, appreciably more fraudulent. In France in 1789, there was extant, visible land freshly taken from the Church for which the currency initially could be exchanged; any German seeking to exercise rights of foreclosure on German property with his rentenmarks would have been thought mentally unstable.

Nevertheless it worked. Circumstances helped. In preceding months the payments under the Treaty had dwindled into insignificance and were not again seriously reasserted. In the end, during the twenties, more was paid to Germany in loans than she paid in reparations,[14] although the principle that the victor should subsidize the vanquished did not become accepted international policy until after World War II. Stresemann, now the Chancellor, abandoned passive resistance in the Ruhr with its heavy drain on the budget. In consequence of these actions the budget could be balanced. The Reichsbank meanwhile stopped discounting the paper of private business firms. After a short, painful passage, such firms were again accommodated at the commercial banks. Unemployment, which had been low during the inflation, rose sharply in the last quarter of 1923, and by Christmas more than a quarter of all trade union members were without jobs. However, recovery was prompt; through all of 1924, unemployment averaged only 6.4 percent of the total labor force. In 1925, it was down to 3.3 percent.[15]

On November 20, 1923, the day the old reichsmark expired, so, by remarkable coincidence, did the head of the Reichsbank, Rudolph Havenstein. His place was taken by Hjalmar Horace Greeley Schacht, who thus became the man behind the miracle of the rentenmark. His reputation as a miracle worker endured. Popular myth held him to be the financial genius who engineered the economic recovery of Germany under Adolf Hitler, financed Germany's rearmament and guided Nazi economic policy in the early successful years of

---

[14]A recent writer, Richard M. Watt, suggests that, over the reparations period, Germany paid 36 billion marks, borrowed 33 billion from abroad. Most of these loans went unpaid. In *The Kings Depart* (New York: Simon and Schuster, 1968), p. 504.

[15]Nineteen twenty-three trade union figures are from Graham, p. 317. Others are from Angus Maddison, "Economic Growth in Western Europe 1870–1957," in Warren C. Scoville and J. Clayburn La Force, *The Economic Development of Western Europe from 1914 to the Present* (Lexington, Massachusetts: D. C. Heath & Co., 1970), p. 56, and are adjusted to include all wage earners.

World War II. For few men have the rewards of financial reputation been so ambiguous, for they made him a vital instrument of Hitler's crimes and landed him in the dock at Nuremberg. Again the fatal association with money.

Schacht was, in fact, like so much else in economics, an accident of timing. If, after 1923, the previous claims on the German budget had continued—the reparations claims and the cost of passive resistance—nothing would have saved the mark or his reputation. Relieved of these costs and given the desire of people who have experienced inflation for a currency they could trust—and their willingness to abide myth if it sustained this trust—everything was possible. Twenty-one years and some months later, American economists, assessing the effects of the World War II air attacks on the German economy, interrogated Schacht in his postwar prison; he had been lodged in a place of containment near Frankfurt for the more technical and professional members of the Nazi high command which the British Army was operating under the code name of Dustbin. Schacht protested energetically his lack of influence in the Nazi years. This, he said, derived from his inability to persuade Hitler of the need to balance the budget, restrain bank lending and otherwise adhere in good times and bad to the immutable laws of orthodox finance. The economists returned convinced that Schacht was, indeed, a man of limited and frozen mind who, plausibly, had little influence on the much more pragmatic National Socialist economic policy. With this conclusion the judges at Nuremberg later agreed, and he was acquitted.

In 1948, the reichsmark, which in the meantime had again replaced the rentenmark, was again largely worthless. Prices this time had not run away; instead, the entitlement to goods was by possession of ration cards or coupons rather than currency. Everyone had enough money; it was the ration card that was scrutinized by the seller. The reichsmark, at the rate of ten to one, was now replaced by the deutschemark. Money suddenly became scarce and important again. Goods held back in anticipation of the new currency became available overnight. They no longer had to be rationed. This was the new German miracle. The planning of the currency conversion was the work of two Americans of German-Jewish origin, Gerhard Colm and Raymond Goldsmith. The largely innocent bystander was Economics Minister Ludwig Erhard. Erhard was, however, the man in position, and so *he* became the new miracle worker. Not even the phrases were changed. Alas, Erhard went on to be Chancellor where his performance made it plain that he also was, if in lesser degree, an accidental man.

That the great German inflation, like the ones elsewhere in central Europe, produced a large transfer of wealth from those who possessed savings accounts, money, securities or mortgages to those who had debts or tangible property is assumed. And, despite a shortage of affirming statistics, that such transfer occurred does seem plausible. The loss so involved, the parallel loss by people of their stake in the social order and the companion anger and frustration were, in turn, thought to have much to do with the rise of Fascism or Communism. These are matters on which there is no proof, and it is unbecoming, however customary, to substitute certainty of statement for hard evidence. But the simple facts are worth a glance. All of the countries of central Europe that suffered a collapse of their currencies following World War I were eventually to experience Fascism, Communism or in most cases—Poland, Hungary, East Germany—both. The countries that did not experience such a breakdown in their money were almost uniformly more fortunate.

What is not in doubt is that the German inflation left

Germans with a searing fear of its recurrence. And whatever the effect of inflation in paving the way for Fascism, measures taken later out of fear of inflation were certainly not without effect. We have noticed, and will see again, that the strongest action is taken against inflation when it is least needed. On December 8, 1931, with one-sixth of the total German labor force out of work, the government of Heinrich Brüning decreed a reduction of from 10 to 15 percent in most wages, this being a rollback to the level of four years earlier. It decreed also a reduction in industrial prices of 10 percent, a similar reduction in rents, railway fares, rail freight charges and charges for municipal services. Earlier, wages of public employees had been reduced by a fifth, and taxes on wages, salaries and on incomes had been sharply increased. Unemployment benefits were also reduced. In the following year unemployment rose to one-fifth of the German labor force, and in the next year came Hitler.[16,17]

---

[16]Unemployment figures are from Maddison, p. 56. Guillebaud, who excludes some nonindustrial categories, puts unemployment in 1931 at around one-quarter of the labor force and in 1932 at one-third. C. W. Guillebaud, *The Economic Recovery of Germany* (London: Macmillan & Co., 1939), p. 31.

[17]Later in the '30's, Brüning joined the Harvard faculty as Professor of Government. At a welcoming seminar one evening I asked him if his Draconian measures at a time of general deflation had not advanced the cause of Adolf Hitler. He said they had not. When, unwisely, I pressed the point, he asked me if I disputed the word of the former Chancellor of the German Reich.

CHAPTER XIII

The Self-Inflicted Wounds

As FRANCE CHOSE the line of least resistance in the decade of great monetary dispersion, so Britain chose that of the greatest. The French experience was better, although this is not proof of superior wisdom. France, as we have seen, has a tendency to rise above all misfortune. Britain, with her heavy dependence on external trade, is a difficult country to manage. British economic policy, accordingly, needs to be better than that of most other countries, and what is often taken to be poor British performance reflects, in fact, the far greater difficulty of the British task. However, in the decade of the '20s, the British, after considerable thought and discussion, did what made things worse.

In Britain, as elsewhere, prices receded in 1920 and 1921 as the wartime shortages were overcome, the budget was brought back under control and the boom came to an end. Unemployment, which of course had been negligible in the preceding years, rose to 12.6 percent of the labor force in 1921. It averaged above 10 percent the following year. Thereafter it fell, prices firmed or rose, as did also wages. All seemed on the way back to normal or what, following President Harding's great solecism, Americans were then calling normalcy. (After President Nixon's departure in 1974, one lexicographer spoke of a return to normality.) In 1925, the decision was taken to return to the gold standard.

This was a less remarkable decision than much subsequent discussion has made it out to be. In the greatest days of Britain, sterling and gold were interchangeable, and the one was not thought inferior to the other. For a nation bent on retaining its past eminence, economic and otherwise, to re-establish this identity was a natural step. None was more open to the thought of these past glories than the then Chancellor of the Exchequer, Winston Churchill, for whom the past was part of life itself and also a rich source of family prestige and personal income. His address to Parliament on April 28, 1925, announcing the return to gold was a Churchillian occasion. The self-governing dominions, he observed, had moved or were moving to re-establish the gold standard, so over the whole of the British Empire there would be "complete unity of action." The success of the step was being ensured by American support—$200 million from the Federal Reserve Bank of New York, $100 million from J. P. Morgan. The consequence would be a great rivival in international and intra-imperial trade. Henceforth nations united by the gold standard would "vary together, like ships in harbor whose gangways are joined and who rise and fall together with the tide." As a minor defect, gold could be had only for export. There would be no more gold coins. The *New York Times* reported next day that, "according to opinion expressed in the lobby," the Chancellor's speech was one of the "finest in a long line" and "fully up to his own high reputation as a parliamentary orator." Its headline said that Churchill's proposals had carried "PARLIAMENT AND NATION TO HEIGHT OF ENTHUSIASM."[1] Sixteen years later Churchill would be well cast; no man was so well equipped to make the lion roar. In 1925, both he and his oratory were, without doubt, a misfortune.

The error they defended was in restoring the pound

---

[1] The *New York Times,* April 29, 1925.

to its prewar gold content of 123.27 grains of fine gold, its old exchange rate of $4.87. In 1920, the pound had fallen to as low as $3.40 in gold-based dollars. Though it had since gained and was still gaining, the prewar gold content and dollar exchange rate were far too high. That was because, for these rates, British prices were far too high. Because of the high British prices anyone possessed of gold or dollars could do better by exchanging them for the money of one of Britain's competitors and buying there. And Englishmen likewise could do better by exchanging pounds for dollars, gold or other currencies at the favorable Churchillian rate and buying abroad. In 1925, the price advantage in doing so was about 10 percent. Exports, as always, were essential for Britain. So, other things equal, British coal, textiles and other manufactured goods could only become competitive at the new exchange rates if their prices were to come down by approximately 10 percent. A very uncomfortable process.

The case of coal was especially disagreeable, for the pits, still in private hands, were poorly equipped, often indifferently managed and manned by an ill-used, angry and highly intelligent labor force. Lower prices for coal would require lower wages. Agreeing that there would be problems in the coal industry, Churchill attributed these difficulties to the poor condition of the business. In a bold substitution of metaphor for thought he averred that the exchange rate had no more to do with the troubles of coal than with the Gulf Stream. Keynes promptly described this assertion as of "the feather-brained order."[2]

Although others had doubts—including Reginald McKenna, the Chairman of the Midland Bank and former Chancellor of the Exchequer, who was

---

[2]John Maynard Keynes, *Essays in Persuasion* (New York: Harcourt, Brace & Co., 1932), p. 246.

brought on board the gold policy only with difficulty —the case against Churchill was led by Keynes. It was a simple one.[3] By returning to gold at the old parity, Britain accepted the need for a painful depression of prices and wages with accompanying stagnation and unemployment, all of which would be a rich source of social stress. But Keynes made his case with compassion. He was anxious to discover why Churchill, a man of considerable reputation, was impelled to do "such a silly thing." And, after a fashion, he exculpated him. Churchill, Keynes explained, had "no instinctive judgment to prevent him from making mistakes." And "lacking this instinctive judgment, he was deafened by the clamorous voices of conventional finance; and, most of all . . . he was misled by his experts."[4] The quality of mercy can sometimes be a trifle strained.

Keynes was not, in fact, forgiven for his compassion, and later events made him even less eligible for absolution, for men of reputation naturally see the person who has been right as a threat to their own eminence. In the next four years prices in Britain remained under pressure and unemployment remained high—from seven to more than nine percent of the labor force. It was a British trademark. In these years Samuel Dodsworth, Sinclair Lewis's retired motor magnate, came to England. He wanted to see, along with Westminster Abbey, the Lancashire textile workers on the dole.

---

[3] Although not even Keynes made it with complete foresight. Before the return to gold, Keynes thought, for a time, such a return would cause American prices to rise with possible inflationary consequences. And his case was solely against returning to gold; neither he nor others urged the simple solution of reducing the gold and dollar value of the pound. That was rejected as one would reject the removal of Stonehenge. On the antecedent discussions see Charles P. Kindleberger, *The World in Depression 1929–1939* (Berkeley and Los Angeles: University of California Press, 1973), p. 43 et seq.
[4] These quotations are from Keynes, pp. 246, 248–249.

It is not easy, half a century later, to imagine a time when organized workers could be advised forthrightly of a wage reduction. It was not entirely possible in 1926. When the miners were advised that their wages would be reduced as the monetary policy required, they, not surprisingly, prepared to strike. The owners anticipated the action with a lockout. In support of the miners came the general strike. The general strike did not last very long and, in the manner of many British misfortunes, was enjoyed by much of the population. Among those taking a rewarding stand for law, order and constitutional government and against the tyranny of the mob was Winston Churchill. Still the Gulf Stream. But the miners' strike lasted through 1926 before it was finally defeated. All during the twenties exports remained sluggish, the gold position of the Bank of England remained perilous, and further support had to be solicited from the United States.

Keynes was still under a cloud for his defection on the Versailles Treaty, although by now it was also conceded that his position on this had much merit. Now for his foresight he was required to content himself with heading an insurance company, writing, cultivating the arts, teaching in a somewhat casual way and speculating ardently on his own behalf and that of King's College, Cambridge, of which he became the bursar. Not until World War II did matters become sufficiently serious to allow of his readmission to the Establishment. Churchill, on the other hand, fared better. The convention that makes monetary misjudgment merely interesting error operated even in his uniquely obvious case. That he had made a mistake all came to agree. But it had none of the adverse effects on his career of his earlier and possibly more defensible stand on behalf of the campaign at the Dardanelles.

By 1929, unemployment was falling, output increasing, though both still at a modest rate. The gold position of the Bank of England was still thin. Then came the American crash and slump. In consequence at least in part of the adversity that followed the 1925 decision, Britain now had a Labour government. It was not greatly more immune than its predecessors to the clamorous voices of orthodox finance. On August 23, 1931, Ramsay MacDonald was advised that a hoped-for loan from an American bank consortium would most likely be possible, assuming that proposed budget cuts, including a cut in the dole, received Cabinet and public support. A Cabinet minority then proved recalcitrant. So MacDonald resigned and formed a coalition ministry with Liberals and Tories. In September the obligation to pay gold under the Gold Standard Act was suspended.[5]

In a sense, Churchill had triumphed. Aided by the inferiority complex of socialists in such matters, his 1925 action had destroyed all threat from the left for another fifteen years. The 1925 return to the gold standard was perhaps the most decisively damaging action involving money in modern times.

In the United States the postwar boom continued through 1919 and well into 1920. Then came severe depression. The Federal Reserve System, its role as the guardian against boom and bust in abeyance, at a minimum facilitated both. While prices were rising and speculation in commodities and land was proceeding, it kept interest rates low. The commercial banks borrowed freely from the Federal Reserve Banks to meet the speculative as well as the other needs of their clients. The U.S. Treasury, which still had to sell bonds, supported the soft policy, although much must also be attributed to the fear of cautious men that they

---

[5]Cf. R. Bassett, *Nineteen Thirty-one* (London: Macmillan & Co., 1958), p. 127 et seq.

would prick the bubble. Then they would be blamed personally for the collapse. Better let it come by itself. Soon it did.

Early in 1920, with military needs at an end, wartime scarcity overcome and overseas orders no longer being sustained by American loans, prices leveled off and began to fall. Once the turn came, the Federal Reserve recovered its courage. The rediscount rate was raised to an unprecedented 6 percent. Loans by the Reserve Banks to banks, which had been increasing, tapered off and then fell sharply. In 1921, they were less than half the 1920 level. From mid-1920 on, the United States suffered what many believe to have been the sharpest depression to that time in its history. The Federal Reserve, facing its first major test, could not be said to have passed with flying or any other colors. By common agreement it assisted the boom and worsened the bust. This has always been considered an especially interesting error.[6]

The depression of 1920–1921 was soon over. In its brief passage, however, it showed a pattern of price behavior that was rich in portent. The American economy was no longer responding in homogeneous fashion to deflation and depression. The prices of farm products were showing a tendency to drop much faster and farther than industrial products. In 1921, wholesale prices of nonfarm products averaged 158 percent of their 1914 level. Farm products were only 124 percent

---

[6]His failure to act more aggressively to end the 1919 boom may have explained the nonreappointment in 1922 of W. P. G. Harding as Chairman (or Governor as then styled) of the Federal Reserve Board. However, as Professor Friedman has observed, he did not suffer too severely for his error. He became head of the Boston Federal Reserve Bank—the salary standard there, as earlier noted, being that of bankers rather than civil servants—at twice his Washington salary. Cf. Milton Friedman and Anna Jacobson Schwartz, *A Monetary History of the United States, 1867–1960.* Study by the National Bureau of Economic Research (Princeton: Princeton University Press, 1963), p. 229.

of that level.[7] Clearly, different forces were at work on these prices, and an obvious difference was that farm prices were made in the uncontrolled markets of many sellers and buyers. Industrial prices, made in markets of few sellers, were under much better private control. The consequences of this difference and this control would eventually be great.

An immediate consequence was a decade of agricultural discontent. Another was the birth of the immortal parity formula. Soon it was evident to farm leaders that it was not the level of farm prices that was important but their level in relation to other prices. From this came the thought that the prewar relationship of prices paid and received by farmers, which had been rather favorable, was the natural and just goal of agricultural policy. The prewar price of a farm product, increased by the increase since then in prices paid by the farmer, was parity. A final, less important consequence was a suspicion that maybe the Federal Reserve had contributed to the farmers' distress—a modest revival of the age-old fear of what a central bank might do to the farmer.

The depression of 1920–1921 was the first to test the nation's weariness with the anarchy of unregulated banking and the resulting failures and the ability of the Federal Reserve to cope. This test also was failed. In 1921, 505 banks suspended, a more than threefold increase over the year before. And the number of failures continued high—in only two of the years through 1929 was the number smaller than in 1921. Most of the failures were of the small nonmember state banks. The old compromise, which allowed the rural areas to have the casual lending, deposit- and money-creation that they believed to fit their needs and to have also the consequences, was still in being. But an appreci-

---

[7]U.S. Bureau of the Census, *Historical Statistics of the United States, Colonial Times to 1957* (Washington, D.C., 1960), p. 117.

able and growing number of failures were of members of the Federal Reserve System. And these were larger; they accounted through the '20s for from a third to, in some years, a half of all the deposits of the failed banks.[8]

The great expectations notwithstanding, the United States was still without an agency for watching bank performance and for rescue when too many people came for hard money. In fact, during these years, the Federal Reserve seemed not to suppose that bank failures were within its purview. "Each year the Board reported the melancholy figures . . . and confined itself to noting that suspensions were in disproportionate number of nonmember rather than member banks, of banks in small communities . . . of banks in agricultural rather than industrial areas."[9] This too had portent when in the next decade banks everywhere, large and small, member and nonmember, fell like trees in a cyclone.

The first test, then, of the new American monetary arrangements was not ambiguous. There was no improvement on the experience of the nineteenth century. Now a much more severe test was put in train. Those who arrange life for men of financial reputation and eminence are not favorable to rest.

Following the depression of 1921 came the eight fat years. These were not fat for all. Farmers were disgruntled and articulate. Workers whose unions had been effectively broken by and during the 1921 slump; blacks and other minorities; women, needless to say— were all voiceless, and none could tell the extent of their dissatisfaction.

What is certain is that beneath the pleasant façade

[8]U.S. Bureau of the Census, *Historical Statistics,* p. 117.
[9]Friedman and Schwartz, pp. 269–270.

there were flaws. Wages and prices from 1922 to 1929 were almost stable.[10] Since both output and productivity were expanding (output per worker in manufacturing in the '20s increased by an estimated 43 percent),[11] this meant that profits were increasing. Net income for a sample of 84 large manufacturing firms nearly tripled between 1922 and 1929; their dividend payments doubled.[12] Assisted by successive reductions in the income tax, this meant that the share of income going to the affluent for consumption and investment greatly increased. This income had to be spent or invested. Were anything to interrupt this consumption or investment, there would be a failure of demand—and trouble.

Both the spending and the investment were vulnerable. The spending of the rich could decline were they subject to a bad fright—as, for example, from a bad slump in the stock market. A considerable share of their investment was in foreign loans—to German cities, South American republics. Many things could happen to this kind of investment—revolution, repudiation, difficulty in acquiring the requisite gold or dollars for payment of interest or principal—which would cause fright to investors. Much of the domestic lending was to the promotions of the current generation of financial geniuses—the railroads of the Van Sweringens, the utilities of Samuel Insull and Howard C. Hopson, the more diverse and shadowy operations of Ivar Kreuger. All of these involved a complex, and on occasion incomprehensible, structure of holding compa-

---

[10]The trend of wholesale prices, a point stressed by Professor Friedman in noting that this was not a time of general inflation, was very slightly down. Cf. Friedman and Schwartz, p. 296 et seq.

[11]John Kenneth Galbraith, *The Great Crash, 1929* 3rd ed. (Boston: Houghton Mifflin Co., 1972), p. 180. From W. Arndt, *The Economic Lessons of the Nineteen-Thirties* (London: Oxford University Press, 1944), p. 15.

[12]U.S. Bureau of the Census, *Historical Statistics*, p. 591. Based on computations of the National Bureau of Economic Research.

nies in which the upstream corporations issued bonds (and preferred stock) to buy and hold the stock of those downstream toward the operating companies. This gave control with minimal investment. It also meant that if anything interrupted the upward flow of dividends—from which the interest charges on the upper-level bonds had to be met—the bonds would go into default, the whole structure collapse in bankruptcy. No more outside money would be invested then. And not much would be invested elsewhere by those who so lost.

The holding-company promotions together with the investment trusts were the wonder of the '20s, and those who brought them off were the giants of the time. Both the promotions and the promoters were, in all respects, the precursors of the conglomerates, performance funds, growth funds, offshore funds and real estate investment trusts, and their builders and unbuilders who were to grace and then ungrace the financial scene of the '60s and '70s.

Finally, and derived in part from the profits of the period and in fact from the seeming genius of the great promoters, was the stock market boom. Stocks started going up in the last half of 1924 and continued on up in 1925. There was a brief setback in 1926. In that year two hurricanes and the exhaustion of the supply of new buyers that is needed to keep any speculation going brought the collapse of the great Florida land boom. But in 1927, the upward movement was resumed, and it continued to gain momentum through that year, through 1928 and until September 1929. The *New York Times* average of twenty-five industrials, which had been 134 at the end of 1924, 245 at the end of 1927, was 331 at the beginning of 1929. It went from 339 to 449 in the three summer months of that year, a gain of 32 percent. As before, individuals and institutions, notably the new investment trusts, the forerunners of the mutual funds, were buying because they expected prices to go up. Their buying caused prices to go up, caused their expectations to be realized and fostered new and yet greater expectations and the resulting rush to buy. This rush, let it be said once more, would last until the supply of new buyers that affirmed the expectations ran out or something happened to reverse the expectations. When this happened, as following the collapse of foreign lending or the failure of the big holding-company structures, investors could be expected to yield to their fears. Both investment and consumer expenditures would fall.

In financing the sale of bad securities and in nourishing the stock market speculation, a leading part was played in these years by the new monetary system.

The underwriting of securities in the '20s was extensively financed by the commercial banks, and much of it in this period was done by the affiliates of the commercial banks. The speculative purchase of securities by individuals was similarly financed. Much of this, being in anticipation of gains, was done on margin. This is to say that the banks provided the funds for the purchase of the stock and took the latter as collateral.

The commercial banks that were lending money for these operations were, in turn, borrowing substantially from the Federal Reserve. Thus the Federal Reserve System was helping to finance the great stock market boom. It would be wrong to say that it was the cause; men and women do not speculate because they have the money to do so. But the Federal Reserve System did nourish the speculation, and it did not stop it.[18]

---

[18]In earlier writing on this period I have argued, as here, that speculation does not occur merely because money is available for such use. Professor Friedman has noted against me that one can exempt the System from responsibility for causing the boom without relieving it of responsibility for stopping it. This correction I would accept. Cf. Friedman and Schwartz, p. 291.

The nourishment to the boom by the Federal Reserve was, according to the accepted legend, the result of another interesting error. On July 1, 1927, the *Mauretania* arrived in New York with two notable passengers, Montagu Norman, Governor of the Bank of England, and Hjalmar Schacht, the head of the Reichsbank. (It was not a moment of general prescience. Alexander Kerensky, ending an American visit that day, told the papers that the Soviet government was on its last legs and would disappear within a few months.) The secrecy covering the visit was extreme and to a degree ostentatious. The names of neither of the great bankers appeared on the passenger list. Neither, on arriving, met with the press, although, according to the *New York Times,* Dr. Schacht, on emerging from the dining room on the way in from quarantine, "paused long enough to announce that he had nothing to say."[14] Sir Montagu hurried upstairs, waving his hand, and was altogether less cooperative.

In New York the two men were joined by Charles Rist, the Deputy Governor of the Banque de France, and they went into conference with Benjamin Strong, the Governor of the Federal Reserve Bank of New York. By this time the doubts as to who was running the Federal Reserve System—the Board in Washington, the spaciously and democratically distributed District Banks, the New York Federal Reserve Bank—had narrowed down to a gentlemanly struggle between New York and Washington. The Old World bankers, as they were called by the *Times,* had no doubt that power lay with Governor Strong. On ensuing days there was much speculation as to the matters being discussed, nearly all of it wrong. These matters were, admittedly, of public consequence. Those discussing them were, in fact if not in precise law, public servants. That the public should be excluded from all knowledge

[14]The *New York Times,* July 2, 1927.

of their negotiations was, however, assumed. To a remarkable degree, that assumption where international monetary policy is concerned still holds.

The principal, or in any case the ultimately important, subject of discussion was the persistently weak reserve position of the Bank of England. This, the bankers thought, could be helped if the Federal Reserve System would ease interest rates, encourage lending. Holders of gold would then seek the higher returns from keeping their metal in London. And, in time, higher prices in the United States would ease the competitive position of British industry and labor. Thus the continuing shadow of Winston Churchill. If some of the gold went to Berlin which was still in the aftermath of the great inflation or to France which was seeking to make the Poincaré stabilization stick, that too was all to the good.

The Federal Reserve obliged. Soon after the meeting the rediscount rate was reduced from 4 to 3.5 percent. The reserves of the commercial banks were replenished in the next few months by open-market operations— by the purchase by the Federal Reserve Banks of $340 million in government securities. This, according to the common view (one still largely accepted), was the error that led to the great stock market speculation. At the moment when restraint was called for, the foreigners had persuaded the American authorities to be liberal for their benefit but at American expense. Adolph C. Miller, a member of the Federal Reserve Board who had disapproved, later described this action as "the greatest and boldest operation ever undertaken by the Federal Reserve System, and . . . [it] resulted in one of the most costly errors committed by it or any other banking system in the last 75 years!"[15] Professor Lionel Robbins of the London School of Economics, a high-

---

[15]Lionel Robbins, *The Great Depression* (New York: Macmillan Co., 1934), p. 53. Miller's statement is from testimony before the Senate Committee on Banking and Currency.

ly prestigious observer of these events, later said: "From that date, according to all evidence, the situation got completely out of control."[16]

In the American financial pantheon, along with Hamilton, Biddle, Jay Cooke and Salmon P. Chase, a more than minor niche is reserved for Benjamin Strong. More than any other American of his time he was thought able to meet the sophisticated financiers from the Old World on their own terms.[17] Nothing is more interesting than that the transaction with which his name is principally associated is this concession to Montagu Norman and Hjalmar Schacht. Such are the sources of fame. Not that they are peculiar to economics. Except for the Watergate scandal H. R. Haldeman and John Dean III would not have made the history books. Nor would Gordon Liddy. John Mitchell would have been a minor footnote. Both John Foster Dulles and Dean Rusk were distinguished by the magnitude of their mistakes in foreign policy. Save that he was associated with the worst-conducted war since that of 1812, no one would ever have heard of William C. Westmoreland. If all else fails, immortality can always be assured by adequate error.

In fact, there was a certain logic on Governor Strong's side—those who celebrate his historic mistake have oversimplified matters. The circumstances are again instructive.

Given the contemporary monetary disorders or difficulties of Germany, France and Britain, it was not surprising that, in the early '20s, many possessors of gold sought refuge for their hoards in the United States. Stocks, which were an unimaginable $2.9 bil-

---

[16]Robbins, p. 53.
[17]A theme of Lester V. Chandler, his very competent biographer, in *Benjamin Strong, Central Banker* (Washington: The Brookings Institution, 1958).

lion at the end of 1918, were $4.2 billion at the end
of 1926,[18] just prior to the arrival of the *Mauretania*
pilgrims. The gold was deposited, on arrival, in commercial banks where, had it been allowed to do so, it
could have sustained a major expansion in loans, notes
and deposits (always assuming that there were people
and firms in search of loans) with great inflationary
effect. This effect the Federal Reserve forestalled in
the '20s by open-market operations—by selling off
government securities acquired during the war for
gold and thus transferring the latter from the vaults of
the banks, where it would serve as reserves for loans
and deposits, to its own vaults. (In March 1923, it
established the Federal Open-Market Investment
Committee, Professor Samuelson's citizens of unique
power, to coordinate these operations. (Once the gold
was safely in the possession of the Federal Reserve, it
no longer had any necessary relation to commercial-
bank lending and deposits, and thus to the supply of
money. The Federal Reserve kept its lending to the
banks well below what its gold reserves would have allowed. What was lent depended on the interest rate it
charged the banks and, to some extent, on whether it
encouraged or discouraged bank borrowing. This lending, in turn, was what affected commercial bank reserves and the capacity of the commercial banks to
lend.

Thus, though the United States was on the gold
standard, the stock of gold did not greatly matter. Now
in peace, as earlier in war, the country had a managed
currency. Since the inflow of gold no longer had any
necessary effect on American loans, deposits, prices or
interest rates—since these were now determined by
Federal Reserve action—the classical forces redistribut-
ing gold under the gold standard no longer operated.
When gold came, there was no necessary fall in interest

---

[18]U.S. Bureau of the Census, *Historical Statistics*, p. 649.

rates; no expansion of loans and business activity; no rise in prices; nothing, in sum, to check the inflow of gold and encourage a new outflow as the operation of the classical gold standard required. A case could thus be made that Governor Strong, an unquestioned man of gold, in yielding to Schacht, Norman and Rist, was only doing what the gold standard was meant to do automatically. It is possible that he so saw matters, although such insight is more likely to come after the fact.

Nor is it wholly certain that a more severe policy in 1927 and thereafter would have stopped the stock market speculation. Other things might have been stopped first. Banks lend for ordinary commercial, industrial and agricultural purposes as well as for speculation. In the '20s the increase in aggregate lending by the commercial banks, that on real estate apart, was relatively moderate—from $23.0 billion in mid-1921 to $30.0 billion in mid-1929.[19] (Loans on real estate, where there was considerable speculation, increased by a much greater percentage.) But within the aggregate just mentioned, loans to brokers for carrying securities on margin, i.e., for speculation, went up hugely—from $810 million at the end of 1921 to $2.5 billion at the beginning of 1929, with as much more being contributed by corporations and other nonbank lenders. There was a further vast increase—in the summer months by around $400 million a month—in 1929.[20] The rate on brokers' loans, for which no offsetting allowance for rising prices had in those days to be made, was wonderful—it ranged from 6 to 12 percent and sometimes even more. This was 12 percent with nearly perfect safety, and the money available on immediate notice. Twelve percent is 12 percent. Accordingly, had the Federal Reserve tightened its rates and its lending, the banks, unless astonishingly im-

[19]U.S. Bureau of the Census, *Historical Statistics*, p. 631.
[20]U.S. Bureau of the Census, *Historical Statistics*, p. 660, and Galbraith, pp. 72–74.

mune to 12 percent, would have cut back on their far less profitable, much less safe, much more pedestrian borrowers for ordinary commercial, housing, industrial or agricultural purposes. These would have been the loans that would have been curbed. The fear that this would indeed happen greatly afflicted the mentally susceptible members of the Federal Reserve Board in Washington. Also a diminishing share of the stock market credit was coming from the banks. Corporations were increasingly being attracted by the high rates on call loans.[21]

The alternative was to warn, and possibly cut off, those banks specifically that were borrowing from the Federal Reserve to lend in the stock market. Unfortunately for this solution the worst offenders were the largest New York banks. And the big New York banks, in turn, lived cheek by jowl with the Federal Reserve Bank of New York. The National City Bank, with the Chase National one of the two largest, was then headed by one Charles E. Mitchell, an ebullient and, as later events established, remarkably obtuse man who was himself heavily involved in the market. Were the boom to collapse, so would Mitchell, a relationship that he was capable of seeing.

At the beginning of 1929, Mitchell, of all men, became a director of the New York Federal Reserve Bank. In February of 1929, the Federal Reserve Board in Washington, over the objections of the New York Federal Reserve Bank, issued a warning against using Federal Reserve funds to finance speculation. It was one that by no means threw caution to the winds: "A member [commercial bank] is not within its reasonable

---

[21]Business loans from the banks could also be recycled to the stock market. "With call rates at 10%, 15% and even 20%, it was profitable, for instance, for a businessman to pledge his inventories and other physical assets for a bank loan of 6%, 7% or 8% and lend the proceeds to a broker." Harold Barger, *The Management of Money* (Chicago: Rand McNally & Co., 1964), p. 91. It is my impression that the volume of this recycling was not great.

claims for re-discount facilities at its reserve bank when it borrows either for the purpose of making speculative loans or for the purpose of maintaining speculative loans."[22] It then hastened to say that what the banks did with their own, i.e., their depositors', money was their own business. This was an abject abdication of the basic responsibility of the central bank, which is to keep all bank lending under surveillance and any necessary control. The market quavered in response to this warning but soon recovered.

The Board turned to the consideration of further action or nonaction. In March word came that meetings were in progress at Federal Reserve headquarters in Washington; there was word even of an unprecedented Saturday session. The banks now took fright and began to curtail their stock market loans; on March 26, the call rate, i.e., the rate for carrying the securities on margin, reached 20 percent. The market tumbled on heavy trading. Now Mitchell took over. He announced that he felt an obligation "which is paramount to any Federal Reserve warning, or anything else, to avert any dangerous crisis in the money market."[23] Suiting action to his words and his personal needs, the National City the next day committed $25 million to brokers' loans to be fed out in $5 million chunks for each point that the call rate went above 16 percent. The market promptly recovered; Mitchell, though he did not escape criticism, continued with no known rebuke as a director.[24] The Federal Reserve Board made no further effort at restraint.

<hr />

[22]Quoted in Galbraith, p. 38.

[23]Quoted in Galbraith, p. 42.

[24]Mitchell did not survive. He was hit hard by the crash that autumn and was subsequently arrested for income tax evasion and sacked by the Bank. He was acquitted on the tax charge but was the subject of a long and costly civil suit seeking recovery of $1,100,000 in unpaid taxes. He had company; the fatal effects of association with money (as well as the rule in American life that those who, without visible qualification, achieve the greatest heights are also marked

Something in this sad performance must be attributed not to design but to incompetence. The American belief that anyone can become a central banker by the act of appointment has been sufficiently noticed, and it was operating with full force in the '20s. Herbert Hoover, who had described the Board members of the period as mediocrities, was not much more agreeable about Strong. He called him a mental annex to Europe. However, in 1927, things had slightly improved. Roy A. Young, a modestly more competent man, had replaced Daniel Crissinger, the steam-shovel lawyer. Young pressed for restriction on the bank lending that was for stock market speculation. However, during the course of 1929, he largely gave up; he concluded, as he later said, that the "hysteria," though it might be somewhat restrained, would have to run its course.[25]

There was yet another reason for keeping hands off which neither Young nor anyone else mentioned. That once again concerned blame. If the Federal Reserve moved strongly to limit lending for speculation, not only would it be responsible for ending the boom, it would also be responsible for the consequences. This would include the loss of hundreds of millions of dollars by hundreds of thousands of speculators, many of whom considered themselves wise, prudent and deserving investors. Plausibly, too, it would mean a de-

---

for the greatest depths) operated powerfully against Mitchell's two most distinguished colleagues of the period, Albert H. Wiggin, the head of the Chase, and Richard Whitney, then Vice-President and later President and principal defender of the New York Stock Exchange. Wiggin was fined for, among other things, going short on the stock of the Chase with money borrowed from the Chase, which he justified by saying that it gave him an interest in his work. Whitney, whose inadequacy, more juvenile than criminal, had not been noticed because of his social position, Harvard education and family connections, was convicted of stealing securities and sent to Sing Sing.

[25]Seymour E. Harris, *Twenty Years of Federal Reserve Policy,* Harvard Economic Studies, Vol. XLI (Cambridge: Harvard University Press, 1933), Part II, p. 547. This book is a valuable guide to the contemporary view of these important matters.

pression. Who would wish to incur the resulting anger?
Who would wish for the rest of his life to be so blamed
—and scorned? In the early summer of 1929, Paul M.
Warburg, who, in addition to being an architect of the
System and an initial Governor, was one of the most
prestigious figures in the financial community, warned
against the current orgy of "unrestrained speculation."
In a prescient comment he suggested that, if it continued, it would "bring about a general depression involving the entire country." He called for stronger
action by the Federal Reserve. The reaction was fierce;
the friendliest commentators said he had not caught
up with the spirit of the times. More candid ones
charged him with an act of sabotage—with "sandbag-
ging American prosperity." There were suggestions
that he might be short in the market. Warburg afterward told friends that it was the most difficult experience of his life.[26] How much better, as seen from the
Federal Reserve, to let nature take its course and thus
allow nature to take the blame.

The end came late that October. On Thursday,
October 24, after a succession of bad days, the bottom
was thought to have dropped out of the market. The
following Tuesday it did.

In subsequent days the panic eased but the market
continued to go down. There was a short-lived recovery
in the spring of 1930 and then a further decline. On
July 8, 1932, the *Times* industrial average was at 58
—a little more than an eighth of the level of three
years before. By then almost everything else was similarly scraping bottom. Gross National Product—the
total production of the economic system—was down
by more than a quarter from 1929 when measured in
prices of that year and by not much short of half in

---

[26]Galbraith, p. 77.

value. In 1929, unemployment—the estimates are after the fact and less than perfect—averaged 1.6 million through the year or 3.2 percent of the labor force. In 1932, it averaged 12.1 million or just under a quarter of the labor force. The following year it was even greater. There was no unemployment compensation; provision for the indigent, in accordance with a grave constitutional principle much cited by the affluent, was held to be a local responsibility. All prices had fallen by about a third from the 1929 level but farm prices had taken an especially ghastly slide. In 1929, wholesale prices of nonfarm products had averaged 92 percent of the 1926 level (1926 = 100). In 1932, they were down to 70, a drop of around one-fourth. Wholesale prices of farm products were 105 in 1929; in 1932, they averaged 48 percent of the 1926 level, a drop of more than half in three years.[27] Once again, for further reference, the different forces working on different parts of the economy are to be noted.

Output continued low, prices continued low and unemployment continued high for all the rest of the decade. Not until 1937 was Gross National Product again as high as in 1929, and not until 1941 did unemployment, as then calculated, fall to less than 10 percent of the labor force.[28] The 1920–1921 depression was sharp but short. That of the '30s was sharp and very, very long.

---

[27] U.S. Bureau of the Census, *Historical Statistics,* pp. 73, 116, 139.
[28] In these years those employed on WPA and other work relief projects were counted as unemployed. As this work was regarded and compensated, this may well have been appropriate.

CHAPTER XIV

When the Money Stopped

THERE IS A CASE that, for its effect on the anxieties of people and in consequence on their behavior, the Great Depression is the most important event in the century so far—at least for Americans. Neither of the two wars had a similar effect on so many; the release of atomic energy, while it may have induced some added measure of caution among the pathologically belligerent, was of yet less consequence. The journeys to the moon were a detail in comparison. Few who lived through the Great Depression were unchanged by the experience.

In contrast to the wars, very little attention has been given to the factors which converted the uncomfortable and distressing crises of the previous century into this profound and enduring tragedy. For Marxists it was simply another manifestation of the fateful tendency of capitalism; it was worse than its predecessors because the capitalist crisis was meant to get worse until the ultimate apocalyptic collapse. For orthodox scholars of the time it was another downturn in the business cycle, one that was quite possibly prolonged by misguided efforts of governments to bring it to an end.

Neither the stock market crash nor the antecedent speculation has usually been thought a decisive cause. The market was a response to deeper and more fundamental forces; it was not itself a major cause of change. "Prosperity began to fade in early 1929, although the public did not begin to realize it until after the sensational stock market crash in October."[1] There was something superficial in attributing anything so awful as the Great Depression to anything so insubstantial as speculation in common stocks. And perhaps, also, a certain protective instinct was at work. The stock market has usually been considered by the righteous to be morally depraved. Why give the enemies of Wall Street more ammunition than they already have? Why make the speculation socially significant too?

In a mature view the speculation of the late '20s and the stock market collapse were matters of importance. As earlier noted, the prosperity of the '20s was strongly skewed in favor of the earnings of business and the incomes of the rich. In consequence, continued prosperity depended on continuing high investment expenditures by business, continuing high consumer expenditures by the affluent. The stock market crash struck a mortal blow at both. As share values came rushing down, prudence in all investment decisions rose as a reciprocal. Solid enterprises began to reconsider their investment commitments. The jerry-built structures of Hopson, Kreuger, the Van Sweringens, Insull and Foshay were forced to retrench, for soon their creators were without the cash to pay interest on the huge bond issues by which they had constructed their pyramids. Banks were suddenly cautious. Borrowers had been caught in the market. Soon depositors might take fright. Better to have plenty of cash. And individual investors, their fingers badly scorched, were also poor prospects for the new issues of securities.

The blight on consumer expenditures was equally severe. Those who until October had been spending capital gains no longer had them. Many not directly affected thought it prudent to behave as though they had been. Not much happened to business in the weeks

---

[1]Paul Studenski and Herman E. Krooss, *Financial History of the United States* (New York: McGraw-Hill Book Co., 1952), p. 353.

before the October storm; in the weeks following, the retreat was devastating. In recent years Charles P. Kindleberger, an economist and historian with a useful resistance to cliché, has re-examined the evidence. His cautious conclusion: "In the light of the sudden collapse of business, commodity prices and imports at the end of 1929, it is difficult to maintain that the stock market was a superficial phenomenon . . ."[2] The stock market crash was not a slight affair. The economy was vulnerable to its blow, and given that vulnerability, the blow was a most important thing.

Once the devastation that followed the crash was fully in process, the monetary history of the previous decade was repeated with remarkable precision in mirror image. It is possible that the Federal Reserve could not then have stopped the deflation and depression as, before the crash, it could not safely have arrested the speculation. But, as during the upsurge, what it did made things worse. As in 1919 through 1921, monetary management heightened the boom and accentuated the bust.

In the months following the crash the Federal Reserve Banks did reduce interest rates—the rediscount rate of the New York Federal Reserve Bank (as noted, the rate that it charged the member banks for loans), which had been 6 percent before the crash, was reduced by .5 percent steps to 1.5 percent in 1931. This, none could doubt, was a less than usurious figure. However, the downward steps were widely spaced, a very slow response to the ghastly reductions in output, employment and prices that were now taking place. And the other Federal Reserve Banks, exploiting their

---

[2]Charles P. Kindleberger, *The World in Depression 1929–1939* (Berkeley and Los Angeles: University of California Press, 1973), p. 127.

admired autonomy, lagged far behind. More important, open-market purchases of securities were not encouraged but avoided. Increasingly in these years depositors, individually or in droves, were descending on banks for cash. The obvious course for the Federal Reserve was to buy government securities, flood the banks with the resulting funds. These the banks could loan if they were wanted; in any case, they would be there when, as sooner or later happened to most, the dreaded lines formed and a run was on. But not until 1932 did the Federal Reserve Banks undertake open-market operations on any appreciable scale.

The reason for this obtuseness—all authorities agree that it was an especially interesting error—is one for which the reader will by now be prepared. In the making of monetary policy we have seen those involved react with the utmost reliability not to the current but to the most striking recent experience. In the 1930s, the vivid recent experience of economists, financial experts, bankers and politicians was with inflation. A mere fifteen years before, during World War I, prices had doubled. The reaction was deeply adverse. And only a decade earlier in Germany and eastern Europe, prices had run away, money had become worthless. In the '20s and '30s, also, there was the great migration of economists from Austria, Germany and central Europe to England and the United States. All had had first-hand experience of hyper-inflation. In normal consequence then, the reputable warnings in these years of extreme deflation were of the grave danger of inflation. The perception of this nonexistent danger was especially sharp in the Federal Reserve Banks; these, above all, were the approved centers of the conventional financial wisdom.[3] This

---

[3]On this see Lester V. Chandler, *America's Greatest Depression, 1929–1941* (New York: Harper & Row, 1970), p. 113 et seq.

perception kept the Federal Reserve System from easing more adequately the position of the increasingly beset commercial banks.[4]

Although the fear of inflation was the most important force immobilizing the financial mind, two other factors were strongly at work in these years. One was the purgative conception of economic policy. This held that the boom built damaging, though often unspecified, distortions into the economic system. Recovery could only come as these were eliminated. Deflation and bankruptcy were the natural correctives. Joseph Schumpeter, his country's Finance Minister during much of the Austrian inflation, was now emerging as a major figure on the American economic scene. He argued that the economic system had, through depression, to expel its own poisons. Looking at the history of business cycles, he concluded that no recovery was ever permanent until this happened and that any public intervention to speed recovery merely postponed the therapy and therewith the recovery. Lionel Robbins, as noted the most admired voice of British orthodoxy, offered essentially the same advice in the most famous book on the Depression: "Nobody wishes for bankruptcies. Nobody likes liquidation as such . . . [But] when the extent of mal-investment and over-indebtedness has passed a certain limit, measures which postpone liquidation only tend to make matters worse."[5] A rather cruder formulation came from Secretary of the Treasury Andrew Mellon. To promote recovery, he ad-

---

[4]There were exceptions. A man with a notably differing view was Eugene Meyer (father of Katharine Meyer Graham) who became head of the Federal Reserve Board in 1930. He used his post to press for a less restrictive policy. Against the weight of orthodox opinion he did not prevail.

[5]Lionel Robbins, *The Great Depression* (New York: Macmillan Co., 1934), p. 62 et seq., especially p. 75.

vised, the country needed to "liquidate labor, liquidate stocks, liquidate the farmers, liquidate real estate."[6]

Finally there was the business confidence syndrome. This, a powerful thing at the time, of which traces still remain, held that the views of bankers and businessmen had to be respected even when they were wrong and positively inimical to recovery. For, if action were taken in opposition to these views, business confidence would be impaired. Impaired confidence would mean reduced investment, reduced output, reduced employment and worsened depression. It followed therefore that the right steps, if taken in opposition to the views of businessmen and the financial community, would be the wrong steps. Since the more reputable bankers and businessmen feared action by the government to provide relief for the indigent, employ the unemployed and otherwise expand demand, the confidence syndrome powerfully favored inaction.

Herbert Hoover was deeply committed to the confidence syndrome and, to the end, sought to convert his successor. Writing to Roosevelt in early 1933, he expressed his conviction that "a very early statement by you upon two or three policies of your Administration would serve greatly to restore confidence and cause a resumption of the march of recovery." Among the promises that he thought would do most for confidence would be that of a balanced budget with all that implied as regards spending for relief and employment and "no tampering or inflation of the currency."[7]

Once deflation of prices and contraction of output were well under way, further forces converged to keep

---

[6]Herbert Hoover, *The Memoirs of Herbert Hoover: The Great Depression 1929-1941* (New York: Macmillan Co., 1952), p. 30. Hoover's memoirs are no model of accuracy. However, this quotation, if possibly impressionistic, undoubtedly recalls Mellon's attitude.

[7]Arthur M. Schlesinger, Jr., *The Crisis of the Old Order* (Boston: Houghton Mifflin Co., 1957), p. 476.

them going, give them cumulative effect. As noted, singed and frightened individuals reduced their purchases. This affected the prices, output and employment of their suppliers, and that had yet further effect on demand. And singed and frightened investors stopped investing and hung on to cash. So income that was saved was no longer invested and spent, and this too had further effect. And workers lost jobs and reduced their spending. And in consequence prices and output fell, with yet further effect on prices, production and employment. Neither then nor since has anyone attached a precise or even an imprecise weight to these several deflationary forces. However, two with particular bearing on the history of money or its prospect require special attention.

One was the tendency, as the Depression deepened in 1930, 1931 and 1932, for firms with some control over their prices—the kind of control that farmers, for example, lack—to seek a competitive advantage with price cuts and then to reduce wages in compensation for the reduced return. When this happened, others in the industry followed; soon there developed a downward spiral, the obverse of the modern inflationary spiral. Instead of prices pulling up wages and wages pulling up prices, prices forced down wages so that each price cut led to a new round of wage reductions.

President Hoover held out against such wage reductions, though with no strongly evident effect. He believed that they reduced purchasing power, accentuated deflation. With the coming of the New Deal it was the principal purpose of the NRA (National Recovery Administration) to arrest this downward spiral. Its codes were a direct intervention, the counterpart of later wage and price controls, designed to halt the spiral.

Economists at the time gave both Hoover and the NRA poor marks. Such intervention was in conflict with the free and competitive operation of markets. To prevent wage reductions was to preclude normal and desirable reductions in labor costs. Such reductions led to more profitable operations, more employment. That wage reductions adversely affected aggregate purchasing power and demand was not thought important. In the end, the orthodox view of the NRA prevailed. Its going was greatly welcomed.

In the longer light of history, the case for President Hoover and the NRA is much better than it seemed at the time. There is now little doubt that, in the modern industrial economy, prices and wages can interact to produce strong, autonomous movements in money incomes and prices. And direct intervention to arrest these movements, in the forty years after the NRA, has been a recurring issue in economic policy. Hoover and the framers of the NRA were reacting in straightforward fashion to circumstance which was, as often, a better guide to action than the prevailing theory.

The other deflationary force to be noticed in these years was the bank failure. This too operated with cumulative effect. As word spread that a bank was in trouble, people came, as ever before, for their money. And then even the best bank was in trouble. And as the lines formed outside one bank, anxiety developed over its neighbors. In what is the best first-hand account written of such an experience, Marriner Eccles, afterward Chairman of the Board of Governors of the Federal Reserve System but then the head of a group of Utah banks of high reputation, told of what happened at one of his banks when word came that a neighboring institution, the Ogden State Bank, would not open its doors that day:

I told . . . [the staff] what they would have to face in a few hours. "If you want to keep this bank open," I said, "you must do your part. Go about your business as though nothing unusual was happening. Smile, be pleasant, talk about the weather, show no signs of panic. The main burden is going to fall on you boys in the savings department. Instead of the three windows we normally use, we are going to use all four of them today. They must be manned at all times because if any teller's or clerk's window in this bank closes for even a short time, that will stir up more panic. We'll have sandwiches brought in; no one can go out to lunch. We can't break this run today. The best we can do is slow it down. People are going to come here to close out their savings accounts. You are going to pay them. But you are going to pay them very slowly. It's the only chance we have to deal with the panic. You know a lot of depositors by sight, and in the past you did not have to look up their signatures, but today when they come here with their deposit books to close out their accounts, you are going to look up every signature card. And take your time about it. And one other thing: when you pay out, don't use any big bills. Pay out in fives and tens, and count slowly. Our object is to pay out a minimum today."

The tellers and clerks ably carried out their part of the act despite the crowd that surged through the doors of the bank the moment they were opened . . .

. . . The crowd in the bank was as taut as it was dense. Some people had been waiting for hours to draw out their money. If we tried to close at three, there was no telling what might happen. But, as in all other things, a poverty of alternatives made us adopt the boldest one. We decided to make an exception of this one day and to remain open so long as there were people who wanted to get their money.

In the meantime a call had been put through to the Federal Reserve Bank in Salt Lake City to send currency to our Ogden banks as well as to all others in the First Security Corporation. The armored car that brought funds to us in Ogden arrived on the scene as in the movies when the Union cavalry charged in to save all from the Indians. The guards strode through the crush inside the bank, and all made way before them . . .

. . . Mounting the counter, I raised my hand and called for attention:

"Just a minute!"

There was instant silence.

"Just a minute!" I repeated. "I want to make an announcement. It appears that we are having some difficulty handling our depositors with the speed to which you are accustomed. Many of you have been in line for a considerable time. I notice a lot of pushing and shoving and irritation. I just wanted to tell you that instead of closing at the usual hour of three o'clock, we have decided to stay open just as long as there is anyone who desires to withdraw his deposit or make one. Therefore, you people who have just come in can return later this afternoon or evening if you wish. There is no justification for the excitement or the apparent panicky attitude on the part of some depositors. As all of you have seen, we have just had brought up from Salt Lake City a large amount of currency that will take care of all your requirements. There is plenty more where that came from." (This was true enough—but I didn't say we could get it.)[8]

The Eccles bank survived as, with much distinction, has Eccles.

In 1929, 659 banks failed, a fair number after the crash. In 1930, 1352 went under and in 1931, 2294. Failures were still the most numerous among the small nonmember banks of the old compromise. But now when the rumors spread and the lines formed, no bank was safe. Federal Reserve members went down with the rest. And presently it became evident that even the big New York banks were no longer safe. In 1931, it will be recalled, Governor Harrison of the New York Federal Reserve Bank found himself re-examining his uncompassionate belief that the "failure of [the] small banks . . . could be isolated."[9] His thoughts along these lines had almost certainly been stimulated in December 1930 by the failure of the Bank of the

---

[8]Marriner S. Eccles, *Beckoning Frontiers* (New York: Alfred A. Knopf, 1951), pp. 58–60. Quoted with permission.
[9]See Chapter IX, page 138.

United States. With deposits of $200 million, this was the largest commercial bank to fail in American history. The bank played an important part in financing the New York garment industry. And its unfortunate name led numerous foreigners to the belief—so it has always been said—that the credit of the United States government was in some way involved. The New York Federal Reserve Bank had tried to interest the big New York banks in a joint rescue operation. They had thought it better to let the Bank of the United States go. There was some doubt as to whether it was worth saving. More important, it was known in reputable New York banking circles as a Jewish outfit. Thus, in a common attitude of the time, no real loss.

When a bank failed, the depositors no longer had their money to spend. So their spending was reduced. And loans and deposits were no longer created on behalf of borrowers. So their investment and further spending fell. And the balances of the failed bank in other banks were called as liquidation proceeded. So the loans of those banks fell and were called, as therewith also investment and spending. And other banks were suffused with caution and called and denied loans with similar effect. "Banking failures were survived only by those banks which were most quick and expert in converting themselves into safety deposit institutions."[10] Both bank failures and the fear of bank failures thus had the same effect. Both were forces of compelling power to induce deflation—to contract consumer spending, investment spending and therewith sales, output, employment and prices. In these years the monetary system became an engine with such effect. Not that cause and effect ran only from the monetary system to the economy. While failing banks were bringing down the economy, falling prices, output, earnings and employment were ruining good loans,

---

[10]Remark of Jacob Viner, one of the most distinguished economists of the time. Quoted in Studenski and Krooss, p. 379.

spreading alarm and bringing down the banks. Economic life, as always, is a matrix in which result becomes cause and cause becomes result.

In 1932, the Federal Reserve finally overcame its fear of inflation and began open-market operations. Government securities were purchased; cash, accordingly, flowed out to the banks. It was too late. The frightened bankers held on to the currency so received as added insurance against the day when their depositors came. Partly from this fear they would soon come to hold reserves far in excess of requirements, and this would be so for many years to come.

Nor did this change of heart mean that the Federal Reserve System was now ready to assume the classic role of lender of last resort. If a bank was in good shape with plenty of cash on hand, its loans might be rediscounted at its Federal Reserve Bank. If it desperately needed money, this suggested trouble, and its assets were examined with a detached eye. Walter Bagehot, in a famous account of the functions of a central bank, said that in moments of great crisis it should loan liberally but at high interest. In these years the Federal Reserve reversed this classic advice. It loaned illiberally at low interest rates.

By the end of 1933, nearly half of all the nation's banks had disappeared. And as early as the beginning of 1932, there were few whose officers did not wonder if they would be among the casualties. Under such circumstances, the concept of a lender of last resort was no academic detail that could be left to the cautious preferences of the Federal Reserve. It was something for which every banker urgently yearned. The Federal Reserve remaining in default as regards this duty, a special lender of last resort had to be created. This was done in 1932; the Reconstruction Finance Corporation was brought into existence.

The RFC, desperate though was the need, also got off to a slow start. By now many banks had few viable assets to use as collateral. They needed capital as well as loans. And there was the fear, if not of inflation, at least of unduly energetic action. "Our private credit structure is inextricably bound to the credit of the United States government," Ogden L. Mills, then Secretary of the Treasury and a cherished voice of financial wisdom, told a radio audience in March 1932, adding, "Our currency rests predominantly upon the credit of the United States. Impair that credit [as by unduly precipitate action] and every dollar you handle will be tainted with suspicion."[11] That a declining number of Americans had any dollars at all to handle was a point that, characteristically, escaped the Secretary's mind.

The first head of the RFC, former Vice-President Charles G. Dawes, was also less than ideal. Pre-eminently he was that peculiarly American persona, the free-lance, cliché statesman. These are men of impressive self-confidence and great predictability of thought —John W. Davis and John J. McCloy are famous examples—who are called upon by Presidents when either wisdom or action must be simulated. Though he accomplished little else, Dawes did succeed in wonderfully dramatizing the role of the lender of last resort. In June of 1932, he abruptly resigned, announcing that he was returning to tend to the affairs of the Central Republic Bank of Chicago from which he was on leave. These affairs needed attention. A few days later the Central Republic got a loan of $90 million from the RFC. The bank was in singularly weak condition. Its deposits at the time were $95 million. The assets previously available to support the deposits must have been truly negligible.[12]

The RFC notwithstanding, the runs continued. And

[11]Quoted in Chandler, p. 123.
[12]Schlesinger, p. 238.

by late 1932 and early 1933, they had ceased to involve individual banks and small banks and now spread over whole communities and even states. They also extended into the principal financial centers and to the big banks. The remedy that now occurred to the authorities, as the runs became pandemic, was to close up all the banks in the community before their depositors closed them up anyway. At the end of October 1932, all the Nevada banks were thus placed on vacation. In early February 1933, word came that the Hibernia Bank and Trust Company of New Orleans was in bad shape. To provide a plausible excuse while the bank won time to go to the RFC, Governor Huey P. Long considered proclaiming a holiday in honor of Jean Laffite, the distinguished pirate. He was dissuaded and, in a thoughtful gesture, commemorated instead of breaking of diplomatic relations with Germany sixteen years before. A fortnight later the storm hit Michigan. One of the two bank-holding companies that did much of the banking in the state, the Union Guardian Trust, was in deep trouble and pleading with the RFC for help. James Couzens, the liberal Republican who, more than Ford himself, made Henry Ford, saw no reason to use taxpayers' money to bail out a badly managed bank in his home state or anywhere else. Nor did Henry Ford. He was asked, as the largest individual depositor, to subordinate his claims to a rescue loan. It was a public duty. Ford felt no such duty. So all the Michigan banks had to be closed. In other states people heard the news and started en masse for their money. More holidays were proclaimed. Three weeks later when Roosevelt was inaugurated, only the banks in the Northeast were still doing business. On March 6, 1933, by Executive Order deriving its authority from the Trading with the Enemy Act of World War I, the holiday was made nationwide. In previous weeks citizens had been supplying themselves with cash in a precautionary way—in February the currency in circulation rose from $5.7 billion to $6.7 billion.[13] This money was a trifle, however, as compared with the more than $30 billion of deposits[14] now unavailable in the vacationing commercial banks.

In 1923, Germany had had so much money that it was worthless. Now ten years later in the United States there was almost none. Clearly there was something still to be learned about the management of money.

In Germany early in 1933, Adolf Hitler came to power. Much of his success must be attributed to the massive unemployment and the deeply painful contraction in wages, salaries, prices and property values following on Brüning's manic defense of the mark. In the United States in March, Roosevelt came to power. His predecessor had been unseated from the Presidency, unusual after only one term, because he, his advisers and his central bank had been for so long immobilized by the fear of inflation. Whatever the importance of money, none could doubt the importance of the fears it engendered.

The banks did not remain closed long enough to reveal how a modern economy might function—or fail to function—without money. Those who were known to have jobs or assets were given goods against a later promise to pay. Those who had neither jobs nor money were given no such help. But they had had neither money nor help before the banks closed. The economy operated during these days at a very low level. But it had been operating at a very low level before the bank holiday began. There was certainly more deprivation and more suffering in the United States when the money stopped than in Germany when it flooded into

---

[13]*Federal Reserve Bulletin,* Vol. 19, No. 4 (April 1933), p. 215.
[14]U.S. Bureau of the Census, *Historical Statistics of the United States, Colonial Times to 1957* (Washington, D. C., 1960), p. 632. The figure for June 30, 1933, was $32 billion. This was down from $49.4 billion on June 30, 1929, an indication, among other things, of the amount of money extinguished by the bank failures.

worthlessness. But both experiences lingered long in the national memories.[15]

With the arrival of Roosevelt the gold standard was suspended—notes and deposits ceased to be exchangeable at the banks for gold coin. This was an act of choice, not necessity. Although in the months before Roosevelt's inauguration there were substantial foreign and domestic withdrawals of gold, reserves in the United States were still large. In World War I, Frenchmen and Englishmen had been asked to turn in their gold. Now a sterner American government instructed its citizens and business firms to do so. Most complied. A noted Harvard professor of finance who contested the right of the government to sequester his treasure was fired, his tenure notwithstanding. There were rumors, however, that he also had been involved in some dubious utility promotions. There will be occasion for another word about gold in the next chapter.

By legislation in 1933, 1934 and 1935, the Federal Reserve System was extensively reformed. All doubt as to where power lay was now brought to an end. The Secretary of the Treasury and the Comptroller of the Currency were deleted from the Federal Reserve Board; the seven members of the Board of Governors of the Federal Reserve System, as henceforth it was styled, were given fourteen-year terms, forbidden reappointment and placed in full authority over the District Banks, including their personnel. Not since then has the name of the head of a District Bank been celebrated, and, except to their wives and neighbors, the names of few are known. ". . .[S]ince 1933, one of the strongest trends has been the erosion of the

---

[15]The banks, those that seemed reasonably solvent, were reopened by March 15. Many remained closed for reorganization or eventual liquidation.

power of the regional Federal Reserve Banks."[16]
Among the new powers given the Board were those to
change the reserves that the commercial banks were
required to keep in their Reserve Bank and to
specify the margin required of those who were speculating in securities.

Now, at long last, in all important respects the
United States had a central bank. Predictably this was
the achievement of the Democrats, the party that, being
most suspicious of such centralization and such power,
could authorize it without being suspected of evil. It
has been suggested that any organization that has
been perfected as to form is already in decline. After
1933, the Federal Reserve could be thought evidence
in this case. For the next quarter-century it was very
much out of the mainstream of economic policy.

In the banking legislation passed in 1933, there was
one provision that was opposed by conservatives and
the new Administration alike. This was authored by
Representative Henry B. Steagall of Alabama, who
had a reputation for eccentricity, even crankiness,
where money was concerned, and by Senator Arthur
Vandenberg of Michigan; it provided for the insurance
of bank deposits. A special corporation, the Federal
Deposit Insurance Corporation, would be chartered
and capitalized by the Treasury and the Federal Reserve Banks. Insurance would be available to the depositors of all banks—state or national, members or
nonmembers of the Federal Reserve—which chose to
join. The dangers of the proposal were evident to all.

---

[16]Sherman J. Maisel, *Managing the Dollar* (New York: W. W.
Norton & Co., 1973), p. 158. Professor Maisel, a former member of
the Board of Governors, places the power of the regional bank
fourth after the Chairman of the Board of Governors, the staff and
the members of the Board of Governors.

The best banks would now have to accept responsibility for the recklessness of the worst. The worst, knowing that someone else would have to pay, would have a license for reckless behavior that the supervision authorized by the legislation could not hope to restrain. The American Bankers Association led the fight against the plan "to the last ditch," holding it to be "unsound, unscientific, unjust and dangerous"[17] as well as otherwise unsatisfactory. Perhaps it would even mean a return to the wildest days of wildcat banking.

In all American monetary history no legislative action brought such a change as this. Not since, to this writing, have the lines formed outside one bank and then spread ineluctably to the others in the town. Almost never have the lines formed at all. Nor was there reason why they should. A government insurance fund was now back of the deposits; no matter what happened to the bank, the depositors would get theirs. And since the insuring agency, the Federal Deposit Insurance Corporation, had to pay for recklessness, it had an iron-clad reason for the supervision and intervention that would preclude recklessness. In a further sense the FDIC was what the Federal Reserve had not succeeded in being—an utterly reliable lender of last resort, one that would immediately and without cavil come forward with whatever money was needed to cover the insured deposits. In 1933, 4004 banks failed or were found unfit to reopen after the bank holiday. In 1934, failures fell to 62, only nine of which were insured. Eleven years later, in 1945, failures in all of the United States were down to one.[18] The anarchy of uncontrolled banking had been brought to an end not by the Federal Reserve System but by the obscure, unprestigious, unwanted Federal Deposit Insurance Corporation.

---

[17]Arthur M. Schlesinger, Jr., *The Coming of the New Deal* (Boston: Houghton Mifflin Co., 1958), p. 443.
[18]U.S. Bureau of the Census. *Historical Statistics,* pp. 636–637.

CHAPTER XV

The Threat
of the Impossible

IN THE MOST QUOTED LINE of his First Inaugural Address, Franklin Roosevelt adverted to the highly operative role of fear in economic affairs. He had reference to the way in which fear of loss of jobs, farms, dwellings, bank deposits or a business was causing people to behave with an unreasoning caution that made everything worse. Even on March 4, 1933, he could have adverted to the continuing effects of the fear of inflation which, in its own way, had an even more paralyzing effect on public action and which, in the months ahead, would be his own principal hazard. This fear, by excluding any action that might increase the supply of money, any action that might increase expenditures and thus the uncovered deficit, any action that might seem to threaten to do these things and thus impair business confidence and involve the confidence syndrome, was capable, so far as it might prevail, of excluding all public action to promote recovery. There was, for example, very little that could be done outside the field of oratory that did not, in some degree, increase public expenditures.

The election of Roosevelt had, in fact, deepened the fear of inflation. As the Depression continued and worsened, there had stirred in Congress the old flame. Senator Key Pittman of Nevada, chairman of the Senate Foreign Relations Committee, was a devoted exponent of silver. Senator Elmer Thomas of Okla-

homa, once a soldier in the Bryan ranks, was a voice
for any form of currency expansion. "We must have
more money in circulation. I care not what kind—silver, copper, brass, gold or paper."[1] Their support was
growing in both Houses for, as it turned out, the last
time. And, as things worsened, the inflationists had
allies even in reputable circles. The Committee for
the Nation, headed by Frank A. Vanderlip, for some
years previously the head of the National City Bank,
and James Rand of Remington Rand, provided a foothold in the banking and business community, one
that was viewed with grave suspicion as possibly having designs on democracy as well as the dollar. Charles
E. Coughlin, the radio priest from Michigan, was a
highly articulate bridgehead in the Church. A few
economists were now beginning to argue for the commodity dollar—for a currency that owed its merit
not to its gold content but to its constant purchasing
power. This constant purchasing power, it was argued,
was true currency stabilization. And since such stabilization required that prices now be raised—the purchasing power of money by any calculation being
currently excessive—a man could be for stabilization
of the dollar and raising of prices at the same time.

However, the vast majority of economists, as also
the reputable bankers and businessmen, remained
faithful to the fears on which they had been raised. Later in 1933, forty of the most prestigious economists
would join under the leadership of Edwin W. Kemmerer
of Princeton in the Economists' National Committee
on Monetary Policy to combat any and all monkey-
ing around with the money. (Professor Kemmerer in
previous years had led monetary missions to Mexico,
Guatemala, Colombia, Chile, Ecuador and other remote precincts where, invariably, he had urged his
client governments to adopt some approximation to the

---

[1]Arthur M. Schlesinger, Jr., *The Coming of the New Deal* (Boston:
Houghton Mifflin Co., 1958), p. 41.

gold standard, always with highly impermanent effect, for, without exception, they later abandoned it. From this affinity for gold he had earned much fame and some money. It is possible that, however innocently, he was caught up in a conflict of interest.) With the arrival of Roosevelt the fears, and the sense of needed vigilance, deepened. Everything that Roosevelt had said during the campaign was reassuring. But who could be certain that he meant it? It was obvious that many in Congress hoped he didn't mean it.

From the earliest days the lines were drawn on the question of inflation not only outside but also within the new Administration. No one of any importance in the Administration was willing to describe himself as an inflationist. An American politician can yearn for freedom from dull marital ties. He does not wish to be a proclaimed adulterer. So with inflation. At most there were proponents of the aforementioned stabilization in the sense that the dollar should neither rise nor fall in value, the most prominent of these being Secretary of Agriculture Henry A. Wallace. And there were wholly outspoken defenders against inflation. The leaders were Lewis W. Douglas, Roosevelt's budget director; James Warburg[2], son of Paul M. Warburg and newly arrived in Washington as an adviser at the Treasury; Dean Acheson, also of the Treasury and much subsequent fame; and, for the moment, Bernard Baruch. "People who talk about gradually inflating," said Baruch, "might as well talk about firing a gun off gradually . . . Money cannot go back to work in an atmosphere filled with the threat to destroy its value."[3]

In the weeks immediately following March 4, the sound-money men, as they did not hesitate to call themselves, had the play. The week after the Inaugura-

---

[2]In later years his views were greatly modified.
[3]Schlesinger, p. 196.

tion, the House of Representatives, at Roosevelt's request and to Douglas's design, passed a sweeping economy bill cutting salaries of public officials, civil servants *and* congressmen *and* reducing pensions. Some liberal Democrats protested but they were swept aside. There was more trouble with an amendment by Senator Thomas to the Agricultural Adjustment Act calling for—among other things—the free coinage of silver; the acceptance of up to $200 million worth of silver in payment of obligations of foreign governments; the issue, subject to some restrictions, of up to $3 billion in greenbacks; and the conferring of authority on the Executive to reduce the gold and silver content of the dollar by up to half. Back of these ideas was all of the ancient passion. Not being sure that it could defeat the Thomas amendment, the Administration had the authority made permissive rather than mandatory, and in this form it was passed. Although the threat was thus averted, it was at the price of making Roosevelt's authority over monetary policy all but unlimited. Thus it increased even more the concern over Roosevelt's views. Should he yield to the inflationists now that he had this vast discretion, all would indeed be lost.

In the summer and autumn of 1933, there was a major change; the sound-money men lost power. The turning point in the struggle for the Roosevelt mind, more visible and dramatic than most turning points in economic affairs, was the London Economic Conference.

The Economic and Monetary Conference which convened in London in June of 1933 was, with the Potsdam Conference of 1945, one of the truly bizarre international convocations of the century so far. An inheritance of the Hoover Administration, it reflected the hope that international discussion might somehow mitigate the economic problems that beset the world, notably unstable currencies, beggar-my-neighbor tariffs, the dumping of surplus commodities and, beyond these, the terrible blight of depression itself. Sixty-six nations were represented, an assurance that no idea for amelioration, however deplorable, would be overlooked. In practice the much narrower purpose of the conference was to allow the countries that were still on the gold standard—France, Italy, Switzerland needless to say, Belgium, Holland, Poland oddly enough, and, at the time the conference was conceived under the Republicans, the United States—to persuade those that had departed gold to stabilize their currencies. Such stabilization involved no mystery; it required only that the monetary recreants make gold available on request whenever their currencies fell below a certain rate of exchange for the gold currencies. Then their money would fall no further. Were this not done, the countries that had left gold and whose currencies could be acquired at a favorable rate of exchange would enjoy an unfair advantage in selling their goods over the countries still on gold. The latter countries would lose gold as it was exchanged for the cheap currencies and be forced sooner or later to abandon the gold standard themselves. For countries that were fresh from the struggle to stabilize their currencies—those which even more than the United States lived in the backdraft of inflation—this was a most unwelcome prospect. France, with her especially arduous struggle for stabilization so recently over, was, not surprisingly, the leader of the gold bloc.

When the conference was planned, no one could have doubted what country would be the ally, even the mentor, of the French. The United States was firmly on the gold standard, amply supplied with gold reserves and led by men for whom gold was a religion. By the time the delegates assembled in the Geological Museum in Kensington, the United States had abandoned the gold standard. Its position, in consequence, was ambiguous. Was it still committed to its recent faith? Or might it not now wish the dollar to go down, with consequent advantage in selling American products, notably farm products, in overseas markets with the further effect of improving American prices? In the weeks before the conference, Roosevelt, in keeping with his initial orthodoxy, had given numerous visiting statesmen the impression that he was for stabilization of the dollar—for making available the gold that, beyond a certain point, would arrest its decline in relation to other currencies. However, the American delegation sailed without this rather basic question being resolved or, for that matter, considered. It was a significant but, as things were being handled, not an unusual oversight.

The members of the delegation—it was led by Cordell Hull with James M. Cox, head of the Cox-Roosevelt ticket in the presidential election of 1920, as vice-chairman—included men with both points of view on stabilization, and these were balanced by some with no point of view at all. One of the latter, Ralph W. Morrison of Texas, was included at the last moment as a reward for his financial support of the Democrats. Another, Senator Key Pittman, was interested only in the remonetization of silver and a vacation from the tedium of national Prohibition. He astonished his colleagues by his ability, even when drunk, to hit a distant cuspidor with a large effusion of tobacco juice and to become suddenly, if briefly, sober whenever silver was mentioned. At the official reception he greeted George V and Queen Mary with exceptional informality. "King, I'm glad to meet you. And you too, Queen." One night at Claridge's a floor waiter asked James Warburg to accompany him to the floor pantry. Pittman, quite naked, was sitting in the sink under the impression that he was a statue in a fountain. The waiter had failed in the effort to persuade him otherwise.[4]

Of the numerous delegations the American had some claim to being not only the most colorful but also the most confused, and, as the conference proceeded, the members also developed a total and well-justified dislike for each other. However, the British delegation, led by Ramsay MacDonald, was deeply unclear as to whether it was a defender of gold, as seemed proper, or of an inconvertible pound at a rate of exchange with other currencies that did not again punish British exports. It was only that being British, as someone said, their confusion was better organized. In the months before the conference American political opinion had become firmly insistent that the British, French and lesser Allied powers pay their wartime debts to the United States. The Allies, now without hope of collecting first from the Germans, as firmly refused. Were this subject mentioned, it would, it was feared, pre-empt the conference. It was agreed, accordingly, that it would not be discussed at London. Ramsay MacDonald, as Schlesinger tells with much pleasure, "briskly launched the business proceedings on a note of bad faith by calling in his opening address for a reduction of war debts."[5] His associates then explained his aberration by his advanced mental and physical deterioration.

On convening, the French promptly pressed for a preliminary agreement on stabilizing the exchanges— an interim action which, they hoped, would pave the way for more permanent agreement. This made stabilization in terms of gold the first order of business. Nothing much else could be done until this issue was resolved. The position of the United States was, of

---

[4]The story was told to me by James Warburg. A slightly different version, as well as Pittman's greeting to the King, are in Warburg's autobiography, *The Long Road Home* (Garden City: Doubleday & Co., 1964), pp. 128–129.

[5]Schlesinger, p. 213.

course, critical. Back in Washington the President's
sound-money men—Acheson, Lewis Douglas, Baruch,
as well as Secretary of the Treasury Woodin—were all
favorable to stabilization, as was James Warburg, who
was with the delegation. Roosevelt was thought by
now to have doubts about stabilization but no one
could be completely sure, for he was away sailing off
the New England coast. To pull things together, and
also it is believed because he wanted the trip and associated rendezvous with destiny, Raymond Moley,
senior Roosevelt Brain Truster and now Assistant
Secretary of State, visited Roosevelt on his boat. Moley
succeeded, it would appear, in not learning Roosevelt's
views and then departed for London to bring this
further uncertainty to the attention of the delegation
for its guidance.

Moley's arrival was awaited with vastly publicized
suspense—and with something less than amusement
by Cordell Hull who did not respond well to the widespread impression that he was being superseded. After
his arrival and a hurried round of conferences, Moley
concluded that the French were right, that a temporary stabilization arrangement was a defensible
thing. The pound was then around $4.40, having re-
cently risen a bit. This Moley believed the President
would find acceptable. He urged stabilization of the
dollar at this rate in relation to the pound.

The error of the President's sound-money advisers
may well have been in allowing him to go off by himself and think—and, it has been said, read a book on
the neostabilization or commodity-dollar idea. In any
case, on July 1, as the delegates were being received at
Cliveden, the Thames Valley house of Viscount Astor
and through the '30s the principal watering place of
what was there first called the Establishment, word
came that Roosevelt was against stabilization. He
would not, in other words, make gold available whenever the dollar fell appreciably below its current ex-

change value with sterling and the franc, with the effect of guaranteeing against further fall. And a day or so later, in a message to the conference, he made his position wholly, many thought appallingly, clear:

> I would regard it as a catastrophe amounting to a world tragedy if the greatest conference of nations, called to bring about a more real and permanent financial stability and a greater prosperity to the masses of all nations, should, in advance of any serious effort to consider these broader problems, allow itself to be diverted by the proposal of a purely artificial and temporary experiment affecting the monetary exchange of a few nations only . . .
>
> . . . old fetishes of so-called international bankers are being replaced by efforts to plan national currencies with the objective of giving to those currencies a continuing purchasing power which does not greatly vary in terms of the commodities and need of modern civilization.
>
> Let me be frank in saying that the United States seeks the kind of dollar which a generation hence will have the same purchasing power and debt-paying power as the dollar value we hope to attain in the near future. That objective means more to the good of other nations than a fixed ratio for a month or two in terms of the pound or franc.[6]

Thus had Roosevelt's position changed. And thus was it proclaimed. The immediate, most publicized but in many ways the least important effect was on the conference. Its principal purpose, an agreement on stabilization, ceased to exist. It continued on but mostly for the purpose of saving face. (Roosevelt's repudiation also marked, effectively, the end of Raymond Moley's public career—yet another example of the ruthlessness with which money destroys public men.) The reaction of numerous of the sound-money men to Roosevelt was

---

[6]The *New York Times*, July 4, 1933.

in language that the late Joe McCarthy might have thought harsh. The Manchester *Guardian,* in a typical comment, called Roosevelt's message "a Manifesto of Anarchy."[7] The *New York Times* was more restrained; mouthing its words with exceptional care, it said the message was "of a nature to intensify bewilderment."[8] Ramsay MacDonald was distraught and incoherent but took some comfort in the fact that King George had expressed outrage at the grief Roosevelt had caused him. More important than the reaction was the effect on the Roosevelt Administration. In the next few months the principal defenders of sound money— Douglas, Acheson, Warburg—all departed the Administration.

But there were notable voices of approval. Faithful to the principles of a lifetime, Baruch now moved fearlessly to the winning side. Before there could be stabilization, he told Roosevelt, each nation must put its house in order "by the same Herculean efforts that you are performing."[9] Another man of flexible mind, or anyhow not disposed to make the same mistake twice, was Winston Churchill. Now out of office, the boats moored together on the golden tide forgotten, Churchill said it was wrong to tie policies to the "rarity or abundance of any commodity [such as gold]" and "quite beyond human comprehension" that this should be done out of love for France.[10] In Germany, Konstantin von Neurath spoke of Roosevelt's "fearlessness," and Hjalmar Schacht was even more helpful in a certain way. He told the *Völkischer Beobachter,* the voice of National Socialism, that FDR had adopted the philosophy of Hitler and Mussolini.[11] Walter Lippmann,

---

[7] The reaction of the *Guardian* is from Schlesinger, p. 224.

[8] The *New York Times,* July 9, 1933.

[9] Schlesinger, p. 224.

[10] The reaction of Churchill is from Schlesinger, pp. 223–224.

[11] John A. Garraty, "The New Deal, National Socialism, and the Great Depression" *The American Historical Review,* Vol. 78, No. 4

a more acceptable observer, also approved. Irving Fisher, professor of political economy at Yale, wrote a special article for the *New York Times* applauding the President's action. "Had President Roosevelt's critics any real understanding of what constitutes monetary stability, his statement last Monday would not have proved the bombshell it did."[12] He went on to suggest that the President certainly did not oppose stabilization. But, being a sensible man, he sought stabilization of the purchasing power of the dollar, not of the exchange. Roosevelt, in other words, had merely accepted the neostabilization formula of those for whom stabilization in the immediate situation meant higher prices.

Even stronger words of approval came from an even more important voice—on economic matters the most important of the decade and most would say of the age. Writing in the *Daily Mail*, John Maynard Keynes congratulated Roosevelt enthusiastically on his stand. The headline, often to be quoted in years ahead, was: PRESIDENT ROOSEVELT IS MAGNIFICENTLY RIGHT.[13] Not just right but magnificently right.

Most economists would now agree in giving first place to J. M. Keynes and second to Irving Fisher for their contributions to monetary thought and policy in this century. All, regardless of predilection, would give first and second place to one or the other. Nothing better illustrates the changes in attitudes than the contemporary reaction to their applause. The *New York Times* thought that it "should hardly be necessary to say" that the ideas of Fisher and Keynes "have been long before the public, and that both have been rejected by the large consensus of economic and financial judgment."[14]

Fisher, and in lesser measure Keynes, shared with

(October 1973), p. 922. This article offers an interesting comparison of American and German recovery policies.
[12]The *New York Times*, July 9, 1933.
[13]Schlesinger, p. 223.
[14]The *New York Times*, July 9, 1933.

the large consensus of economic and financial judgment the belief that higher prices and associated expansion of production could be rather easily achieved. With Roosevelt they did not know how difficult that would be to accomplish—how hard it was to be magnificently right or even right. That discovery was now to be made.

In 1848, as told in Chapter III, John Stuart Mill offered an explanation of what governed prices and thus the value of money. In ensuing years it served well, as it has, in a general way, this history. Prices depend on the supply of money in relation to the quantity of goods and services being sold. The more money (the supply of goods and the resulting volume of trade being unchanged), the higher the prices. If the supply of money is infinitely great, as in Germany in 1923, the prices will be infinitely high.

By 1933 it had come to be recognized that money included not only hand-to-hand cash but also bank deposits. And when business was good, bank borrowing would be brisk and bank deposits would increase. So, in degree, the supply of money depended on the state of business. Additionally, it had long been recognized that increasing prices stimulated business. So the increase in the supply of money that increased prices could also increase the supply of goods available for sale. This would reflect back with dampening effect on price increases. Finally, allowance had to be made not only for the supply of money but for the rate at which it was spent. Money that was spent immediately on its receipt obviously had a different effect on prices from money that was stored away in the mattress.

Amidst all of these refinements, however, it remained the view of economists and the instinct of most other people that the active factor in the situation was the supply of money. Here cause began; prices were the effect. It was also the handle that, it seemed, could be grasped. The money supply could be increased; higher prices and business expansion would then follow.

The refinements just noted had, early in the century, been added to Mill's formulation, primarily by Irving Fisher. A slender, handsome man with sharp, good-humored eyes and an elegantly trimmed beard, Irving Fisher was the most versatile and, by a wide margin, the most interesting of American economists, Thorstein Veblen (who also received his doctorate from Yale) possibly excepted. In addition to teaching economics at Yale, Fisher was a mathematician, a founder of econometrics, the inventor of index numbers and an enthusiast for eugenics, nutrition, securities specula-tion and Prohibition. Prohibition he regarded as im-portant for raising labor productivity. Early in life he invented a card index file, which he first manufactured and then sold to Remington Rand. From this and later involvement with the stock market he profited hand-somely—something about which he felt no guilt. In the aftermath of the 1929 crash he lost, according to his son, between eight and ten million dollars, a sizable sum even for an economist.[15] In 1944, Keynes, who did not prefer praise to truth, responded to a letter from Fisher approving the recently concluded Bretton Woods agreements: "Your letter has given me the greatest possible pleasure. You were one of my earliest teachers on these matters."[16]

Fisher made prices dependent on the volume of cash or circulating money and the rate at which it turned over, together with the volume of bank de-posits and the rate at which they turned over, all adjusted for the volume of trade. All refinements were

---

[15]Irving Norton Fisher, *My Father—Irving Fisher* (New York: Comet Press, 1956), p. 264.
[16]Fisher, p. 326. The Bretton Woods agreements are discussed in Chapter XVIII.

thus brought within the framework of a single rule. In algebraic form, Fisher's equation of exchange,[17] as it has long been called, still rules in the textbooks, is still the accepted formulation of what is called the quantity theory of money.

Consistent with Fisher's formula, but not much considered, was a terrible possibility. It was that the supply of money could not be increased. The largest part of the supply of money, as by now will be adequately understood, is deposits in banks. These come into existence as people and firms borrow money. If business is sufficiently bad, profit prospects sufficiently dim, gloom sufficiently deep, businessmen may not borrow money. Then no deposits are created, no money comes into existence. The banks can be provided with cash for reserves by purchases of government securities by the Federal Reserve Banks from the banks or their customers. This cash will then lie fallow in the banks. Without borrowing and deposit creation there is no effect on prices or through prices on production. This, it now developed, was not a hypothetical possibility but one that was intensely, miserably real.

Irving Fisher had not, in the past, had doubts. And, having formulated the equation of exchange, he proceeded characteristically to its practical applications. The money supply, he believed, should be varied in such fashion as to keep prices stable. The price index, the other great Fisher contribution, would guide and control the reduction in the gold content—or its later increase, as that was required. A man notably immune

---

[17] $P = \dfrac{MV + M'V'}{T}$ where P is the level of prices, M cash or circulating money, V the velocity of the circulation of this cash or the rate at which it turns over, M' the volume of bank deposits subject to check, V' the rate at which these deposits turn over and T the volume of transactions or, roughly, the level of trade.

to the attractions of the quiet, noncontroversial life, singularly free from the Belmont Syndrome, Fisher had long been an evangelist for this compensated dollar, as it was called, and had organized his converts for its adoption. In 1933, with stabilization of the exchanges no longer a controlling consideration, the way was open for the ideas of Irving Fisher.

Fisher's precise plan called for lowering the gold content of the dollar as prices fell. Banks, including the Federal Reserve Banks, would then have more dollars and more reserves on which to make loans. The expansion in reserves would be automatic, not at the discretion of the Federal Reserve. (Previously people who had owned gold would also have been able to take it to the mint and have it exchanged into an increased quantity of paper—or, conceivably, recoined into a lighter dollar. However, now that Roosevelt had sequestered private gold holdings, this possibility did not exist.) In the event, it was not Fisher's procedure but a slight variant that was followed.

Instead of proclaiming a reduction of the gold content of the dollar, the device employed was to raise the price at which gold was bought at the mint. Since a higher price for gold meant that the dollar contained less of the metal, the result was indistinguishable. The immediate source of this variant was Professor George F. Warren of the New York State College of Agriculture at Cornell University. In association with his longtime colleague, Frank A. Pearson, Professor Warren had shown with great statistical competence that, for approaching a hundred years, there had been a close relationship between prices, production and the increases in the world stock of gold. If production expanded faster than world gold stock, prices fell. If gold stocks went up more rapidly than production, prices rose. From this Warren and Pearson had drawn the obvious conclusion: When you want to increase prices and expand production, get an effective increase in the gold supply by reducing the amount of gold in the dollar. Do this by raising the price of gold in dollars. Warren, like Fisher, would have liked to see this adjustment in accordance with some continuing formula. ". . . to provide some method for making future necessary changes in the price of gold without the necessity of long years of economic distress and political agitation would seem to be a conservative proposal."[18] But he was willing to accept, as was Fisher, a decision, *ad hoc,* to raise the gold price. It did not matter as long as it was increased.

Warren's reference to conservatism in the above statement was not casual. By manipulating the gold price he believed that much other public and reformist action, including most of the New Deal farm program, could be avoided. This he thought highly desirable. He was one of the first in a long line of monetary reformers extending to Professor Milton Friedman in our own day who have hoped that their changes would make other and more comprehensive government action unnecessary. They are monetary radicals because they are political conservatives.

Roosevelt's turn to Warren could not, as viewed by economists, have been more tactless. In the economics profession there is a well-defined order of precedence. At the top are economic theorists, and their professional eminence in the pecking order is shared by those who do teaching and research on banking and money. At the bottom of this hierarchy are agricultural economists and home economists, and within agricultural economics an especially low position is reserved

---

[18]George F. Warren, "Some Statistics on the Gold Situation," *The American Economic Review*, Vol. XXIV, No. 1 (Supplement, March 1934), p. 129. This paper was given at the annual meeting of the American Economic Association in Philadelphia in December 1933 and was the first such session I ever attended. The crowd was dense and very critical of Warren. Reflecting a sound education, I shared these doubts. During the meeting Irving Fisher was loudly paged by the hotel staff.

for professors of farm management. Warren was a professor of farm management. However brilliant the success of his gold-buying plan, it would still have been poorly regarded by scholars of the highest esteem.

Beginning in the autumn of 1933, the government began buying gold at steadily increasing prices. As the Federal Reserve was too reputable for bailing out banks in bad condition, so it was too distinguished for anything as dubious as the monetary vision of George F. Warren. So, as for serving as the lender of last resort for the troubled banks, the RFC was used. Roosevelt himself set the prices at which gold would be purchased. In later times he was criticized for the irresponsibility with which, in casual breakfast conversations with Secretary of the Treasury Morgenthau and Jesse Jones, the head of the RFC, he decided on the next day's price. Once the increase was 21 cents because, being three times seven, it seemed a lucky number. No man alive could say what was the difference between a considered or an unconsidered judgment—or whether one was better than the other. But where money is concerned, solemn consideration is required even if the reasons for the choice are enveloped in ignorance. The price of gold was gradually raised by this process from its erstwhile level of $20.67 an ounce until, early in 1934, it was approximately $35.00 an ounce. Initially only newly mined gold was bought, later any and all.

The results were disappointing, and partly because of another government action of that busy year. That spring, it will be recalled, the government called in the gold of the citizenry, and this included that of the banks. In consequence, the higher gold price or diminished gold content of the dollars did not increase the cash reserves of the banks. The extra dollar value of the gold accrued as profit to the Treasury. The banks, having no more dollars than before, had no more reserves against which to lend and thus no greater incentive than before to make loans, expand deposits and thus to increase the money supply.[19] Thus there was no clear way in which the gold-buying policy could affect domestic prices. And, in the period over which the policy was pursued, it didn't. In late 1933, wholesale prices fell. The case of export prices may have been an exception. Here the cheaper dollars made American products cheaper abroad. It is possible, accordingly, that the policy did help to sustain exports and their dollar price.

Meanwhile there was much orthodox criticism of the gold-buying experiment. It was one thing to be criticized for a policy that worked, something else for a policy that seemed not to be accomplishing anything. Accordingly, Roosevelt gave up. To the unconcealed satisfaction of his colleagues, George Warren's moment of glory came to an end. A farm management professor after all. In January 1934, under legislation that had been requested by the President, the government took the profit from the higher price of gold and put the proceeds in a fund to buy and sell currencies as might by required to stabilize exchanges. It then returned to the gold standard. Following the fashion of other countries, this was only for international transactions. Americans could not get gold on request and, as an added feature, were still forbidden to possess it.

By this time, as noted, the sound-money men had quit. They did not wish to be associated with the inflation that the gold-buying policy would surely bring. Clearly their fears were misplaced; prices did not rise. But defeated also were the hopes of Fisher, Warren and, in lesser measure, Keynes. Money had dealt impartially with both those who feared inflation and those who wanted some—or, more precisely, wished to recoup past price reductions. All had been shown

---

[19]As gold later came in from abroad, a given weight did buy more dollars, provide more reserves.

to be wrong. A country seeking inflation was like a woman of exceptional virtue deciding, after many adverse warnings of conscience and friends, to take a lover, only to discover that the lover was both unwilling and unable.

There remained a more orthodox possibility. As earlier noted, the Federal Reserve by 1932 had sufficiently suppressed its fear of inflation so that it was able to go into the market and buy government bonds and thus substitute cash for securities in the vaults of the banks. This policy it continued in ensuing years. The consequences of this action too were deeply disappointing. Before, it had been supposed and taught that when banks had reserves in excess of requirements, they would, some minor periods or examples of caution excluded, expand their loans and therewith their deposits and the money supply. The history of the small banks on the frontier suggested that this expansion would be undertaken not with an excess of caution but in a reckless absence of caution.

Now the banks simply sat on the cash. Either from a shortage of borrowers, an unwillingness to lend or an overriding desire to be liquid—undoubtedly it was some of all three—the banks accumulated reserves in excess of requirements. Already in 1932, member banks of the Federal Reserve averaged $256 million more in reserves than was required for their deposits. In 1933, these excess reserves were $528 million; in 1934, they were $1.6 billion. In 1936, they were yet a billion more. In 1940, augmented by large shipments of gold sent to the United States for safekeeping, excess reserves averaged $6.3 billion.[20]

Within a matter of five years or so, the circle of fail-

[20]Lester V. Chandler, *America's Greatest Depression, 1929–1941* (New York: Harper & Row, 1970), p. 174.

ure on monetary policy had come complete. In 1928 and 1929, the Federal Reserve had been unable to check the boom, for to do so was to be nailed with the responsibility for the ensuing collapse. Now it was helpless in counteracting the Depression, for the banks would not lend or the borrowers would not borrow. In a metaphor that gained currency at the time, monetary policy was like a string. You could pull it, though with incalculable results. But you could not shove it at all.

Not surprisingly, after 1933, monetary policy in general and the Federal Reserve System in particular sank into the shadows. Though still celebrated in the textbooks as before, in Washington the Federal Reserve System was a backwater. Two of its leaders, Marriner Eccles and Lauchlin Currie, achieved fame not for the monetary policy of the Federal Reserve System but for the Keynesian fiscal policy which was the substitute. There was, however, one glowing moment. As the excess reserves increased after 1934, some durably anxious officials considered what a huge volume of loans and deposits they would sustain were they ever used. Thus there was a renewed concern about inflation. In 1936 and 1937, with the economy making a very gradual recovery, the new power to raise the reserve requirements of the member banks was invoked. This was a forthright way of reducing the seemingly dangerous excess. In consequence, the banks stiffened their interest rates and reduced their outstanding loans. In the same months steps were being taken to bring the Federal budget back into balance—the deficit was cut nearly in half in the fiscal year ending June 30, 1937, and by half again the following year. The combination of restrictive monetary policy and restrictive budget policy brought a sharp new recession within the arms, as it were, of the larger depression. It was another interesting error. "With the benefit of hindsight it is now clear that the increase of member bank reserve requirements in the spring of 1937 was a mistake."[21]

. The 1937 action was the last error of the Federal Reserve for a long time. That was because it was its last action of any moment for fifteen years. The problem with monetary policy was now clear. It could make reserves available. It could not cause them to be borrowed, bring about the resulting deposit creation. On the old question of how causation ran, it was plain that, in depression at least, it was the state of trade that ruled. The supply of money did not affect prices and trade nearly so much as the state of trade affected the supply of money and the level of prices. The answer —obvious enough here but rather less obvious at the time—was to make the creation and use of money not permissive but obligatory. Money must be not only manufactured but spent—made to operate directly on the state of trade. This was the policy that was now, though with great caution, pursued. This was fiscal as distinct from monetary policy. It is tied irrevocably to the name of Keynes.

---

[21]Chandler, p. 180. Professor Chandler was himself, for many years, a Director of the Philadelphia Federal Reserve Bank.

CHAPTER XVI

The Coming
of J. M. Keynes

In 1935, at the age of fifty-two, John Maynard Keynes might well have been considered at the peak of a reasonably remarkable career. His views of the Versailles Treaty had been vindicated, although they had also encouraged the Germans in resisting the reparations which had helped the vindication. He had assuredly been right on Churchill and the return to gold. In 1930, he had published what he had intended as his masterwork, the two-volume *A Treatise on Money*.[1] Tall, angular, arrogant, very English, he was very much a figure in the London intellectual world.

In fact, most of his reputation was still to be made, a circumstance of which he was wholly aware. Writing to George Bernard Shaw on New Year's Day, 1935, he said: "To understand my state of mind, you have to know that I believe myself to be writing a book on economic theory which will largely revolutionise— not, I suppose, at once but in the course of the next ten years—the way the world thinks about economic problems."[2] So it developed.

What made the book, and Keynes's further reputation, was his instinct that there were forces in the

---

[1] John Maynard Keynes, *A Treatise on Money* (New York: Harcourt, Brace & Co., 1930).

[2] R. F. Harrod, *The Life of John Maynard Keynes* (London: Macmillan & Co., 1963), p. 462. Keynes was responding to a suggestion of Shaw that he interest himself in something on, or by, Marx.

modern economy that were frustrating the most important assumption made by men of orthodox mind—the
assumption that, left to itself and given time, the economic system would find its equilibrium with all or
nearly all its willing workers employed. More than the
orthodox views were involved. Were Keynes's instinct
right, the hopes of the monetary radicals would also be
destroyed. A change in the gold content of the dollar
or an increase in banks' reserves would not mean
more borrowers, more deposits, more money and a
surge of the economy back to full employment. The
level of trade might be indifferent to the supply of
money. The loans might be available in the banks; the
returns from borrowing, given the natural tendency of
the economy to low performance and unemployment, might be such that no one would want to borrow.
It followed, as the failures of the gold-buying policy
and open-market operations were beginning in the
mid-'30s to suggest, that monetary policy would not
work. It was essentially passive or permissive. What
was needed was a policy that increased the supply of
money available for use and then ensured its use. Then
the state of trade would have to improve.

The conclusion as to the proper policy was one to
which Keynes came well before he got around to its
theoretical justification. In the late '20s he helped persuade Lloyd George, in the latter's last effort at a come-
back, to support a major program of borrowing for
public works to cure unemployment. The borrowing created the money; its use for public works ensured its expenditure and the effect on production.
And at the end of 1933, as the American gold-buying
program was negating both the hopes of its supporters
and the fears of its opponents, he urged the same
course on Roosevelt. "I lay overwhelming emphasis on
the increase of national purchasing power resulting
from government expenditure which is financed by

loans."[3] The New Dealers should not content themselves with making funds available to be borrowed and
spent; they must borrow and spend. Nothing could be
left to hope or chance.

The theoretical justification came in the book Keynes
mentioned to Shaw, *The General Theory of Employment Interest and Money*,[4] published in Britain in
February 1936, and in the United States a few months
later. Keynes had long been suspect among his colleagues for the clarity of his writing and thought, the
two often going together. In *The General Theory* he
redeemed his academic reputation. It is a work of
profound obscurity, badly written and prematurely
published. All economists claim to have read it. Only
a few have. The rest feel a secret guilt that they never
will. Some of its influence derived from its being extensively incomprehensible. Other scholars were needed
to construe its meaning, restate its propositions in in-
telligible form. Those who initially performed this
task—Joan Robinson in England, Alvin Hansen and
Seymour Harris at Harvard—then became highly effective evangelists for the ideas.

The belief that the economy would find its equilibrium at full employment depended partly on what had
long been called Say's Law—for J. B. Say, the French
counterpart and interpreter of Adam Smith—and
partly on the corrective movement of wages, prices and
interest rates when there was unemployment. Say's
Law, not a thing of startling complexity, held that,
from the proceeds of every sale of goods, there was

---

[3]Letter to the *New York Times,* December 31, 1933.
[4]John Maynard Keynes, *The General Theory of Employment Interest
and Money* (New York: Harcourt, Brace & Co., 1936). Reflecting
some unstated preference, Keynes's title had no commas. Editors
and proofreaders have ever since inserted them.

paid out to someone somewhere in wages, salaries, interest, rent or profit (or there was taken from the man who absorbed a loss) the wherewithal to buy that item. As with one item, so with all. This being so, there could not be a shortage of purchasing power in the economy. Movements in prices, wages and interest rates then validated J. B. Say and also ensured that the fundamental tendency of the economy would be to operation at full employment. People and firms saved from their income, and this saving had, obviously, to be spent. This happened when it was invested in housing, plant, capital equipment. If people saved more than was invested, the surplus of savings would bring down interest rates. Investment would thus be stimulated and saving (at least in theory) discouraged. So the excess of savings would be eliminated and Say sustained. Prices of goods would also fall in consequence of any short-fall in purchasing power that resulted from an excess of savings. This would encourage buying and, by reducing the income from which savings were made, also reduce savings. Again Say was sustained.

Until Keynes, Say's Law had ruled in economics for more than a century. And the rule was no casual thing; to a remarkable degree acceptance of Say was the test by which reputable economists were distinguished from the crackpots. Until late in the '30s no candidate for a Ph.D. at a major American university who spoke seriously of a shortage of purchasing power as a cause of depression could be passed. He was a man who saw only the surface of things, was unworthy of the company of scholars. Say's Law stands as the most distinguished example of the stability of economic ideas, including when they are wrong.

Supplementing Say, as noted, were the forces that kept the economy at full employment. These too were relatively straightforward. Were there unemployment, the competition for jobs would bring a fall in wage rates. Prices would be less immediately affected by the unemployment. The relationship of prices to costs would thus be made more attractive—real wages would fall—and workers whose employment was previously unprofitable to employers would now be hired. The fall in wages would not affect purchasing power; because of Say, that was always sufficient. Employment would continue to expand until the approach to full employment raised wage costs and arrested the hiring. Thus did the economy find its equilibrium at or very near full employment. From this also came the one decisive recommendation of the orthodox economists for ending unemployment. Do nothing to interfere with the reduction of wages in a depression. Resist all siren voices, including that of Herbert Hoover, who, it will be recalled, urged against wage cuts. On no matter was compassion so softheaded, for to keep up wages merely perpetuated the sorrow of unemployment and the sorrows of the unemployed.

This was the doctrine, perhaps more accurately the theology, that Keynes brought to an end. There are numerous points of entry on his argument; perhaps the easiest is by way of the rate of interest. Interest, he held, was not the price people were paid to save. Rather it was what they got for keeping their assets in plant, machinery or similarly unliquid forms of investment—in his language, what was paid to overcome their liquidity preference. Accordingly, a fall in interest rates might not discourage savings, encourage investment, ensure that all savings would be used. It might cause investors to retreat into cash or its equivalent. So interest rates no longer came to the support of Say's Law to ensure that savings would be spent. And if Say's Law was no longer a reliable axiom of life, the notion of a shortage of purchasing power could no longer be excluded from calculation. It might, among other things, be the consequence of a reduction in wages.[5]

What people sought to save, in Keynes's view, had still to be brought to equal what they wanted to invest. But the adjustment mechanism, he argued, was not the rate of interest but the total output of the economy. If efforts to save exceeded the desire to invest, the resulting shortage of purchasing power or demand caused output to fall. And it kept falling until employment and income had been so reduced that savings were also reduced or made negative. In this fashion savings were brought into line with investment—which also, meanwhile, would have fallen but by not so much. The economic equilibrium so established, it will be evident, was now one in which there was not full employment but unemployment. Thus unemployment for Keynes was a natural condition of the economy.

There was much else. And not all of Keynes's argument survived. The liquidity-preference theory of interest, for example, though it served Keynes's argument, did not gain permanent acceptance as a description of reality. But on two things Keynes was immediately influential. Say's Law sank without trace. There could, it was henceforth agreed, be oversaving. And there could, as its counterpart, be a shortage of effective demand for what was being produced. And the notion that the economy could find its equilibrium with unemployment—a thought admirably reinforced by the everyday evidence of the '30s—was also almost immediately influential.

If Keynes seemed radical to some in his time, he was, in one important respect, completely orthodox. The

---

[5]This is a complex point in Keynes. For a full discussion (and much else that is important in Keynes), see Robert Lekachman's admirable *The Age of Keynes* (New York: Random House, 1966).

economic structure which he assumed was that which economists had anciently avowed—that of competition, freely moving prices and the ultimate, uninhibited control of economic behavior by the market. There were unions but they made relatively little difference to Keynes. Corporations and corporate power made no real difference at all. In fact, both unions and corporations, as Keynes wrote, were acting to affirm his thesis. He had support for his ideas that he did not use.

Thus, during the fifty years before Keynes, in all of the industrial countries, corporations had gained greatly in influence and market power. It was the textbook time of what was coming to be called corporate concentration. With the United States in some measure the exception, there had been also the rise of the modern trade union. And in the latter '30s, under the aegis of the New Deal and in response to the organization drive of the CIO, the United States had come abreast of other countries in union organization. The effect of both corporate concentration and union strength was to make radically more unreliable the adjustments which were assumed to sustain Say's Law and the full-employment equilibrium.

In 1920, it has been noticed, farm prices fell more rapidly and much more severely than did prices of industrial products. The reason, not subject seriously to debate, was that the industrial corporations had the power in their markets—the power normally associated with monopoly or oligopoly—to temper or arrest the decline. Farmers and other small entrepreneurs lacked such power. Again, from 1929 to 1932, farm prices at wholesale fell by more than half. Nonfarm prices fell by less than a quarter.[6] This disparate movement was influentially studied by Gardiner C. Means, at the time employed in the United States De-

---

[6]U.S. Bureau of the Census, *Historical Statistics of the United States, Colonial Times to 1957* (Washington, D.C., 1960), p. 116.

partment of Agriculture.[7] To the better-controlled industrial prices he gave the enduring term administered prices.

The Keynesian adjustment to an excess of savings is through a reduction in aggregate demand. When demand falls, something must give, and what gives must be either prices or production. If prices can be held up by the market power of the corporation, it is production that must fall. When production falls, so will employment. With corporate market power, unemployment will thus become a highly distinctive feature of the Keynesian adjustment. And the reduced spending of those who lose their jobs or who fear that they will lose their jobs can be expected to have a further depressing effect on output and employment. Plausibly this effect on output and employment will be far greater than that which might come, in a competitive economy, from the reduction in prices and wages that Keynes, in the main, envisaged.[8]

The difference in production and employment during the Depression years between the corporate and competitive sectors was great—although, as always, not everything can be attributed to a single cause. Between 1929 and 1933, the nonfarm product of the economy fell from $88.6 billion to $57.8 billion in 1929 prices. Agricultural output rose slightly—from $10.7 billion to $11.0 billion. Nonagricultural employment fell from 37 million in 1929 to 29 million in 1933. Agricultural employment showed only a negligible change—from 10.5 million to 10.1 million.[9]

The rise of the trade union also made hash of the orthodox hope that wage reductions would serve as a

[7]Louis H. Bean, J. P. Cavin and Gardiner C. Means, "The Causes: Price Relations and Economic Stability," in U.S. Department of Agriculture, *Yearbook of Agriculture 1938* (Washington, D.C., 1938).

[8]More precisely, that he should have envisaged, given his view of the economy. The matter is less than clear in his writing.

[9]U.S. Bureau of the Census, *Historical Statistics*, pp. 70, 140.

stabilizing influence, act to correct unemployment.[10] Whatever the merits of wage reductions to increase employment, they would not so serve if they did not occur. And one of the first purposes of a union was to resist such reductions. The adjustment in money wages that Keynes thought of dubious corrective value was something that was increasingly less likely to occur. But the unemployment which was now the alternative to wage reductions could have an even greater effect in reducing aggregate demand than the adjustment Keynes did discuss.[11]

The rise of the corporations and the unions had another importance for the Keynesian system. They were to be the prime instrument of its failure when inflation, as well as depression, became the problem.

A disputed question concerning the Keynesian Revolution had long been how much credit should accrue exclusively to its namesake. Many scholars have argued that more attention should be given to his numerous precursors[12]; that, in fact, their preparation of the ground went far to explain the acceptance of Keynes. These scholars have a point.

A century earlier Malthus had argued the case for a

---

[10]This, in the right time and competitive or small-enterprise setting, was not as barren a hope as later theory has come to regard it. It was, for example, the willingness, if that is the word, of American farmers to accept a lower return for their toil—and their ability to impose a similar reduction on their hired hands—that kept agricultural output and employment high during the Great Depression. Had farmers and their hired men refused to accept any reduction in their income—withdrawn their services in some miraculous way once income fell below pre-Depression levels—agricultural output and employment would have been much smaller.

[11]Again an ambiguous point in Keynes. He did foresee efforts by unions to maintain wages.

[12]Cf. a forthcoming article by George Garvy, "Keynes and the Economic Activists of Pre-Hitler Germany," *The Journal of Political Economy.* As this goes to press, it is still to be published. I am indebted to my old friend for letting me see this interesting paper.

general deficiency in demand. And a generation before Keynes, J. A. Hobson had developed the case that economic crises were caused by oversaving. (So great was his heresy that in 1899 he was not allowed to teach it even to consenting adults. ". . . in appearing to question the virtue of unlimited thrift I had committed the unpardonable sin.")[13]

For some years before the publication of *The General Theory* innovative and highly responsible economists in Sweden had been developing and, in degree, applying the same ideas. To them belongs specifically the notion that the budget of the national government should be based on revenues accruing at full employment and that it should not be reduced as expenditures fall during depression. This, in elementary form, is the idea that, in more recent times, has been called the full-employment budget.

Also, by the time of Keynes, Major C. H. Douglas had, for some years, been winning lowbrow converts to the concept of Social Credit. The operative feature of Social Credit was a social dividend, meaning the equivalent of cash payable to citizens at large—a reprise of the pioneering idea of colonial Maryland. The social dividend would surely be spent. It involved none of the passiveness of monetary policy. So Douglas anticipated Keynes—as Keynes himself observed.

Keynes was also anticipated by one of the miracle men of the 1920s—Waddill Catchings. With John Foster Dulles and others, Catchings was an architect of three of the great investment trust promotions of the period —Blue Ridge, Shenandoah and Goldman Sachs Trading Corporation—achievements not different, except in the extreme respectability of their promoters, from those crafted more recently by Bernard Cornfeld. About the time he became so engaged, Catchings foresightedly

---

[13]Hobson told of this in "Confessions of an Economic Heretic," an address delivered in London in 1935. Cited in Keynes, *The General Theory*, p. 366.

gave thought to the causes of business depressions, in the next of which he would be a spectacular loser. With William T. Foster, erstwhile president of Reed College, he produced two notably persuasive books, one of which especially, *The Road to Plenty,* achieved, when the Depression did come, a large audience. It held, in opposition to J. B. Say, that oversaving—a shortage of purchasing power—was possible, even normal. The solution was for the government to borrow and spend— the Keynesian remedy. At Harvard during the early '30s, the most lucid teacher concerned with money and banking was John H. Williams, a conservative but no mossback. To the surprise of nearly everyone he told his students that the Foster and Catchings thesis on oversaving and the cure could not automatically be dismissed. Other economists were less tolerant, and noneconomists were not necessarily more sympathetic. Roosevelt read the book before going to Washington as President and wrote in his copy: "Too good to be true—You can't get something for nothing."[14]

At a higher level of academic reputability in these years, Lauchlin Currie, an instructor at Harvard, published, in 1934, *The Supply and Control of Money in the United States.*[15] In significant respects Currie anticipated Keynes; it was an unwise academic strategy, for the book caused doubts as to Currie's soundness as an economist.

Also, well before Roosevelt came to office, the Hearst papers had been strongly, even violently advocating a $5 billion government loan—a breathtaking sum in those days—to be spent on public works. With the advent of the New Deal had come public works and public employment programs—PWA, CWA, WPA— though on a smaller scale than urged by Hearst.

---

[14]Arthur M. Schlesinger, Jr., *The Crisis of the Old Order* (Boston: Houghton Mifflin Co., 1957), p. 136.
[15]Lauchlin Currie, *The Supply and Control of Money in the United States* (Cambridge: Harvard University Press, 1934).

These were perceived not as a step on from monetary policy—a way of enhancing demand by creating money and then ensuring its use—but as an imperative remedy for joblessness. It was, however, a policy in search of a rationalization, the rationalization that Keynes provided.

Finally, as early as 1933, Irving Fisher had proposed feeding borrowed funds directly into private payrolls; he urged FDR to have the government borrow money and lend it to private employers without interest, two dollars per day for 100 days for each man they added to the payroll. This too would ensure the expenditure. Other plans were in circulation for paying people money for services, pensions or simply because they existed. These had the further provision that the currency, if not spent within a decent period of time, would become worthless. Thus also would spending be enforced.

By the mid-'30s there was also in existence an advanced demonstration of the Keynesian system. This was the economic policy of Adolf Hitler and the Third Reich. It involved large-scale borrowing for public expenditures, and at first this was principally for civilian works—railroads, canals and the *Autobahnen*. The result was a far more effective attack on unemployment than in any other industrial country.[16] By 1935, German unemployment was minimal. "Hitler had already found how to cure unemployment before Keynes had

---

[16] ". . . the Nazis were . . . more successful in curing the economic ills of the 1930s [than the United States]. They reduced unemployment and stimulated industrial production faster than the Americans did and, considering their resources, handled their monetary and trade problems more successfully, certainly more imaginatively. This was partly because the Nazis employed deficit financing on a larger scale . . . By 1936 the depression was substantially over in Germany, far from finished in the United States." John A. Garraty, "The New Deal, National Socialism, and the Great Depression," *The American Historical Review*, Vol. 78, No. 4 (October 1973), p. 944.

finished explaining why it occurred."[17] In 1936, as prices and wages came under upward pressure, Hitler took the further step of combining an expansive employment policy with comprehensive price controls.

The Nazi economic policy, it should be noted, was an *ad hoc* response to what seemed overriding circumstance. The unemployment position was desperate. So money was borrowed and people put to work. When rising wages and prices threatened stability, a price ceiling was imposed. Although there had been much discussion of such policy in pre-Hitler Germany, it seems doubtful if it was highly influential. Hitler and his cohorts were not a bookish lot. Nevertheless the elimination of unemployment in Germany during the Great Depression without inflation—and with initial reliance on essentially civilian activities—was a signal accomplishment. It has rarely been praised and not much remarked. The notion that Hitler could do no good extends to his economics as it does, more plausibly, to all else.

Thus the effect of *The General Theory* was to legitimatize ideas that were in circulation. What had been the aberrations of cranks and crackpots became now respectable scholarly discussion. To suggest that there might be oversaving now no longer cost a man his degree or, necessarily, his promotion. That the proper remedy for oversaving was public spending financed by borrowing was henceforth a fit topic for discussion—although it continued to provoke bitter rebuke. The way was now open for public action.

The Keynesian ideas passed into the domain of public policy by way of the universities. If this was a revolution, it was not of the streets or of the shops but of the seminar rooms. Keynes was taken up, in the main,

---

[17]Joan Robinson. Quoted by Garvy.

by younger scholars. Economists are economical, among other things, of ideas; most make those of their graduate days do for a lifetime. So change comes not from men and women changing their minds but from the change from one generation to the next. Keynes's great contemporaries, almost without exception, reviewed his book and found it wrong. This conviction they then, with a few exceptions,[18] carried into retirement and perhaps beyond.

The principal British center of Keynesian discussion was, as might be expected, the University of Cambridge; here the ideas were brilliantly examined and explained by two younger colleagues of Keynes, R. F. Kahn and Joan Robinson. It was through Harvard that the Keynesian ideas reached the United States. In the months following the appearance of *The General Theory* the discussion was nearly continuous—an interested student could attend a seminar, formal or more often highly informal, on *The General Theory* almost any evening. Students who had been at Cambridge, England, and had known Keynes became minor oracles in Cambridge, Massachusetts—valued courts of appeal on what Keynes really meant.[19]

In time, Harvard alumni became aware of the Keynesian ferment and were distressed. (In later years a small organization, the Veritas Foundation, was formed to combat the menace.) The older faculty members, though tolerant, were not approving. In the autumn of 1936, the University celebrated its three-hundredth an-

---

[18]The most notable exceptions were Alvin H. Hansen, presently to be mentioned, and A. C. Pigou of Cambridge and King's College, whom Keynes singled out as the man whose writings represented the best in what was wrong. Pigou's last writing reflected strongly the influence of Keynes.

[19]The leading such authority was Robert Bryce, recently from the University of Cambridge, who went on from Harvard to thirty years and more of service as a senior Canadian official concerned with economic policy.

niversary. It was known that honorary degrees would be given to the greatest men in the various fields of science, social science, arts and public life, and that Franklin D. Roosevelt, to the distress of many distinguished graduates, was to give one of the principal speeches. The younger members of the Departments of Government and Economics offered suggestions to their elders as to proper recipients of the degrees; the thought was to propose names that, by their plausibility, would cause the maximum of embarrassment. The name so chosen by the political scientists was Leon Trotsky; by the younger economists, it was Keynes. Neither man was honored. Those who were are mostly forgotten.

From 1938 on, however, a senior member of the Harvard faculty, just arrived from the University of Minnesota, was vital for winning acceptance for Keynes. This was Alvin H. Hansen. Hansen's initial reaction to *The General Theory* as a reviewer was cool; however, he had a notable, even exceptional, capacity to change his mind. Soon his seminar on fiscal policy was a major focus of both theoretical and practical discussion. In the late '30s it was joined by a steady flow of Washington officials. Thus it became, in appreciable measure, the avenue by which the Keynesian ideas went on to Washington. Hansen also wrote lucidly and indefatigably on Keynesian policy. Less lucid but even more indefatigable was another, somewhat younger Harvard professor, Seymour E. Harris. Hansen, Harris and, with his pioneering textbook, Paul A. Samuelson were the men who brought the Keynesian ideas to Americans.[20]

---

[20] In these years a young group of Harvard and Tufts economists also published a small but influential tract on Keynesian policy. Richard V. Gilbert, George H. Hildebrand, Jr., Arthur W. Stuart, Maxine Yaple Sweezy, Paul M. Sweezy, Lorie Tarshis and John D. Wilson, *An Economic Program for American Democracy* (New York: Vanguard Press, 1938).

However, Washington in the second half of the '30s was also fertile ground. The failure of monetary policy, along with the folding up of the NRA, had left the Administration with no clear design for ending unemployment and promoting recovery. One possibility was an attack on monopoly. Monopolies were wicked; something good would surely come from harassing them. More logically, the market power of monopoly, as just noted, meant that prices remained higher in face of falling demand. It was output and employment that suffered. To restore competition would presumably reduce the influence of administered prices, diminish the importance of this cause of unemployment. In the later '30s there was a marked revival of interest in antitrust enforcement in Washington. It proceeded from this view of matters.

The difficulty was that market power and price administration were not a problem of a few firms; they were pervasive in the American economy. So the remedy required a complete restructuring of that economy. To spend money, as the experience of the early '30s with public works was by now showing, took time. But it was a marvel of immediacy as compared with the time that would be needed to bring the antitrust laws to bear on all American corporations that had power over their prices. And not many in the New Deal were willing to propose the logical companion step, which was to disintegrate the trade unions. So there remained only Keynes.

From the time of the publication of *The General Theory* forward, the center of Keynesian evangelism in Washington was the Board of Governors of the Federal Reserve System. History seemed to be proceeding in an exceptionally logical way. Monetary policy resulted only in an increase in excess reserves. Those responsible were turning, accordingly, to the less passive, more certain fiscal policy that ensured that the money would be spent. In fact, the role of the Federal Reserve was mostly an accident. Lauchlin Currie, having anticipated Keynes, was notably open to his ideas. He was now Director of Research for the Board. And the Chairman was Marriner Eccles, whose description of a bank run we have read. Eccles, reflecting on his own perilous experience as a banker and the deprivations and perils of Utah farmers and businessmen during the Depression, had been led quite independently to the view that the government should intervene in the economy along Keynesian lines. Thus the emergence of the Federal Reserve, after the publication of *The General Theory,* as the entering Washington wedge of Keynes.

Currie proceeded in a more practical way. In 1939, he moved from the Federal Reserve to the White House as, in fact though not in title, economic adviser to FDR, the first such in a long line. At the White House he constituted himself an employment agency and general dispatcher for government economists. As openings of importance developed anywhere in the government, he endeavored to see that they were filled by people of assured Keynesian convictions. By the end of the '30s he had established an informal network of such converts extending into all of the fiscally significant agencies. All remained in close communication on ideas and policies. Neither Currie nor any of those involved regarded this as a conspiracy. It merely seemed the necessary and sensible thing to do.[21]

---

[21]In the summer of 1940, a few days after the fall of France, I was summoned to Washington by Currie. Leon Henderson had just been placed in charge of prices in the recently revived National Defense Advisory Commission. It was potentially—and, as matters developed, in practice—a powerful position. Henderson was not, however, a fully ordained Keynesian. Currie wanted a reliable disciple to be at hand. I was such. From this came my wartime responsibility for price control. A couple of years earlier, also at Currie's behest, I had directed a large review of the public works experience of the '30s for the National Resources Planning Board ("The Economic Effects of the Federal Public Works Expenditures, 1933–1938" [with G. G. Johnson, Jr.]). The report, not surprisingly, took a strong stand for Keynesian policy—for use of public works and the

Thus were Keynesian ideas brought to bear in the second half of the '30s. It was on Washington rather than on London that they had their first impact. On the whole, however, it was more on thought and hope than on practical policy. Arrayed against the Keynesian ideas in a stout phalanx were all the practical men. When not able to grasp an idea, practical men take refuge in the innate superiority of common sense. Common sense is another term for what has always been believed.

What had always been believed, as against Keynes and the Keynesians, was an inordinately powerful thing. For two hundred years Americans of the truest blood had displayed a penchant for paper money. For seventy years they had agitated for silver. Monetary experiment in the United States was thus in an ancient and politically most acceptable tradition. It also retained a large political constituency. A congressman or senator, returning to Oklahoma or Iowa after urging an issue of greenbacks to enhance prices and advance social justice, could be a hero. No such tradition and no such constituency supported the idea of deficit financing, a deliberately, promiscuously unbalanced budget. A man returning to Iowa after advocating this in Washington might be thought dangerously insane.

---

requisite borrowing, not merely to give jobs and get buildings but as part of a broad policy for inducing recovery and increasing output: ". . . [U]nemployed men and materials," it stressed in unmistakable Keynesian vein, "[are] the normal or equilibrium situation in the modern economy . . . [T]he construction of public works, so financed as to offset otherwise idle saving, represents one of the devices for escaping a persistently low level of private investment and a persistently high level of unemployment." (P. 4.) Later in the '50s when Currie came under heavy (and richly unjustified) attack as an alleged Communist agent, I came across letters from him, long forgotten, urging the importance of getting "our people" into one or another agency of the Administration. "Our people" meant Keynesians. It occurred to me that I would have difficulty persuading one of the congressional committees then searching out Communists of this meaning. The occasion did not arise.

Wise governments had always sought to balance their budgets. Failure to do so had always been proof of political inadequacy; things need not be any more complicated than that. Also politicians had always sought to excuse failure to make ends meet and sometimes had displayed no slight ingenuity in the effort. However ingenious the explanations, all were ultimately meretricious—a cover for spending too much, taxing too little, managing too badly. Keynesian rationalization of deficits and deficit financing was surely more of the same. Advising Roosevelt in February 1933, President Hoover had said it would "steady the country greatly" were it made clear ". . . that the budget will be unquestionably balanced, even if further taxation is necessary; that the Government credit will be maintained by refusal to exhaust it in the issue of securities."[22]

Roosevelt did not disagree; in his first post-convention radio speech he said the country must "stop the deficits," adding that "Any Government, like any family, can for a year spend a little more than it earns. But you and I know that a continuation of that habit means the poorhouse."[23]

The beliefs so affirmed by the two Presidents were still powerful five years later—still a formidable barrier against the ideas of a distant English don. There was also explicit in Roosevelt's position what has come to be called the fallacy of composition. This too was a staunch bar to the Keynesian ideas—and it remains influential to this day.

An engagingly plausible mode of thought, the fallacy of composition extends the economics of the family to that of the government. A family cannot indefinitely spend beyond its income. So neither can a government.

[22]William Starr Myers and Walter H. Newton, *The Hoover Administration: A Documented Narrative* (New York: Charles Scribner's Sons, 1936), pp. 339–340. Cited in Schlesinger, p. 476.
[23]Schlesinger, p. 420.

A parent who borrows to live leaves debts, not a competence, to those who come after. A government that borrows does the same. Both are morally deficient.

The comparison between family and state, on second thought, is implausible. That anything so massive, diverse, complex, incomprehensible as the United States government (or any national government) should be subject to the same rules and constraints as a wage-earner's household is a matter that, to say the least, requires proof. Nor is it proof, as often said, that it *should* be so. Additionally it should be observed that the wealth and solvency of a nation depend on what its national economy produces. If borrowing and spending enhance production, as the Keynesian ideas held, then such borrowing and spending enhance solvency. Only rarely do borrowing and spending enhance wealth for a family. It was an enduring complaint of Keynesians that their opposition did not understand what they were trying to do. It was equally the case that the Keynesians did not understand the depth of the tradition to which their opposition was subject or the power by which it was governed.[24]

Keynesian policy in these years was also circumscribed by the small role available for taxation. Partly this was circumstance. Before World War II, the government of the United States was a small thing; in 1930, total expenditures were $1.4 billion; in 1940, still less than $10 billion. Purchases by the Federal government of goods and services were 2 percent of Gross National Product in 1930 and 6 percent in 1940.[25] In the latter '50s and '60s, in comparison, they ranged from 10 to 12 percent.[26]

Federal expenditures being small, so were the taxes

---

[24] A failure of understanding in which, needless to say, I shared.
[25] U.S. Bureau of the Census, *Historical Statistics*, p. 142.
[26] *Economic Report of the President, 1974*, pp. 249, 329.

to cover them. In later years Keynesian policy would come to depend heavily on two types of tax changes. One is the tendency of both the corporate and the personal income taxes to adjust themselves in a fortuitous way. When output and employment fall, so do profits and incomes, including those incomes subject to surtax. And as incomes fall, so, and more than proportionately, do the taxes paid. The reverse holds when output, employment, profits and incomes increase. In the '30s, taxes being small, this effect was negligible.

In later years also, the idea of tax reduction to increase the deficit and thus expand borrowing and spending from borrowed funds would gain acceptance. In the 1930s, with the budget out of balance, a tax cut in order to increase the deficit seemed a far too radical step even to the most persuaded Keynesians. Currie, and perhaps a few others, saw the failure to urge taxes as a flaw in the policy.[27] In general, however, Keynesian policy was considered identical with increasing public spending.

This, too, had an adverse political effect. Spending was not then for such socially reputable purposes as national defense. Rather it had the spendthrift aspect invariably associated with outlays for the average citizen or the poor. And Keynesian policy shared this reputation. In later times, when Keynesian policy to expand output came to lay greater emphasis on the use of taxes, attitudes would greatly change. Among the beneficiaries of tax reduction would be the affluent and the rich. Economic stimulation that works through the increased outlays of the affluent has, inevitably, an aspect of soundness and sanity that is lacking in expenditures on behalf of the undeserving poor. The shift from use of spending to use of tax reduction would have much to do with making Keynesian stimulation of the economy respectable.

---

[27]He once expressed this belief to me.

So, as far as the '30s went, the practical effect of Keynes was not very great. In 1932, 1933 and 1934, the revenues of the Federal government had been less than half of expenditures—a greater relative imbalance than in any peacetime year since. In the fiscal year ending June 30, 1932, revenues were $1.9 billion, expenditures $4.7 billion. But in relation to the economy these magnitudes were, as noted, far from impressive. Then, after 1934, revenues gained relatively on expenditures. By the fiscal year ending in June 1938, the deficit was only $1.2 billion on expenditures of $6.8 billion. It rose again in consequence of the recession of 1937–1938, and part of the increase was deliberate. It was then, for the first time, that the deficit was justified, at least by policy-makers to themselves, by Keynesian policy. But the magnitudes were still small. In the 1939 fiscal year the deficit, for example, was only $3.9 billion, the same amount as in the year following. This was only marginally greater than the $3.6 billion deficit in 1934.[28] Clearly the triumph of Keynesian policy was not overwhelming. "Fiscal policy . . . [was] an unsuccessful recovery device in the 'thirties—not because it did not work, but because it was not tried."[29]

The Great Depression did not, in fact, end. It was swept away by World War II. This was, in a grim sense, the triumph of the Keynesian policy. But the problem it posed was not employment and output; it was inflation. And for this, as was to be learned again a quarter-century on, the Keynesian system did not answer.

---

[28]U.S. Bureau of the Census, *Historical Statistics*, p. 711.
[29]E. Cary Brown, "Fiscal Policy in the 'Thirties—A Reappraisal," *The American Economic Review*, Vol. XLVI, No. 5 (December 1956), p. 863.

CHAPTER XVII

War and the Next Lesson

THE EDUCATIONAL ROLE of catastrophe in the first half of the present century was obviously considerable. The First World War showed how fragile was the monetary structure that had been erected on gold—a structure which, by 1914, nearly all who presumed to expert knowledge on the matter believed to have solved the age-old problem of money. With the August guns the gold standard disappeared; it was never in any satisfactory way to be restored. The great boom of the 1920s showed how futile was monetary policy as an instrument of restraint, at least when employed by men who did not wish to be blamed for the crash that, not unreasonably, it was supposed might follow from its effective use. The Great Depression showed the patent ineffectuality of monetary policy for rescuing the country from a slump—for breaking out of the underemployment equilibrium once this had been fully and firmly established. For this only fiscal policy would serve. Only fiscal policy ensured not just that money was available to be borrowed but that it *would* be borrowed and *would* be spent. This was the lesson of John Maynard Keynes.

Now came the lesson of another war. It was that fiscal policy, however useful for expanding output and employment and overcoming depression or recession, was, by itself, ineffective in reverse. In the modern, highly organized, industrial economy it could not pre-

vent inflation except at the price of far more unemployment, far more idle capacity than was tolerable in
peacetime or could even be contemplated in war.

These were the lessons. The learning was, in all
cases, imperfect. The hope that monetary policy would
work, the faith in the magic of men managing the modern economy from around a polished table, would survive in economic pedagogy and have a disastrous resur-
gence in practical policy a full quarter century on. The
lesson of World War II that general measures for restraining demand do not prevent inflation in an economy that is operating at or near capacity was also
resisted for another quarter century. The wartime experience, it was said, was *sui generis;* what could be
done in a peacetime economy was very different. Nos-
talgia combines regularly with manifest respectability
to give precedence to old error as opposed to new truth.

The Second World War came gradually to both
Britain and the United States. From the fading summer
days of 1939 until the invasion of France the following
May it was possible in Britain to believe, however
improbable it might seem in retrospect, that full-scale
conflict could be avoided. And in the United States,
until the fall of France, the dominant hope was for
remaining out. Only gradually, in ensuing months, did
this hope give way to fear that the United States might
not be involved, that Hitler might triumph. The consequence was that, in both countries, there was a
period for planning, when, indeed, there was a compulsion on the part of their governments to show by
way of public reassurance that such planning was in
process. Not a little of this had to do with economics.

In both countries the economic planning reflected
strongly the new Keynesian fiscal design. What was
urged as the policy against peacetime unemployment
would work against wartime inflation; instead of public

expenditure to increase employment there would now be higher taxes to restrict civilian demand and consumption. This restriction would make manpower, plant and materials available for military use. This was the heart of the matter; all else was detail.

That British planning conformed to the Keynesian design was not wholly surprising; the most influential architect was Keynes himself. During the months of anticipation he published his views in detail first in the *Times* (London), then in a widely circulated booklet called *How to Pay for the War*.[1] The basic needs of life—food, rent, elementary clothing—would be supplied in adequate quantity at stable prices. If costs rose, subsidies would be employed to keep prices stable. This, in turn, would remove the justification for wage increases. Wage stability was important. For the rest, aggregate demand or purchasing power would be kept in rough equilibrium with the supply of goods available for purchase at current prices. This would be accomplished partly by taxation, partly by a Keynesian novelty, which was compulsory saving. A levy would be made against all wages, salaries and other incomes, which would be returnable, with interest, after the war. Given the dark experience of the '30s, this refreshment to postwar purchasing power would then be a most welcome stimulant.

The curtailment or removal of purchasing power was the basic reliance. Keynes said, ". . . the only way to escape from this [inflation] is to withdraw from the market, either by taxation or by deferment, an adequate proportion of consumers' purchasing power, so there is no longer an irresistible force impelling prices upward."[2] Only a subordinate role was assigned to direct control of prices or to rationing— ". . . some measure of rationing and price control should play a

---

[1] John Maynard Keynes, *How to Pay for the War* (New York: Harcourt Brace & Co., 1940).
[2] Keynes, p. 51.

part in our general scheme and might be a valuable *adjunct* to our *main* proposal."[3]

In Washington, as in previous years, the response to Keynes was more prompt and reverent than it was in Whitehall. Accordingly, a substantially similar design was envisaged. In Washington, however, there was an alternative. Calling on his World War I experience, Bernard Baruch was insisting that only a comprehensive control of wages and prices would serve in the event of another war. "I think you have first to put a *ceiling* over the whole price structure, including wages, rents and farm prices . . ."[4] The prestige of Baruch in the Congress was very great—an eminence that was derived less from his wisdom or exceptional physical presence than from his relentless subsidy of those southern senators who were best assured of re-election and in whom, therefore, such investment involved no serious risk of pecuniary loss.[5] Accordingly, the issue was not met in forthright debate. It was proposed that, by means of taxation, demand would be kept roughly in line with what the economy could produce at the going price when plant and labor force were fully employed. This would be the main reliance for preventing inflation. But as production expanded from the Depression levels under the stimulus of wartime demand, bottlenecks could be expected for certain products and materials. These would be particularly serious for items —metals, machine tools, chemicals—which would be under the special pressure of military need. Here price

---

[3] Keynes, p. 51. The italics are added.

[4] Testimony before the House Banking and Currency Committee, September 19, 1941. Cited by Bernard Baruch, *The Public Years* (New York: Holt, Rinehart & Winston, 1960), p. 287. Italics added.

[5] According to common calculation, twenty or so received a campaign contribution from Baruch of $1000 each election, with $5000 for James Byrnes of South Carolina who acted as whipper-in. Required only were regular speeches affirming the wisdom of Baruch. At an estimated $4000 to $5000 a year, this was a superb and extremely economical investment in public relations.

ceilings would be used and controls placed, as necessary, on use or consumption. The word ceiling was
adopted in the hope that Baruch, who had used the
term, would be pleased and give his blessing. It was
thought also to give a useful (if quite fraudulent) impression of flexibility. Prices could always fluctuate
downward from the ceiling, although it was certain in
the circumstances in which they would be imposed that
they would not. In a paper that had influential circulation in Washington in 1941, it was noted that "the
best-remembered lesson of our World War [I] experience concerns inflation"; that "whatever the state of
feeling about the present war, any sort of poll would
show a grim [sic] determination to defeat inflation."
It argued, as did Keynes, that the ultimate reliance
for preventing inflation must be on measures which
"seek to check the increase or to reduce the volume
of spending in the economy as a whole."[6]

In these preliminary designs no role was assigned to
monetary policy—after the failures of the previous
decades it was considered, at best, futile. And, in the
event, it had no significant role during the war. The
rediscount rate was set for the duration at the modest
level of 1 percent, with a lower preferential rate for
short-term loans to the government. Access to this bargain by the banks was limited by the wartime regulations and restraints limiting the demand for bank loans,
including direct controls over consumer credit. In the
years from 1940 on, the Federal Reserve became, as
noted, a Washington backwater. Its most signal contri-

---

[6]John Kenneth Galbraith, "The Selection and Timing of Inflation
Controls," *The Review of Economic Statistics*, Vol. 23, No. 2 (May
1941), p. 82 et seq. The importance to be attached by a historian to
a paper written by himself is a troublesome matter and one on
which anything but extreme modesty must invite skepticism. However, in this case there is some redeeming proof. The views expressed
in the paper led to my being placed in charge of the organization
and administration of wartime price control, a post that I held,
amidst steadily mounting criticism, from April 1941 for the next
two years.

bution to wartime operations in 1940 and early 1941 was in housing in its gleaming new Washington headquarters the National Defense Advisory Commission which was planning and, in a manner of speaking, organizing the initial economic mobilization.

In late May 1940, just before the fall of France, President Roosevelt established—in fact, revived from World War I—the agency just mentioned, the NDAC; its purpose was to plan and organize for military production or, as many suspected, to reassure the citizenry by simulating such action. One of its seven members, Leon Henderson, an exceptionally intelligent and exceptionally energetic public official, was charged with directing efforts "at price stabilization in the raw materials field."[7] Henderson interpreted the term raw materials broadly to include the prices of everything except farm products, where for twenty years public policy, in rhetoric or in fact, had been committed not to stabilizing prices but to increasing them. This commitment was not altered by the prospect of war. Henderson and a small staff held what was mainly a watching brief on prices until April 1941, when, by Executive Order, the Office of Price Administration and Civilian Supply was established, also under Henderson. This office was authorized to establish ceilings on prices; however, legislative authority was lacking, and only verbal condemnation could be visited on violators. (It was during these years that, to describe such oral punishment, the word jawboning entered the language.)

In early 1942, following the attack on Pearl Harbor and after exceptionally extended legislative hearings and debate, price control received full legislative sanction with special courts for enforcement and duly established penalties for violation. Authority for the control of

---

[7] The *New York Times,* May 29, 1940.

wages was not sought; throughout the war this remained a matter for relatively informal, although not for that reason less firm, control. Farm prices were made subject to effective control only in mid-1943.

With the passage of the Emergency Price Control Act of 1942 just described, the way was open for the full application of the, by now, approved Keynesian design. There would be firm control of those prices that were under particular pressure; fiscal restraint on demand would keep prices in general stable. As the new price-control legislation became effective, it became evident that the overall design was sadly defective. It has sufficiently been observed that economic ideas that are admirable in their supporting theory can prove sadly deficient in practice. It is a tendency that does not spare even authors of a history such as this. However, the intended World War II design was deficient both in theory and in practice.

The practical failure involved the oldest problem of war finance—the tendency of expenditures, under the imperatives of military need, to outrun the best-intentioned efforts to increase revenues. By any earlier standard, taxes were increased astringently in World War II; by 1944, the revenues of the Federal government were six times the 1939 level, an impressive expansion. But outlays increased even more rapidly; in 1942, the first year of conflict, they were more than twice revenues. In all later years of the war expenditures were between twice and three times revenues.[8] No more than in earlier conflicts did it prove possible to keep taxation abreast of outlays. With less wishful thinking or even a better knowledge of history, this might have been foreseen.

---

[8] Figures as given in the *Economic Report of the President, 1974,* p. 324. All subsequent figures on Federal revenues and expenditures, unless otherwise indicated, are those from the national income and product accounts. These are the revenue and expenditure figures that show most accurately the effect of government operations on the economy.

The selective fixing of prices also encountered intensely practical difficulties. Prices in the modern industrial economy are inconveniently numerous; those in different parts of the economy had to be given to different people to monitor. The speed of the reaction of different people to price increases varied as inevitably as that of runners in a road race or lovers to love. Additionally, there was a marked difference in the ease or difficulty with which ceilings for different products were set. Some products come in only a few grades, qualities, sizes, at F.O.B. prices without special discounts. In other cases the product is a thing of breathtaking variety, and the prices likewise. This difference affected the reaction time of price-fixers. The differing reaction time meant, in turn, that one industry might easily get away with a price increase that for another would be forbidden. Such differences in treatment did not escape notice; they certainly did not if the price of the uncontrolled industry, e.g., coal or scrap, was the cost of the controlled one, e.g., steel. This difficulty should also have been foreseen.

Such were the practical problems of the Keynesian design. The deeper problem of economic principle was even more serious and would survive to plague policy for the next thirty years. It resulted from market power; it meant that, long before full employment was reached, corporations had the power to raise their prices, and it was greatly to their earnings advantage to do so. Unemployment (including those on work relief projects), which averaged nearly 20 percent of the civilian labor force in 1938, fell sharply under the influence of military spending—to 14.6 percent in 1940 and to 9.9 percent in 1941.[9] This reduction was an impressive demonstration not only of the efficacy of the Keynesian remedy for unemployment but also of the differing reaction to military as opposed to civilian expenditure.

---

[9]U.S. Bureau of the Census, *Historical Statistics of the United States, Colonial Times to 1957* (Washington, D.C., 1960), p. 73.

An outlay for civilian purposes only a fraction as large just a few months before would have brought cries of the deepest alarm from conservatives and, among the susceptible, symptoms of severe cardiac arrest. Now it was greatly welcomed.

But price increases did not wait for full employment. In late 1941, with unemployment still substantial, prices began to rise, and the increase quickened in the early months of 1942. Farm prices rose, and considering their previous low level, this was inevitable. But industrial prices also began to go up and in face of expanding output and good and improving earnings. It was clear that, very soon, price advances would be large and general. And wage increases would soon be stimulating and justifying yet further price advances. In later years there would be much discussion among economists of the Phillips Curve,[10] a statistical function showing, on the basis of past experience, the price increase that would have to be accepted to bring unemployment down to any particular level. The experience of 1941 showed what was later to be learned, that the relationship between inflation and unemployment was highly unattractive—that below a certain rather high level of unemployment the cost of a further reduction of unemployment was a very substantial rate of price increase, one considerably greater than Phillips foresaw.

There was, happily, a solution for both the practical and the theoretical problems. That was to go back to Baruch and fix all significant prices at the same time. This required only that previously and quite eloquently

---

[10]Named for A. W. Phillips of the Australian National University and the London School of Economics. Though a subject of much fashionable discussion, the calculations underlying the curve were considered suspect by more perceptive economists, for they depended on information antedating, in part, the rise of modern corporate and union power. A. W. Phillips, "The Relation Between Unemployment and the Rate of Change of Money Wage Rates in the UK, 1861–1957," *Economica,* Vol. XXV, No. 100 (November 1958).

argued positions be quietly but completely reversed. This, once the need was faced, was accomplished with exemplary speed and with almost no public rebuke or even comment.

On April 28, 1942, the General Maximum Price Regulation placed a ceiling over all prices (farm prices substantially excepted until 1943) at the highest levels reached during the previous month. The GMPR, known also as General Max, remained, with much refinement and modification, the basic control until the summer of 1946 when regulations were lifted. Rents were also controlled.

A myth to the contrary, assiduously cultivated by devout friends of the market, these controls were highly effective. From 1942 through 1945, the wholesale prices of industrial commodities were virtually stable —the overall increase from 50.7 to 53.00 (1967= 100) compares with an increase of from 135.3 to 166.1 in the single year of 1974. From 1943, when ceilings became applicable to food, the wholesale index was wholly stable. (Increases in the farm prices of some foods were also offset by subsidies.) The Consumer Price Index increased between 1943 and 1945 from 51.8 to 53.9. During 1974, it increased from 139.7 to 155.4.[11] Given the scale of the military effort and the associated budget deficit, it is beyond doubt that, in the absence of controls, there would have been large, accelerating and, ultimately, vertical increases in prices. By the end of the war prices and wages would almost certainly have been doubling, perhaps trebling each year, maybe more. It is also part of the adverse legend that there was a serious black market and a sharp deterioration in quality. These the indexes did not measure. In fact, the proportion of all transactions in the black market was small even at the end of the war. And quality

---

[11] All price data from the *Economic Report of the President, 1975*, pp. 300, 305.

deterioration poses technical problems. It is not easy, even with determination, much to reduce the quality of gasoline, coal, electricity or even numerous foods.

When controls were lifted in 1946, there was a substantial bulge in prices. The Consumer Price Index went from 53.9 in 1945 to 58.5 the following year and to 66.9 in 1947. After a further gain of five points it then leveled off and fell.[12] This increase is the further case against the efficacy of controls; it showed that the wartime inflation was only postponed. It would be more sensible to take it as an indication of what would have occurred, in vastly greater magnitude, during the war, had there been no controls. And some of this bulge could have been avoided, had the wartime controls been less abruptly canceled in 1946.

The controls were not popular with those whose prices were fixed. Their unpopularity was almost certainly enhanced by the youth of those administering them and by the tendency to equate effectiveness of control with inflexibility of administration. Also, in the common view, those responsible did not entirely conceal a certain administrative sadism where the large corporation was involved or their conviction that they had not only a monopoly of economic wisdom but of patriotism as well. Controls remained highly popular, however, with the public. Chester Bowles, an effective executive and accomplished advocate who became OPA Administrator in 1943, was one of the first public officials to use polls to test public reaction to policies. In November 1945, he received the following analysis of public attitudes:

> According to the countrywide survey which we have just completed, the public support we have had for the last three years is undiminished. The way in which OPA has handled not only price controls but rationing is still overwhelmingly approved by the women

---

[12]*Economic Report of the President, 1974*, p. 300.

who do the shopping. Ninety-one percent say that OPA has done a "good" or "fairly good" job in handling price controls and only 9% say it has done a "poor job." The support of what remains of rationing is almost equally great.[13]

The social memory of World War I in the United States was of inflation. It is significant that the memory of World War II, a much greater convulsion in economic terms, was not of inflation. When that war ended, the memory was still of the depression that had preceded it.

The theoretical miscalculation concerning price stabilization policy in World War II in the United States turned on the market power of the great corporations and the not unrelated role of the unions. Corporations, as noted, could raise prices well before full-employment output was reached. The resulting higher profits and living costs then led—or would have led—to enhanced union demands. This use of power effectively defeated all hope of a nice balance between aggregate demand and aggregate supply at stable prices and approximately full-employment output. However, it may be that the penalties and rewards of error in economics are impartially distributed. Corporate power made comprehensive price control necessary in World War II but it also contributed signally and unexpectedly to its success.

That was because it proved relatively simple to fix prices in industries where there was market power. And such industries—those of the large corporations—being common to a large part of the economy, the task of controlling prices was, in the aggregate, much simplified.

---

[13]Chester Bowles, *Promises to Keep* (New York: Harper & Row, 1971), p. 136.

Specifically in markets of many sellers and many buyers—those where there is no market power—there is no mechanism by which, if there is a shortage at the going price, the supply that is available can be distributed equitably among the claimant buyers. Some buyers get all they want; some get nothing. In these circumstances the incentive to pay something to the seller to avoid total deprivation is very strong. And the temptation to the seller to accept is not weak. And the number of buyers and sellers being great, the chances of detection are small. Also, since in the small enterprise records are meager or nonexistent and employees few and often reliable, the illegal transaction leaves few tracks, does not risk exposure by a telephone call to the government from a patriotic, righteous and indignant employee. In the competitive market of small sellers and buyers, controls are very difficult to enforce.

With the large corporation everything is vastly easier. There is, first, the effect of excess capacity. The small competitive firm operates, in effect, at capacity. The large corporation, in contrast, usually operates with some excess capacity. This was notably the case in 1941 and 1942; where in agriculture the effect of the diminished demand in the preceding Depression years had been on prices, in corporate industry, as repeatedly noted, it had been much more on output. Accordingly, when the prices of the large corporation were fixed, it could continue to expand output and could therefore continue for a substantial period to supply all of its customers. The shortage and resulting temptation to noncompliance did not soon develop. And with the expanding output went expanding profits which removed the justification (though not the pleas) for higher prices.

Even when capacity operations were reached, controls on the large firm were easier to administer than on the small, competitive enterprise. The large firm knew its customers; it could distribute scarce supplies more or less equitably between them or it could be ordered to do so. The number of firms to be watched for violations was small. Each had elaborate records which simplified the search for illegal transactions. Employees or unions volunteered information on corporate hanky-panky. Along with all else there was the wholesome vulnerability of the large firm to adverse publicity. There is sympathy for the small lawbreaker in economic matters, much more rarely for the large.

That price control for the large firm with market power was a far simpler matter than for those in the classical competitive market was not a discovery after the fact. It was well observed at the time and, like most of the lessons of the wartime experience, little studied and soon forgotten. It was summarized not long after the war as follows:

> Over the great range of manufactured producers' and consumers' goods, both in World War II and in the recent [Korean War] period, price control has been administered with relatively little public fuss and controversy. There have been relatively few complaints of maldistribution of supplies or of black markets. This, by common observation, is the part of the economy where market imperfection is characteristic. The great problems of price control have been encountered in food and clothing, the part of the economy which, with important exceptions, most closely approaches pure competition. At least two-thirds of the energies of the Office of Price Administration were devoted to these products, and a considerably larger fraction of its failures were in this area. The efforts to hold meat prices, before and after an effective rationing system was in effect, provided an almost classic display of the frustrations of price-fixing *qua* price-fixing in the market of many sellers and buyers.[14]

---

[14]John Kenneth Galbraith, *A Theory of Price Control* (Cambridge: Harvard University Press, 1952), p. 26. This conclusion parallels that of a yet earlier article by the same author, "Reflections on Price

The nature of the economic system of World War II can now be seen as a whole. It is a thing which has rarely been so viewed.

Since prices during the war remained at remunerative levels and thus provided the incentive to production, their function did not entirely disappear. But, along with money, their role was greatly reduced. Specifically and rather obviously, since they were fixed, prices no longer rose to cut back on the use or consumption of products or services in short supply. And such increases no longer advised producers as to where they should invest or expand. Nor were price rises the decisive factor in moving plant, labor and materials into military use, although prices of military items were, of course, at remunerative levels.[15]

Civilian consumption was reduced not by higher prices but by rationing or by allowing shelves to go empty and thus forcing consumers to turn away empty-handed or by giving the supplies to those who arrived earliest of a morning or stood longest in a queue. Not all of these techniques are to be recommended. Needed military production was obtained not by higher prices but by a combination of negative and affirmative controls. Automobile production, most civilian construction, most investment for nonmilitary purposes were forbidden and therewith the use of materials and manpower in these employments. And nonmilitary, nonessential use of steel, copper, other metals, rubber and other such materials was prohibited. Ceilings were also placed on employment in civilian industries. Affirmative controls then allocated the scarcest of the

---

Control," *The Quarterly Journal of Economics,* Vol. LX, No. 4 (August 1946), p. 475 et seq.

[15]Prices of military end-products—tanks, aircraft, ammunition, ships—were subject to whatever control was inherent in control procedures. Despite some initial efforts in that direction they were not otherwise subject to the ceilings. Prices of materials going into military use were, of course, controlled.

scarce materials—steel, copper, aluminum, rubber, a few others—to military or indispensable civilian purposes.

Associated and vitally assisting the foregoing controls was the expansion of the economy. The total output of the economy in constant prices—the Gross National Product—increased from $209 billion in 1939, the last year unaffected by war or the prospect of war, to a peak of $361 billion in 1944. This increase was about the same as that in government purchases for wartime purposes. This meant that aggregate civilian consumption was not reduced during the war; on the contrary, it greatly increased, for there was a decline in civilian business investment. Civilian purchases of goods and services in constant prices were $156 billion in 1940, $171 billion in 1944, another $12 billion more in 1945.[16]

Thus World War II in the United States was fought, broadly speaking, from expanded production—from employing the plant and labor force that had been idle during the Depression, from drawing new workers into the labor force, from working longer hours.[17] Possibly not since the agony of the Christian martyrs under Rome was there so much mention of the grandeur of sacrifice as in the United States during these years. The reference was to goods, not blood. Some goods, such as new automobiles and alarm clocks, became unavailable. But by the end of the war Americans had more to consume, both in the aggregate and per

---

[16]*Economic Report of the President, 1974,* p. 250. These are 1958 prices.

[17]The Twentieth Century Fund, by rough estimate, attributed approximately three-quarters of the increased output from 1940 to 1944 to the employment of the previously unemployed and of workers newly drawn into the labor force. The rest was attributed to natural increase in numbers and to productivity gains. *America's Needs and Resources* (New York: The Twentieth Century Fund, 1947), p. 13.

family, than ever before. Rarely has sacrifice been so rewarded and so rewarding.

There was, however, far more money to spend than could be spent. Though consumer supplies rose, the wages, salaries and profits accruing from expanded output and employment rose much more. The difference was saving; never before and not since have Americans put money aside on such a scale. Partly this was in response to the war-bond drives, and this time no one was encouraged to go to the banks to get the money to buy them. Indeed, the bonds were made ineligible as collateral for loans. Saving also rose because money was difficult to spend: Some goods that were wanted were rationed; some, such as gasoline, that were necessary for spending for other things were scarce or also rationed. (It has often been observed that one saves money by staying home.) Some required standing in line. A few customary objects of expenditure, such as new automobiles and new houses, could not be bought. People also saved because, come the end of the war, they expected prices to go down, the depression to resume, jobs to become scarce. It would be well, then, to have a nest egg.

In 1940, personal savings were 5.1 percent of disposable income. In 1943 and 1944, they were 25 percent.[18] As a moment's reflection will suggest, this was a remarkable design for getting effort during a war. Men and women were working not to obtain services and goods which required manpower and materials and equipment to produce; they were working in return for money which cost nothing to produce. A quarter of all civilian effort in 1943 and 1944 was so engendered. Claims on actual manpower, materials and plant

---

[18]*Economic Report of the President, 1974,* p. 268.

were postponed until after the war. It is too bad that so fortunate an arrangement was also fortuitous; it should have been the fruit of much careful planning.[19]

In Britain, Canada, Australia, as also in Germany, the broad design of wartime administration was similar to that in the United States. In the United States the rationing of scarce or exceptionally indispensable commodities—tires, sugar, shoes, heating oil, gasoline, canned goods, meat—was important but not as in Britain or Germany completely central to wartime economic management. The rationing of foods suffered from the relentless optimism of those responsible for food supply as to what would be available and from their associated desire to cultivate popularity and applause by increasing the allowable ration. In consequence, it frequently happened that supplies were not forthcoming in sufficient quantity to fill the ration. Purchasers then found themselves with money and a ration ticket, both of the requisites for a purchase, but nothing to buy. A principal purpose of a rationing system, which is to provide a smaller amount but to *ensure* that this smaller amount, come what may, is available, was defeated. In Britain rationing was far more comprehensive and administered with superior precision. Rationing was also far more central to the German design.

In both Britain and Germany as the war proceeded, the ration coupons became the decisive currency. Everyone or almost everyone could obtain the requisite pounds or marks; it was the availability of a ration ticket that determined whether or not a purchase, almost any purchase, could be made. In contrast with

---

[19]This design, which I called "the disequilibrium system," I described in some detail in *A Theory of Price Control*. The book, published for a professional audience in 1952, invited a general lack of interest.

the more traditional means of exchange, the ration ticket is, with privileged exceptions, available to all in equal amounts. The rich in property, pay or accumulation of traditional currency are allowed no more of this currency, and thus can buy no more, than the poor. And the rich are not usually allowed to buy ration coupons from others. Accordingly, the use of a ration currency imposes an egalitarianism which is thought necessary for morale during war but which is not deemed at all desirable in peace.

In Britain during the war accumulations of traditional money increased. However, taxes were very high and incomes were kept under tight restraint. In consequence, money did not become an object of contempt; as in the United States it seemed worth holding for expenditure after the war. In Germany, as also in the other European belligerents, the accumulations of traditional money became very large, and for the second time in a quarter of a century the mark became effectively worthless. For access to goods it was only ration coupons or similar entitlement that counted. In these circumstances the fixed prices did not matter greatly; they became, like the money that covered them, an unimportant datum as compared with whether the individual had the requisite ration ticket. It is the peculiar feature of ration currency that it is good for one transaction or (if passed back by the retailer to claim replacement stocks) one set of transactions. No one, in consequence, had an incentive to work to accumulate them; no one could be denied the minimum entitlement. Under this currency regime in Germany in the years immediately following World War II, productive activity proceeded largely under the impulse of habit and momentum.

The suppressed inflation of 1945–1948 was far more damaging to production than its predecessor in 1923. On the other hand, the inflation of 1923, with its euthanasia of the rentier class—of all who held assets denoted and payable in marks—had almost certainly a far greater effect on relative wealth. On the whole, and for this reason, the social memory of Germans of the 1923 inflation was stronger than of the 1945 experience. So it remains. The loss of assets makes a deep impression on an impressionable class of people. The loss of jobs is accepted more philosophically.

The mark being largely useless as a medium of exchange in Germany after 1945, substitutes, as ever, came into use. More precisely, there was a return to one of the classic currencies of the past, namely tobacco. This was now available in a far superior form. Instead of leaf passed awkwardly from hand to hand or the sometimes suspect warehouse certificate, there was the neatly minted, highly standardized cigarette. This was the equivalent, in all respects, of a well-considered coinage. The single cigarette was excellent small change; the package of twenty and the carton of two hundred were convenient multiples for large or major transactions. The decimal form was modified but not to the point of mathematical difficulty. Few forms of money in history have been more difficult to counterfeit. None had within it such an excellent tendency to a self-regulation of its value. If the exchange value of cigarettes had a tendency to fall, i.e., if supply was too great and the price of products in exchange for cigarettes too high, there was a tendency for the holder of this coin to smoke it up or offer it to his addicted friends rather than pass it on. This had the effect of reducing supply, maintaining value. Some abuse came from the collection of discarded butts and their recycling into new but inferior coin. In 1946, in the washroom adjoining the offices of General Lucius Clay and the other senior American military government officials in Germany was a sign, "Do Not Throw Cigarette Butts in the Urinals." A soldier who had observed the diligence with which these were sought for recycling had appended underneath, the further explanation, "It Makes Them Soggy and Hard to Smoke." However, such inferior coin could readily be recognized, and it was accepted only at appropriate discount. The instinct of the early American colonists that tobacco had the makings of an admirable medium of exchange was fully supported by the experience in Germany after World War II.

In 1948, in keeping with the practice of several other countries after World War II, came the German currency reform. Subject to rather complex arrangements to maintain parity of sacrifice as between money and other assets, this consisted, in essence, in bringing the vast currency overhang down to size. This, as earlier described, was by exchange of the old reichsmarks for new deutschemarks at the rate of ten of the first for one of the second—a distinctly more modest ratio than the trillion-to-one exchange of the reichsmark for the rentenmark in 1923. Merchants and producers, as also noted, had heard that the new money was coming. They waited for it. Suddenly, when it arrived, the shops were replete with goods. For the new money it was also worthwhile making more goods. Price controls could now be abandoned, as also rationing. And tobacco as money was once again on its way into the mists of history and legend. The dependable cycle which, in the management of money, causes people to react most strongly against their most adverse recent experience was soon seen at work in Germany. Having suffered again from inflation after World War II and with the memories of 1923 still strong, the Germans in the next two decades were, of all people, the most at pains to prevent inflation. And, in doing so, they made the deutschemark, in time, the new world symbol of sound money

CHAPTER XVIII

Good Years:
The Preparation

THE TWENTY YEARS from 1948 through 1967 may
well be celebrated by historians as the most benign era
in the history of the industrial economy, as also of
economics. The two decades were without panic,
crisis, depression or more than minor recession. In
only two years, 1954 and 1958, did output fail to
expand in the United States. It was during these decades
that the new term Gross National Product, or GNP, entered the language; it was something which, as frequently affirmed, enjoyed what was always called a
healthy growth. As to the health of growth there were,
indeed, no doubts. Unemployment was low in these
years, at least by the standards of the '30s—in only
two years, 1958 and 1961, did it average more than 6
percent of the labor force. And by later standards there
was no appreciable inflation. During the '50s, industrial
prices had a disagreeable tendency to edge upward
as wage settlements were passed along in higher prices
and higher prices led to larger settlements—the familiar
spiral. But this movement, though uncomfortable at
the time, was small in comparison with subsequent misfortune and was partly offset (except for farmers) by
declining farm prices. In 1948, the wholesale price index stood at 82.8; in 1967, it was 100.[1] This increase,
by roughly seventeen points in twenty years, was be-

---

[1]*Economic Report of the President, 1974,* p. 305.

low the annual rate of increase in the same index in the summer of 1974. Beginning in the early '60s and continuing for several years, prices were wholly stable. In these years American business leaders, meeting on occasions of public ceremony and comparing their performance with that of the Communist countries, found themselves all but overwhelmed by their own praise. Economists, while reserving some of the credit for themselves, did not disagree. Nor secretly did many Communists. It was a very difficult time for critics of the capitalist system.

This was especially so in the United States but in other industrial countries things were only slightly less benign. Repair of wartime damage went rapidly. On occasion countries found themselves with imports that were too large, exports that were too small and, in consequence, diminishing means of payment with which to pay for the difference. The problem of Britain in these years was often difficult, partly because the British enjoy economic discussion far more than any other people and thus celebrate their difficulties more fully, and partly because the British economy, with its great dependence on imports and exports, requires, as earlier observed, a far more exact management than that of France or the United States. So at intervals during this period the British were faced with a deteriorating trade balance. In 1949 and 1967, it was necessary to devalue the pound. And, otherwise, after orgiastic discussion repeating more or less verbatim the newspaper headlines and Parliamentary debates of the last crisis, business investment would be moderately restrained, the increase in consumption moderately restricted by higher taxation or tighter controls on consumer borrowing, and the increase in public expenditure would be slowed, often by abandoning another symbol of imperial grandeur. This would bring a suitable readjustment of imports to exports, and Britain would again be saved.

As in the years before 1914, firms traded and people traveled in certain knowledge of what their dollars, pounds, francs, marks or yen would bring when exchanged between themselves or for other currencies. The notion of a floating, i.e., of an erratic and unknown, movement as between currencies had not been invented. Not many would have thought it a good thing. In the early years of this period there were still restrictions on the movement of capital from one country to another—in simple terms, on the amount of money that could be changed from one currency to another at one time. And similarly there were restrictions on trade. But through these years both capital movements and trade restrictions were steadily liberalized as exchange controls were eliminated and tariffs and quotas on the movement of goods were reduced. The European states—France, Germany, Italy, Belgium, the Netherlands, Luxembourg—began their movement to what they hoped would be full economic union. Economists of the widest persuasion have long measured the progress in intellectual perception of many by their ability to see the larger gains of international trade as opposed to the narrower and more selfish rewards of protection. Not the least of the wonders of these years was the evidence that, at long last, in his view of international trade, man had matured. Farmers and a few others were still apostles of the protectionist darkness. For the rest the age of light had arrived.

One idea and two institutions received major credit for the achievements of these years. The idea was, of course, Keynesian fiscal policy. By controlling expenditures in relation to revenues, government made the level of output and therewith the level of employment in the economic system a dependent, not an independent, variable—the product of a positive policy, not the uncertain consequence of the vagaries of the business cycle. And this was all that was changed. The private ownership of the means of production, the private corporation, the classical market all remained as before. The Keynesian system was a highly conservative idea but, seemingly, it worked. In all the industrial countries it was accepted.

The two institutional arrangements, which were thought especially important for the United States, were the Bretton Woods agreements and the Employment Act of 1946. The first brought order to international monetary arrangements. The second, through the Council of Economic Advisers to the President and the Joint Committee on the Economic Report (later the Joint Economic Committee), provided an operative structure for Keynesian ideas in both the Federal Executive and the Congress.

Keynes was a prime mover in the Bretton Woods design. Accordingly, his name is associated not only with the ideas that receive credit for the success of these years but also with both of the institutions. If there is a case for naming the two decades for any individual, they are thus rightly called the Age of Keynes.[2] By now Keynes was no longer a suspect figure on the British scene. As Baron Keynes of Tilton he had become a fully accredited member of the British Establishment. He did not survive to see the achievements associated so powerfully with his name. On April 21, 1946, he died of heart disease from which he had suffered for some nine years. This was thought by some to have been aggravated by his hurrying to catch a train. It would have been appropriate, British postwar austerity notwithstanding, to have provided him with a car and driver.

Beside the ideas and institutions there was an influence of yet further importance. That was confidence

---

[2]The name used, in fact, by my literate and perceptive friend, Robert Lekachman. Cf. his *The Age of Keynes* (New York: Random House, 1966).

—confidence less in the system than in the instruments available for its management and in the capacity for intelligent discretion in their selection and use. To fiscal policy, it may be noted, there was again added in modest form in these years the use of monetary policy. Its clouded reputation from the '30s and before was not fully redeemed. But in 1951 it was brought partly out of its decade-long retirement. By the terms of an accord reached between the Treasury and the Federal Reserve in March of that year, the Federal Reserve System was relieved of the obligation to support the price of government bonds. This is to say it was free to raise interest rates—for so long as past issues of bonds could not be allowed to fall in price, neither their interest rates nor those for other and interchangeable assets could be allowed to rise. The pressure for the release of the Federal Reserve came partly from the banks. For farmers, steel companies, even physicians and professors, higher prices are assumed to be rewarding and something that, in pursuit of self-interest, firms or persons will seek. Bankers also like higher prices, at least to a point, and their price is the rate of interest. The shelving of monetary policy in the previous decade had left interest rates very low. It was rightly felt that, with a revival of monetary policy, rates would be higher. However, the unpegging was not defended for its effect on the earnings of the banks. It was an act exclusively in the national interest.

Numerous economists also supported the revival of monetary policy; the intricacies of central-bank operations were still being described in the textbooks, and it was sad that what was so excellent in theory should be in limbo in practice. So in the early '50s the passive role of the Federal Reserve—its low interest rate and its obligation to acquire whatever securities sustained that rate—came to be described by numerous economists as an "engine of inflation." Why it had not been so described in the vastly more inflationary years before is something of a mystery. In any case, though very gradually, monetary policy was again added to fiscal policy as part of the "kit of tools," as they were denoted, by which the economy was to be guided. There was high confidence among economists that, at long last, they had mastered the judicious use of these tools.

In fact, in the good years, with one brief exception when they did not work, these tools were not tried by their final test—that of controlling inflation. In all but one or two of these years economic policy worked against the one condition for which they were effective —which was not inflation but unemployment and depression or recession. During these twenty years, most propitiously, the economy had more often to be propped, not restrained. When it had to be restrained, the success evaporated. But first the history.

The Internationl Monetary Fund, along with its companion organization the International Bank for Reconstruction and Development, had its origins, albeit after much preparation, in New Hampshire at the Mount Washington Hotel at Bretton Woods in July of 1944. It was thus that a small mountain resort took leave of its sylvan personality and became, worldwide, the symbol for enlightened international monetary policy and assistance to the poor and ambitious peoples of the planet. A total of 730 persons from 44 countries attended the conference during those summer days; there can have been few international meetings in the history of such convocations where public comprehension of what was occurring or even of what was being attempted was so slight. This was far from a handicap. What people do not understand, they generally think important. This adds to the prestige and pleasure of the participants and to the fear of politicians that, in rejecting the resulting action, they may be doing serious damage.

Although the conference had to extend its sessions beyond the originally scheduled period, to the considerable inconvenience of the hotel which had taken reservations for its first season of the wartime years, agreement was eventually reached on a multitude of infinitely technical details concerning the two proposed organizations. This was assisted by the uncertainty of numerous of the participants as to what they were discussing; if one is pretending to knowledge one does not have, one cannot ask for explanations to support possible objections.

But more of the agreement was to be attributed to the dominant role of two exceptionally talented men, each of whom had previously produced a detailed proposal. One, of course, was Keynes; the other was Harry D. White, Assistant Secretary of the United States Treasury. Of the two, White, backed by the resources of the United States (which would be indispensable for success), was possibly the more powerful. Impolite and irascible, and like Keynes also arrogant, he was accused not long afterward of being the protector and agent of the Communists.[3] On August 13, 1948, he answered the charges to the Un-American Activities Committee of the House of Representatives with poorly restrained contempt, omitting to mention only that had he been a Communist, he would have been not their servant but their master—a fact to which all who knew him would attest. Then, a day or so later, he too died of heart disease from which he also had previously suffered. At Bretton Woods, agreement between Keynes and White was not quite tantamount to agreement by all but it went far.

The mystery surrounding the Bretton Woods discussions notwithstanding, both the purpose and the basic design of the International Monetary Fund—the IMF, as it has come to be called—were exceedingly simple.

---

[3] And the Bretton Woods institutions were soon to be attacked as instruments of capitalist imperialism.

In 1944, the world's supplies of gold were even more
egregiously ill-distributed than before. And the gold
standard was itself in ill repute. The Bretton Woods
arrangements sought to recapture the advantages of the
gold standard—currencies that were exchangeable at
stable and predictable rates into gold and thus at stable
and predictable rates into each other. And this it sought
to accomplish while minimizing the pain imposed by
the gold standard on countries that were buying too
much, selling too little and thus losing gold. This was
done by moderating, making less abrupt, the measures—tighter fiscal policy, tighter monetary policy with
higher interest rates, perhaps a tighter hold on incomes
—by which a country reduced consumer and investment demand and thus prices and so made itself a
harder place in which to sell, an easier one from which
to buy, a better one to keep money at interest, by all
these means reversing the tendency for gold to flow
away.

The moderating element, not surprisingly, was money—a fund, *the* Fund, on which countries could call
until they were able to put things right. To the original
Fund all countries subscribed—partly in gold or dollars, these being, of course, interchangeable, and partly
(and, for most, much more feasibly) in their own currencies. These subscriptions were in accordance with
an elastic calculation of the particular nation's share in
international trade and its general ability to pay. By
far the largest subscribers were the United States and
Britain.

Every country undertook to keep its currency stable
—subject to a thin 1 percent fluctuation—in relation to
that of others. If, under the pressure of, say, too many
imports and too few exports, a country's currency
started to fall, its central bank would buy up that currency and so support its value in relation to the money
of other countries. And if the central bank's often
minimal reserves of currency acceptable to other coun-

tries did not allow of such purchases, the country could turn to the IMF for gold or dollars or other acceptable currencies with which to maintain the support. When it did so, it deposited an equivalent amount of its own currency as security. What it all amounted to was an arrangement for getting quickly a hard-money loan. The amount that the country could so borrow from the IMF was determined by its quota—the amount that it had contributed. A scale of charges rising with the amount and duration of the loan encouraged the country to end the circumstances that had led to the original need. And it now had time to take the remedial action—higher taxes, lower government expenditures, higher interest rates. If the country were small and vulnerable to advice, it would be advised by the IMF as to the desirability of such action, and, in time, IMF missions would acquire a certain reputation for the astringency, even political sadism, of their recommendations. The pain that gold inflicted immediately, the IMF mission inflicted a little later. If the balance-of-payments problems of a country were persistent, it was allowed a onetime devaluation in relation to gold and other currencies of up to 10 percent. If, like Brazil, its currency was endemically subject to depreciation, there was tolerance. Nothing, in fact, happened.

Such was the Bretton Woods system. After further discussion of organization in Savannah in 1946, the Fund began operations in Washington March 1, 1947. The Communist countries, after first contemplating membership, did not join.

For the first several years of its existence the IMF was an amiable academic curiosity, with little relationship to problems as they existed. This was because, as was to be equally evident two decades later, it could deal admirably with small problems but not with large ones. In the immediate aftermath of the war, the war-deprived European members had vast import needs, a negligible capacity to export. The resulting gap was huge. To bring imports and exports into some kind of balance would take time. Keynes had argued for a fund large enough to deal with this gap. The United States delegates had replied out of their greater political knowledge that the Congress would never appropriate the required sums. The United States view prevailed—for a while. But then the money had to be found, the Congress was asked and it responded. A special loan of $3.75 billion was made to Britain under the Anglo-American Financial Agreement of 1945. Then, later, came much more with the Marshall Plan.

The Fund, with its comparatively modest resources —$2.75 billion from the United States, $6.8 billion from all sources compared with total Marshall Plan appropriations of $12.5 billion—remained, in these years, largely inoperative.

By the mid-'50s, however, the European economies had been fully restored and more. Exports were again in a reasonable relationship to imports. The now modest discrepancies the IMF could bridge or help to bridge. So, gradually, it emerged from the shadows. A sensible substitute for the gold standard seemed to have been found. Presently, as with the gold standard before the two wars, the basic arrangements—fully convertible currencies among the major industrial countries, occasional difficulties bridged by borrowing from the IMF, occasional major adjustments—were taken for granted. Thus, as before 1914, although now with a somewhat diminished role for gold, international monetary arrangements seemed, on the whole, to have been solved.

The second development that receives credit for the superior performance of these years was a purely domestic design of the United States government; it was the Employment Act of 1946. The result was to institutionalize professional economic advice and guidance in the Federal Executive. This too had its origins in wartime discussion. One source was the Committee for Economic Development. This body, uniting liberal businessmen with economists of Keynesian disposition, came into being in the war years. It was the product of fears of a severe postwar depression that would be damaging both to the reputation of capitalism and to the revenues it returned to the businessmen concerned. And it was the result also of the well-earned reputation at the time of the two other major business organizations, the Chamber of Commerce of the United States and the National Association of Manufacturers, for deeply principled negativism on all questions of economic policy, even where a positive stand would have served their members' interests. The Committee's first major publication, *Jobs and Markets*[4] appearing in 1946, affirmed the Keynesian thesis without, however, invoking the name of Keynes. The CED formula devised by Beardsley Ruml, a man of great and varied ingenuity, was to ask that the Federal budget be balanced in accordance with all reputable rules but only when the economy was operating at full employment levels or thereabouts. By inescapable inference but not by direct mention, deficit financing thus became the proper policy for dealing with unemployment. A subtle exercise in semantics. This, for a business organization at the time, was a position requiring much courage.[5] However, the CED soon ceased to offend.

---

[4]The Committee for Economic Development, *Jobs and Markets* (New York: McGraw-Hill Book Co., 1946).

[5]Word in those years reached the CED that I was reviewing *Jobs and Markets* for *Fortune* and welcoming its Keynesian enlightenment. The authors called to plead that the references to Keynes be muted or eliminated. In the interest of the larger cause, this seemingly sensible invasion of journalistic freedom and integrity was approved.

The more specific support for the Employment Act came from economists and liberal reformers assembled in Washington for the tasks of the war. These tasks were often routine or uninspiring; relief was found in informal professional discussion of how aggregate wartime employment, output and achievement could be made to last into the peace. The locus of much of this discussion was the National Planning Association, a loose convocation of economists, public officials, trade-union and farm-organization representatives, with a sprinkling of liberal businessmen who provided the financial support. Especially it was the gathering place of the Washington Keynesians—Gerhard Colm and Alvin Hansen (the latter then on temporary duty at the Federal Reserve Board), Richard and Milton Gilbert, cousins with a powerful commitment to the Keynesian ideas and an especial gift for evangelism, Walter Salant (to whom Keynes had written admiringly of his Washington disciples), Robert Nathan, the dominant force in wartime economic planning, Michael Meehan, an energetic and talented statistician at the Department of Commerce, as well as others.

Nathan, Meehan, Milton Gilbert and also Gerhard Colm all reflected a further influence that now became decisive for the advance of the Keynesian ideas. This was the calculations of national income, national product and their components. Though long under development, these had recently been brought to a much higher state of perfection and timeliness by Simon Kuznets, the notable economist and statistician of the University of Pennsylvania and the National Bureau of Economic Research, later of Harvard. (In 1971, Kuznets received the Nobel Prize in economics for this work.) Robert Nathan and Milton Gilbert had been students and coworkers of Kuznets. Under Nathan's guidance the Kuznets calculations achieved major use and prominence during the war years; they showed what increases in total output were possible, what was going to civilian investment and consumption and what, accordingly, could be made available for military purposes. Knowledge of these magnitudes had much to do with making American and especially British wartime planning more rational than that of Germany where such information was lacking. With peace it was evident the same calculations would show what output and employment would be possible, what would be saved from the resulting income, what would have to be invested to offset that saving and thus ensure full employment. The calculations were

> . . . the empirical counterpart of the Keynesian model of the economic system and of the short-term changes in output and employment that it illuminates. It was, indeed, the joint appearance in the mid-1930's of Keynes's general theory and of the early Kuznets report on gross national product and its expenditure components which made it possible to give quantitative expression to the Keynesian revolution in economic thought.[6]

Soon there emerged from the discussion the proposal that a firm legislative commitment to the Keynes and Kuznets ideas be sought. Initially the commitment was very firm indeed. The early drafts of the Full Employment Act, as it was first called, proclaimed the sovereign and indefeasible right of every American to a job. And the government was called upon each year to specify and ensure the investment, public and private, that (offsetting estimated savings at full employment) would ensure such a level of employment. In any year when private investment did not supply the requisite

[6]Moses Abramovitz, "Nobel Prize for Economics: Kuznets and Economic Growth," *Science*, Vol. 174, No. 4008 (October 29, 1971), p. 482.

total, the Federal government would be instructed to borrow and spend whatever was necessary to make up the difference. Initially the legislation named the total investment that most likely would be required—a round $40 billion. In 1945, a draft bill (the $40 billion figure having been deleted) was introduced in the Senate by James E. Murray[7] of Montana as S380. It was widely cosponsored by liberal members.

Already in 1945 it was becoming difficult to be against full employment, although, in the end, a considerable number of legislators rose to the challenge. In the Senate the adverse reaction, led by Robert A. Taft, was relatively mild; much of the effort involved verbal modifications which, in the view of the sponsors of the bill, had the effect of concealing, and, in the view of its enemies, had the effect of discouraging, the use of deficit financing. The bill passed the Senate with its commitment to full employment, the required forecasts of investment and the call for the resulting expenditures largely, though not completely, unimpaired.

The House was then, as often since, far more conservative. And by the time the bill reached this chamber, the opposition had taken notice of the threat and organized to combat it. A scholarly analysis of the legislation was prepared at the behest of the National Association of Manufacturers and Donaldson Brown, a General Motors executive; it concluded that the legislation would enhance government control, destroy private enterprise, unduly increase the powers of the Federal Executive, legalize Federal spending and pump-priming, bring socialism, be unworkable and impractical, promise too much and be open to ridicule. This and similar material was distributed over the country as a whole, with exceptional attention being paid to Senator Murray's constituents in Montana where it was

---

[7]Originally from Elgin County, Ontario, on the north shore of Lake Erie. This liberal Eden is the provenance also of the author.

put around in rural mailboxes and must have been a source of some puzzlement.[8]

In consequence of this opposition, S380 was professionally gutted in committee and then opposed as too liberal by those congressmen who had been appeased by the emasculation. Thus it passed the House. The Conference Committee agreed to remove, as offensive, the reference to full employment. In what may have involved an all-time record in qualification, modification and general verbal retreat, it was declared instead to be the policy of the United States government,

... TO USE ALL PRACTICABLE MEANS ... WITH THE ASSISTANCE AND COOPERATION OF INDUSTRY, AGRICULTURE, LABOR AND STATE AND LOCAL GOVERNMENTS, TO COORDINATE AND UTILIZE ALL ITS PLANS, FUNCTIONS, AND RESOURCES FOR THE PURPOSE OF CREATING AND MAINTAINING, IN A MANNER CALCULATED TO FOSTER AND PROMOTE FREE COMPETITIVE ENTERPRISE AND THE GENERAL WELFARE, CONDITIONS UNDER WHICH THERE WILL BE AFFORDED USEFUL EMPLOYMENT, FOR THOSE ABLE, WILLING, AND SEEKING TO WORK, AND TO PROMOTE MAXIMUM EMPLOYMENT, PRODUCTION, AND PURCHASING POWER.

To accomplish these impressively presented purposes there would be no Keynesian savings and investment

---

[8]Stephen Kemp Bailey, *Congress Makes a Law* (New York: Columbia University Press, 1950), pp. 137–138. This book is an extraordinarily complete and lucid case study of the origins, watering down and passage of the Employment Act of 1946. The adverse analysis was the work of Professor Jules Backman of New York University, considered a handy man for such tasks at the time.

budget, private or public. Nor, needless to say, would there be any obligation to a resulting expenditure. Instead a report would go to a special joint committee of the two houses of Congress at the beginning of each session. It would review the state of economic affairs and confine itself to suggesting such action as might be necessary to foster and promote free competitive enterprise and the useful and maximum employment for "the able, willing and seeking," as urged in the above declaration. The victory of the conservative counter-attack against Keynes—who, along with Henry Wallace, Stuart Chase and William Beveridge, was strongly featured in the debate as one of the devils to be exorcised—seemed reasonably complete.

It was also Pyrrhic. Conservatives in the House, partly as a design for reducing the fiscal powers of the President, partly to substitute apparatus for substance, put in the bill a provision for a special advisory body on economic affairs—the Council of Economic Advisers. This was accepted by the liberals. So unimportant did it seem initially that it was many months before President Truman got around to appointing its three members. When he did so, his choice as Chairman was Edwin G. Nourse, an estimable scholar whose commitment to the Keynesian ideas was not surprisingly negligible, for he had never paid them the slightest attention. However, the Vice-Chairman was Leon Keyserling who had worked on the drafting and passage of the Employment Act. Keyserling was passionately committed to its goals, and he was also exceptionally energetic and thoroughly experienced in Washington evangelism. In November 1949, he became Acting Chairman, the following year Chairman. Keyserling was not deterred by the conservative reservations written into the basic law. He committed the new Council firmly to the original employment goals. And, with Walter Heller, who became Chairman a decade later under Kennedy, he showed that advocacy, both with a President and at large, is no slight instrument of power. Though his claim to a pioneer role in the new organization and policy is not now seriously disputed, for a long time it was not conceded. Keyserling suffered from the serious moral handicap of being a lawyer. By the end of World War II, professional economists were becoming a force in the United States. It was hard that this first expression of their power should be by one not matriculated in the craft. Keyserling did not ease matters by frequently alluding to this source of professional sorrow. Since Keyserling, all members of the Council have been fully certified members of the economics profession.

In the twenty years following the passage of the Employment Act and the establishment of the Council of Economic Advisers there has been published each January[9] the *Economic Report of the President;* it is a professionally competent statement on the recent behavior of the economy and the prospect. These reports have not been without drawbacks; rarely has an administration looked back on its work and found it poor. Never has it assessed the results of its intended policy and found them other than in the right direction. Nonetheless the presence close to the President of men immediately concerned with output and employment and with the further effect of their concern on spending, taxation, Federal Reserve policy, international trade policy, even farm policy, has been important. It is doubtful if those who participated in the first drafting of S380—and who wanted a national budget specifying what would be received, what would be invested or spent, what would be needed additionally to be spent by the government to hire the able, willing and seeking —would, in light of the later history, have asked for much more.

---

[9]On occasion, February. In the early days there was more than one *Report* annually.

CHAPTER XIX

The New Economics
at High Noon

IN THE YEARS following World War II in the United
States, a reference to Keynes, rather more than one to
Marx who was a less relevant menace, was thought to
arouse conservative antagonism that might otherwise be
silent, exclude moderate acquiescence that might otherwise be had. Though the Keynesian result was acceptable, the name of Keynes was a red flag.

In 1947, Seymour Harris of Harvard University, the
most diligent of all the Keynesian evangelists and one
of the most effective, edited an influential series of essays on the ideas. (It began with the stately obituary in
the *Times* [London] on April 22, 1946: "Lord Keynes,
the great economist, died at Tilton, Firle, Sussex
yesterday from a heart attack. By his death the country
lost a very great Englishman. He was a man of genius . . .") Harris entitled his volume *The New
Economics*.[1] In ensuing years this name became the
accepted form of reference.[2] With the Kennedy Administration the commitment of the United States government to the New Economics was openly avowed. In the
Kennedy and early Johnson years the total output of

---

[1]*The New Economics: Keynes' Influence on Theory and Public
Policy,* Seymour E. Harris, ed. (New York: Alfred E. Knopf, 1947).
[2]James Tobin in *The New Economics One Decade Older* (Princeton:
Princeton University Press, 1974) suggests that the popular usage
is to be attributed not to Harris's book but to a separate coinage by
Washington reporters in 1962.

the economy expanded at a steady rate. The resulting employment increased more rapidly than the labor force; in consequence, unemployment went steadily down. And by modest direct effort prices were held stable. This was the New Economics. Nothing seemed wrong.

Nor were those responsible beset by excessive doubts. In the early days of 1968, as the period of postwar prosperity was rounding out its twentieth year, the President's economists were moved to reflect on the more recent record. During these last "years of achievement," they observed, it was "far more than a coincidence [that] fiscal and monetary policy have been actively and consciously employed to promote prosperity . . ." And "no longer," they added, "does Federal economic policy . . . *wait* for a recession or serious inflation to occur *before* measures are taken."[3] There followed then a small concession to modesty, quickly retrieved:

> Fiscal and monetary policies have not been per-
> fectly executed nor perfectly coordinated in the past
> few years. But our policies have remained under con-
> tinuous and coordinated review. And our actions have
> been consistently in the right direction, if not always
> perfectly timed nor in precisely the right degree.[4]

It was, alas, almost the last moment for self-congratulation, however well-deserved. And a better sense of history might have warned against it. In December 1928, Calvin Coolidge had sent his last message on the State of the Union to the Congress. He said: "No Congress of the United States ever assembled, on surveying the state of the Union, has met with a more pleasing prospect than that which appears at the present time. In the domestic field there is tranquility and content-

---

[3]*Economic Report of the President, 1968*, p. 7. Italics added.
[4]*Economic Report of the President, 1968*, p. 7.

ment . . . and the highest record of years of prosperity."[5] The next year came the deluge.

Behind the benign façade of the New Economics in these years were, in fact, four serious flaws. Some were just becoming visible at the time; all are now wonderfully clear with the always invaluable aid of hindsight.

The first was the reliance on prediction and foresight —on taking action before need. Foresight is an imperfect thing—all prevision in economics *is* imperfect. And, even more serious, the economist in high office is under a strong personal and political compulsion to predict wrongly. That is partly because of the temptation to predict what is wanted, and it is better, not worse, economic performance that is always wanted. It is partly because prediction in economics is thought by many to be self-fulfilling. A gloomy prediction on employment and output will, it is imagined, make businessmen gloomy and pessimistic and cause them to retrench. A prediction of higher prices will cause corporations to look again at their own prices and to raise them. And unions will base their wage claims on what the government says is going to happen to prices and living costs—a forecast of higher prices will immediately be an argument at the bargaining table. It follows that *all* official prediction in economics is suspect; everyone reading it should assume a heavy component of wishful thought. In the decade from the mid-'60s to the mid-'70s economic policy was to be extensively guided by prediction that was deeply subordinate to hope.

Additionally, official economic prediction cannot contradict other and yet higher public expectation. In

---

[5]John Kenneth Galbraith, *The Great Crash, 1929*, 3rd ed. (Boston: Houghton Mifflin Co., 1972), p. 6.

1967 and 1968, in the last years of economic success, the economy was under increasing pressure from the expenditures for the Vietnam war. In all official doctrine this war was soon to be over; the light was glowing ever more brightly at the end of the now immortal tunnel. Administration economists, however much they might believe that the war would continue and become more costly, could not make this a basis for public calculation. They could not publicly predict that war expenditures would increase, inflationary pressures intensify. The official expectation as to the end of the war, however wrong or fanciful, was controlling.

The three other flaws were specific and concrete. All had the effect of limiting, even negating, the ability of the government to deal effectively with inflation.

The first of these three further flaws was in the machinery for dealing with the now familiar problem of market power. In the years following World War II, the power and self-confidence of the trade unions increased steadily. If the market power of the great corporations did not increase—as some conservative economists were at pains to aver—it was because, as their statistics showed, it had long been very great. However, in the view of all but the most inspired defenders of the classically competitive market, such power did increase. So now, as capacity operations were approached, it was possible to increase prices over the wide area of concentrated industry. And it was possible for unions, responding to these prices, to win higher wages and for the corporations to pass on the resulting higher wage costs. Thus the familiar spiral. In wartime the spiral could not be arrested by general fiscal policy save at the cost of far more production than could be afforded. In peacetime it could not be arrested except by more unemployment than could be tolerated. The solution that was seemingly achieved during the Kennedy Administration was highly infirm both in machinery and supporting ideas. For a full view of this weakness it is necessary to recur to the earlier of the good years.

A severe test of the ability of the economy to combine high output and stable prices followed the outbreak of the Korean war in the summer of 1950. Prices rose rapidly in the ensuing months, partly in response to the market power just mentioned, partly in consequence of the rush for goods by people who had memories of the recent wartime shortages. In June of 1950, the wholesale index was at 80; by the following January it was at 89 (1967 = 100.)[6] Over the initial resistance of the Truman Administration, the Congress then passed legislation providing for wage and price controls. The Office of Price Stabilization was established under the determined direction of Michael DiSalle and Gardner Ackley, the latter a veteran of World War II price control. A full-scale organization for administration and enforcement was assembled.

Rarely has an economic action had a more immediate and effective result. The upward movement of prices was brought promptly to a full halt. It is possible that the price increases would eventually have moderated as people discovered that the Korean conflict was, in its impact, a small affair—no replay of World War II. But at the time of the action a spiral in wages and prices was fully under way. This, in the absence of controls, would have continued and perhaps accelerated.

Once again it had been shown that direct action was necessary to control the spiral. Once again, however, the experience was not influential. The short-run success of the Korean controls was conceded. But again

[6]Calculated from *Economic Report of the President, 1952*, p. 189, and *Economic Report of the President, 1974*, p. 305.

this was war. The wartime experience was once again dismissed as *sui generis*. No one could say that this small and distant conflict aroused much patriotic emotion or allowed of action that would not be possible in peacetime. But it was not imagined to have relevance for the peacetime experience.

The Korean controls were dismantled in 1953. Thereafter, industrial prices and wages resumed their slow upward climb. This seemed sufficiently troublesome at the time to cause the Eisenhower Administration—first in the mid-'50s and then at the end of the decade—to increase interest rates, restrict monetary expansion and seek budgetary restraint. A budget deficit of just under $6 billion in 1954 was turned into a surplus of about the same size in the two following years. In 1958, the deficit had grown again to $10.2 billion; this was brought down to $1.2 billion the following year and turned into a surplus of $3.5 billion in 1960.[7]

Farm prices fell sharply in both periods of restriction. Not being subject to the market power of corporations or the pressure of union wage claims, they responded as prices are meant to respond. Industrial prices, on the other hand, continued steadily upward until 1960. By then the index of industrial prices at 95.3 (1967 = 100) was a full ten points higher than in 1953 when the Korean controls were removed. In 1960 and 1961, monetary and fiscal restriction did bring the increase in industrial prices largely to an end. But the more spectacular and painful lesson, as by now will be expected, was the amount of unemployment that was required—an average of 6.7 percent of the labor force in 1961.[8] A more than incidental political consequence of the control of prices by unemployment

---

[7]These are the deficits and surpluses in the national income accounts (see Ch. XVII, p. 291, Footnote 8). *Economic Report of the President, 1974,* p. 328.
[8]*Economic Report of the President, 1974,* pp. 279, 305.

was the election of John F. Kennedy in 1960. So minute
was his margin of votes that it is impossible to suppose
that in the absence of so much righteously induced
hardship he would have made it. It was to the measures taken to control inflation in industrial prices that
the Republicans, including Mr. Nixon, attributed their
defeat.

The lesson of its election was not lost on the new Administration. In the '50s President Eisenhower and
his staff had addressed numerous pleas to unions and
corporations to moderate their wage and price demands
in the interest of higher patriotism and greater price
stability. As before, and to a marked degree in the ensuing twenty years, the decisive role of corporate and
union power for inflation was recognized. The pleas
then conceded the need for direct intervention. After
thus conceding the need, it was regularly explained that
more effective intervention was inconsistent with the
free-market system.

The new Democratic Administration accepted, to a
point, the need to intervene. A search immediately began for some mechanism for coming to grips with the
wage-price spiral. The problem was stated explicitly in
the report of the Council of Economic Advisers on the
first year of the new Administration: "There are important segments of the economy where firms are
large or employees well-organized, or both. In these
sectors, private parties may exercise considerable discretion over the terms of wage bargains and price decisions."[9]

The responding action still relied on voluntary
compliance, save as this might be assisted by official
pressure or indirect sanction. Formal limits or guideposts for setting wages and prices were established. Un-

---

[9]*Economic Report of the President, 1962*, p. 185.

der these, unions were asked to hold their wage claims to an amount roughly equivalent to the annual gain in productivity, then estimated at about 3 percent per annum. The productivity gain having increased production per man-hour enough to cover this wage increase, there was, in consequence and on the average, no increase in costs. Costs being stable, firms were asked to keep their prices stable.

In the spring of 1962, the policy was dramatically tested—and publicized. Early in that year Arthur Goldberg, the Secretary of Labor and previously the general counsel of the United Steelworkers, had negotiated a wage settlement with the steel industry that was generally in line with the guideposts. The United States Steel Corporation, with the genius for self-righteous and deeply obtuse self-assertion that has long been a tradition in one branch of corporate public relations, then blandly announced a price increase of $6.00 a ton. As the increase was announced to the public, the head of the Steel Corporation dropped in to announce it to the President. Other firms made ready to follow the lead of U.S. Steel and shortly did. President Kennedy responded with some inspired invective on the character and parentage of businessmen. This, combined with threats of action under the antitrust laws, by the Federal Trade Commission and in respect of government purchases of steel, along with an outraged public, press and congressional reaction, caused the companies to have second thoughts. One or two, more sensitive than the rest, decided not to go along. The rest, including U.S. Steel, were forced to cancel the increase. The voluntary principle in wage and price control, as it was loosely called, was thus saved. For the next four years, a period of steadily expanding employment and output, industrial prices were nearly stable. In a restrained appraisal of the experience, Walter Heller, the principal architect of the economic policy of these years, concluded that ". . . judged both by privately expressed opinions (and public cries of pain) of business and labor and by careful comparative studies of wage and cost trends, the guideposts can fairly take credit for some of the wage-price moderation in the great expansion of the 1960's."[10]

It was not to last. Beginning in 1966, there were large increases in spending for the Vietnam war. To the natural reluctance to increase taxes there was added the greater reluctance to increase them for an unpopular war. Not until 1968 was a surtax for war spending finally voted. Meanwhile expanding demand put pressure on prices and living costs. As these rose, so did the pressure for higher wage settlements. It was part of the bargain, after all, that prices would be stable. At the same time, the moral authority of the government, which had now to recruit support for a widely rejected war, had been sadly weakened. So, as the need for the guideposts increased, their effectiveness diminished. In 1966, a settlement with the New Jersey building trades exceeded by a wide margin the amount allowed by the guideposts, as did a later settlement with the airline mechanics. Soon the restraints both on prices and wages were dead. The economists of the Nixon Administration, taking office in January 1969, made clear their opposition to any such market intervention as a matter of high principle.

For them the principle, however in conflict with circumstance, was important. Nothing is more basic to conservative economic thought than the benign pre-eminence of the market. The market is neither benign nor pre-eminent if there must be government intervention to prevent inflation, and thereby to improve its performance. But action along the lines of the guideposts and associated price restraints was never fully

---

[10]Walter W. Heller, *New Dimensions of Political Economy* (Cambridge: Harvard University Press, 1966), p. 46.

incorporated into the conventional wisdom of liberal economists either. For this also there was good reason. The Keynesian system left the market, and therewith the established microeconomic ideas of the textbooks and their teachers, untouched. Supply and demand found their equilibrium after the requisite management of demand at a higher level of output than before. The mechanism by which demand and supply were brought into equilibrium, prices established and resources distributed among uses remained unchanged. The guideposts conceded that prices and wages *were* subject to the control of corporations and unions. Both were a reflection not of market equilibrium but of corporate and union power. For such power the accepted economics had no place. It was something, in consequence, from which numerous liberal economists tried devoutly to avert their eyes. Some still do.

Liberal members of the Council of Economic Advisers, during their terms of office, could not escape the unpleasantly real effect of unions on wages and corporations on prices and the interaction between the two. But once back in the universities and adjacent suburbs and teaching the young, they were in a position to jettison such messy, contentious and unscientific preoccupations. In their writing and instruction, prices were retrieved once again from the corporations and the unions brought back to the markets. Employment was again assured and inflation prevented by well-considered professional adjustments in monetary and fiscal policy.

Thus the flaw. The experience of the good years showed that economic power—that of the corporations and unions—could defeat efforts to combine high employment with stable prices. So in practice intervention was essential. But the practice never became part of the principle, and the principle remained highly influential. There is a hopeful myth that, on matters as deeply of concern to the citizen as economic policy, the citizen decides. Perhaps in the long run he does; he retains the happy right eventually to expel from public office those who fail. But in the interim before failure becomes evident or the expulsion becomes possible, economic policies, like open-heart surgery, are in the hands of the specialists. Thus what economists believe or wish to believe—the economic principles to which they repair—are not matters of passing detail. They are decisive.

The next flaw was the fatal inelasticity of the Keynesian system. As this system developed during these years, expenditures ceased to be subject to reduction. Taxes still adjusted themselves automatically with increases or decreases in taxable income. But, except in the extreme case of war, they ceased to be subject to legislated increase. If expenditures can be increased but cannot be reduced and taxes can be reduced but cannot be increased, fiscal policy becomes, obviously, a one-way street. It will work wonderfully against deflation and depression but not very well against inflation.

The Keynesian system had always been more inflexible than its proponents imagined. In the '30s, as earlier noted, fiscal policy was perceived as working through public expenditures. These would be increased to compensate for insufficient private expenditure or investment, reduced when the latter was sufficient. Taxes would not be touched. Since expanding output and employment had the effect of removing people from the relief rolls and the work projects and easing the claims of, for example, the farmers on the Federal budget, there was some possibility for reducing expenditures as output and employment expanded. Between 1936 and 1937, Federal expenditures were reduced from $8.5 billion to $7.2 billion or by more than 15 percent

—a large as well as, at the time, distinctly unwise slash.[11] Still no one is likely to think that public outlays are easily curtailed.

In the postwar years spending became much more inelastic. During the Depression public outlays were for economic and social purposes—for expanding output and employment and improving the income of the unemployed. Such being their purpose, they were regarded by men of sound and conservative view with unease or alarm. There was always a strong constituency supporting their reduction.

After World War II, public expenditures were vastly larger—in 1954, some eight times greater than fifteen years before. But now a very large part was for military purposes. This expenditure was manifestly respectable. It had the backing of a powerful military bureaucracy and its supplying industries. And such expenditure was no longer to support income, output and employment, however agreeable these incidental rewards. It was to contain Communism, sustain national security, protect freedom, arm the Free World—ends which conservatives applauded. Accordingly, expenditure was no longer subject to adjustment in accordance with economic need. As was very often said, you do not tamper with national security.

This meant that adjustment had to be found in taxes. In the postwar years, as compared with the years of depression, these had greater in-built flexibility. The great increase in public expenditures had been roughly matched by increased returns from the corporate and personal income taxes. We have seen the benign tendency of these taxes. With expanding output, income and employment, both personal incomes and corporate profits increase. Hitherto untaxed persons then pay taxes, and those in lower surtax brackets are promoted to higher brackets. And corporate profits increase more

---

[11]*Economic Report of the President, 1965*, p. 262. Expenditure for the calendar year in the national income accounts.

than proportionately with a more than proportionate increase in corporate tax yields. Thus tax revenues increase more than in proportion to the increase in output and income. And when output, income and employment fall, these effects go into reverse. The higher the volume of taxes, the greater these stabilizing effects. Tax concessions for the affluent obviously impair the operation of this benign process. However, in the twenty good years numerous such benefits, notably the maximum rate of 50 percent on what, very graciously, is called earned income, were as yet unenacted. And various tax loopholes and shelters were still not fully exploited. The automatic stabilization effect of the income taxes in these years was relatively strong.

Too strong, in fact. By the early '60s it had become the conventional wisdom of the New Economics that, at full employment, the revenues raised by the Federal government were too large in relation to expenditures. The result was "a fiscal drag" upon output, income and employment. To lessen this drag, a horizontal reduction in taxes was deemed necessary. By now, public sophistication allowed of such action; taxes could be reduced and the deficit increased for the deliberate and exclusive purpose of increasing the budget deficit and so improving economic performance. In 1964, such a reduction, amounting to $14 billion in revenues, was enacted. It was "the most overt and dramatic expression of the new approach to economic policy."[12]

Implicit in this action, however, was the need to reverse it should an excess of demand start pulling up prices. And this, as later history would amply establish, was far more difficult. More than the normal political reluctance to impose higher taxes is involved. An increase in taxes at a time when prices are rising appears to all but the most enlightened of citizens as a peculiarly gratuitous action. More is being paid in

---

[12]Heller, pp. 71-72.

prices for goods; now the government adds insult to the injury with higher taxes. Few economic actions seem more unnatural.

Reinforcing this elementary obstacle are the politics of the policy—of using tax increases against inflation. It is the income and corporate taxes that must be used; the impact of these, if they are levied with any approach to equity, is heavily on the affluent. In the past, Ricardo's monied men were notable for their opposition to inflation. But when the measures for controlling inflation have a special impact on the incomes of the rich, this opposition greatly subsides. Perhaps, for those so involved, it is more profitable to have the inflation. In any case, the use of taxes as an anti-inflationary instrument immensely dampens the anti-inflationary ardor of the affluent.

If taxes cannot be increased except under the *force majeure* of war and public expenditures cannot be decreased much for any reason, it follows that Keynesian policy is unavailable for limiting demand. It can expand purchasing power but it cannot contract it. During the twenty good years no reliable method was devised for dealing with the wage-price spiral—with direct market power as a cause of inflation. And fiscal policy was also becoming unavailable for dealing with inflation. The goals were there; the instruments for reaching them were becoming distressingly inoperative.

There was one exception, and that was monetary policy. Nothing in the decline of other instruments was as unfortunate as the increasing faith in this one.

The final flaw was this revival, during these years, of faith in monetary policy. In light of the history of this instrument it was as surprising as it was damaging. The actual use of monetary policy during the good years was, in fact, cautious. And it was still not encouraging.

Moderately restrictive open-market operations, combined with increased rates on bank borrowing at the Federal Reserve, were generally agreed to have brought expansion to a halt in the mid-'50s. And they did not stop the upward increase in industrial prices. Then at the end of the decade, in conjunction with a restrictive fiscal policy, they brought the price increases to an end—but at the price of the fall in output and the rise in unemployment that, among its other consequences, helped elect Kennedy.

Nevertheless, offstage faith in monetary policy was growing. Partly this was the result of the fading memory of earlier failures. Partly it was the normal human hope that salvation might somehow be found in magic, sorcery or witchcraft as these are revealed to experts. Partly it reflected the unsinkable prestige of central bankers in general and the Federal Reserve System in particular, something to which readers of this history will no longer react with surprise. In the small world of economics the failures of monetary policy, though fully conceded, continued to be a reflection not of fundamental fault but of interesting abberation. The textbooks and teaching still told in refined detail of how movement in the rediscount rate and the purchase and sale of bonds, notes and bills could increase or decrease the supply of money, thus encourage or restrain the economy. Discussion of movements in the money supply became especially fashionable, although subject somewhat inconsistently to growing doubts (to be mentioned in a moment) as to what should be included in the monetary aggregates. And best of all was the freedom of monetary policy from interference from any of the inconveniences of public process. Monetary policy ". . . enjoys a degree of flexibility which fiscal policy does not enjoy: The decisions of the Board of Governors are not subject to the time-consuming procedures which characterize congressional action or to the time lapse which may occur between the enacting and the applying of fiscal policy."[13]

But much of the revival was owing to the effective evangelism of the most diligent student of monetary policy and history during these years, Professor Milton Friedman. As a devout and principled conservative, Professor Friedman saw monetary policy as the key to the conservative faith. It required no direct intervention by the state in the market. It elided the direct management of expenditures and taxation, not to mention the large budget, which was implicit in the forgive the errors of the Federal Reserve or minimize role of government—for returning to the wonderfully simpler world of the past. Professor Friedman did not forgive the errors of the Federal Reserve of minimize their importance. On the contrary, he emphasized them, and thus he took no responsibility for past misfortune or nonfortune. It was merely that the task was far simpler than previously assumed; Professor Friedman returned to Irving Fisher and held that attention need be paid only to the quantity of money in Fisher's equation. "Changes in the behavior of the monetary stock have been closely associated with changes in economic activity, money income and prices . . . Monetary changes have often had an independent origin; they have not been simply a reflection of changes in economic activity."[14,15] The money supply, now de-

---

[13]Campbell R. McConnell, *Economics*, 4th ed. (New York: McGraw-Hill Book Co., 1969), p. 332. This is one of the two or three most widely used textbooks in economics.

[14]Milton Friedman and Anna Jacobson Schwartz, *A Monetary History of the United States, 1867–1960*. Study by the National Bureau of Economic Research (Princeton: Princeton University Press, 1963), p. 676.

[15]A more complete summary of the monetarist position, the best I think currently available, is in Tobin, pp. 58–59. It justifies a full, very slightly edited, quotation: "Monetarism, in my understanding of it, encompasses the following . . . (a) Past rates of growth in the stock of money are the major determinants—indeed, virtually the only systematic, nonrandom determinants—of the growth of

noted the monetary aggregates, consists as always of currency in circulation (i.e., outside the banks) and bank deposits subject to check. By later addition, and subject to continuing dispute, it also includes savings accounts, for these can also be readily available for expenditure, and the difference between savings and checking deposits was becoming increasingly unsharp. If these aggregates were so controlled as to allow for a steady moderate increase related in magnitude to the increase in economic activity, the task of economic management was accomplished. There is nothing more. For this simple task the elaborate policy-making apparatus of the Federal Reserve is not really necessary, and on various half-serious occasions Professor Friedman argued for the abolition of the Federal Reserve. What is required, rather, is a set of firm rules and a firm determination to adhere to them. For anyone looking for ease in a complex world nothing could be more agreeable. Professor Friedman's case was not

---

nominal (current-dollar) GNP. (b) A corollary: Fiscal policies do not significantly affect nominal GNP, though they may alter its composition and also affect interest rates. (c) Another corollary: The overall impact on nominal GNP of monetary and financial policies and events is for practial purposes summed up in the movements of a single variable, the stock of money. Consequently monetary policy should be exclusively guided by this variable, to the exclusion of interest rates, credit flows, free reserves, and other indicators. (d) Nominal interest rates are geared to inflation expectations and thus, with a lag, to actual inflation. Although the immediate market impact of expansionary monetary policy may be to lower interest rates, this is fairly soon reversed when premiums for the resulting inflation are added to interest rates. (e) The central bank can and should make the money stock grow at a steady rate equal to the rate of growth of potential GNP plus a target rate of inflation. (f) There is no enduring trade-off between unemployment and inflation but rather a unique natural rate of unemployment that allows for structural change and job search. Government policy will produce ever-accelerating inflation if it persistently seeks a lower than natural rate of unemployment and an ever-accelerating deflation if it seeks a higher rate. If the proper steady-growth monetary policy is followed, the economy will settle into its natural unemployment rate. Since this equilibrium can be achieved with any rate of inflation, the inflation target might as well be zero."

casually advanced; it was supported by massive evidence which, as necessary, was arranged to serve the author's purpose. (Substantial changes in the velocity of money use had especially to be explained away. There was also the serious and unresolved problem just mentioned of what was to be counted as money.) In the years to come, Professor Friedman's breathtakingly simple solution would not, in fact, be tried. But it would powerfully support the hope that all problems could be solved by the magic of monetary management. Alas.

Thus the flaws of Keynesian economics or, to change the metaphor, the sparks that, in the late '60s and early '70s, would become the flame. It was the genius of the Nixon economists that they would now supply the wind.

CHAPTER XX

Where It Went

THE CIRCUMSPECT HISTORIAN ends his work well before the present; then he takes his seat with the others for the day's parade. A solemn reason is offered for this: History cannot be written too soon, perspective must be gained. The tactical advantage of this restraint is even greater. Of current happenings people are often informed. They will question the historian's interpretation, even perhaps his facts. His professional advantage is thus lost. Better then to stay safely with the past.

The circumstances of this essay, alas, do not allow of this careful solution. It seeks to tell of the wisdom and folly of the past but it seeks to use these to illuminate the present. Accordingly, there is no decent escape in these last pages from the perplexities of the present and of a world beset, as so often in the two-and-a-half thousand years since the kings of Lydia, with the tendency for its money to become bad or for the management of money to make much else, including production and employment, bad. Still there are mitigating circumstances. Much that has happened in the recent present is not terribly in dispute. And much was foretold by the events of the near and distant past. Much of what must be done is also foretold—but on this there will be more disagreement.

The good years of economic management in the United States came to an end with the Vietnam war.

343

Wartime spending and resulting demand put pressure on prices. The guideposts succumbed. Prices pressed upward.

Spending for the war and the associated deficit are held especially responsible. In fact these were rather quickly neutralized. In the calendar year 1967, the Federal government had a deficit of $12.4 billion in the national income accounts. Income taxes were then increased by the addition of a surtax; as a principal though not exclusive consequence, the deficit was a modest $6.5 billion the following year. And in 1969, there was a surplus of $8.1 billion.[1] With the ending of the surtax and other tax reduction the deficit then returned.

The sequence of events just mentioned is of importance; in later years the economists of the Nixon Administration attributed the increasingly serious inflation to the fiscal disorder they had inherited. Through repetition the explanation acquired a wide measure of acceptance. There is an obvious convenience in attributing one's shortcomings to one's predecessors in office. Carried to its logical end, it would mean that no administration would have to take responsibility for economic performance until it had been in office for several years. A valuable alibi. But, in fact, the fiscal position inherited by the Nixon Administration was, as such matters are usually described, remarkably sound. This was not so true of the efforts of its economists to make economic causation a branch of archaeology.

Nor, in fact, were the price movements that the new Administration inherited especially alarming. From a base of 100 in 1967, the wholesale index had risen to 102.5 in 1968. It went on up to 106.5 in 1969.[2] In economic matters misfortune is, obviously, a relative thing. However, these price increases seemed sufficient-

---

[1]*Economic Report of the President, 1974*, p. 328.
[2]*Economic Report of the President, 1974*, p. 305.

ly grave so that the new Administration came to office in January 1969 with a firmly announced determination to bring them to an end. For doing so, the new President boldly announced his intention of extending and making more dangerous all of the flaws, real or potential, in the previous economic management. On January 27, 1969, in his first press conference after taking office, and with the uncertainty of syntax that the Watergate tapes were later to celebrate, Mr. Nixon said: ". . . what we are trying to do without, shall we say, too much managing of the economy—we're going to have some fine tuning of our fiscal and monetary affairs in order to control inflation. One other point I should make in this respect. I do not go along with the suggestion that inflation can be effectively controlled by exhorting labor and management and industry to follow certain guidelines."[3]

All possible damage was here. Management of the economy, though ever more demanding as to need, was to be minimized. The mention of fine tuning, a phrase from his economists, gave currency to a ridiculous cliché. As well fine-tune a Mississippi flood. While the reference was to both fiscal and monetary policy, it had to mean a heavy reliance on monetary policy. By no stretch of the imagination of even a new presidential adviser could Federal expenditures or taxation, both subject to congressional action, be thought susceptible to sensitive adjustment. Present also was the thought that the success of both fiscal and monetary policy depended not on superior wisdom but on superior technique. This, all will know by now, has never been so. Were it the happy case, the economic problem would have been solved long since, for in all fields of endeavor good technicians abound.

And as the hopeless course was emphasized by the President, the important power was rejected. There

---

[3]The *New York Times*, January 28, 1969.

would be no interference with prices and wages. The previous hope for restraint was replaced by an invitation to corporations and unions to exercise whatever market power they possessed and might find immediately rewarding. In dealing with Mr. Nixon, it is not easy to be unfair. He invites and justifies all available criticism. However, something must be reserved in this case for the most reputable of his subordinates. Testifying a few days later on the guideposts which, if straightforward results be accepted, had helped keep prices stable during the Kennedy years, Secretary of Labor George Shultz held that:

> ... (1) ... they had not been very effective while in force; (2) they may well have strengthened the forces of inflation in the long run by diverting attention away from the fundamental weapons of monetary and fiscal policy and manpower policy; (3) they may have contributed to more labor unrest and to higher wage settlements after their demise than would otherwise have occurred. Further, (4) they are contrary to the spirit of competition and subvert the forces of the market; and (5) when combined with jawboning they are possibly in defiance of the nation's antitrust law.[4]

Not much remained to be said in favor of direct restraints on prices and wages. Mr. Schultz was soon to emerge as the dominant voice of the Administration on economic policy.

This policy in the next two years reflected with remarkable precision the President's projection. Fiscal policy was tight in 1969. Then, as noted, with the

---

[4]This summary of the Shultz position is from an essay by Neil de Marchi, "Wage-Price Policy in the First Nixon Administration: Prelude to Controls," which is included in a volume on the development of wage-price policy in the United States, published by the Brookings Institution in 1975.

phasing out of the surtax, other tax relief and increased expenditures, it greatly eased. The Federal deficit in the national income accounts was $11.9 billion in 1970, a large $22.2 billion in 1971.[5] For resisting inflation, reliance was on monetary policy; this was tightened, with sharply increasing interest rates, in 1969, and kept so until the closing months of 1970. So much for the fine tuning.

In mid-1970, the long period of boom and euphoria in the stock market came to an end. There was nothing here for which the Nixon Administration could be much blamed. The causes of any collapse are always imbedded in the previous boom. In 1929, those who were believed to have unlocked the secret of the market were found to have unlocked only the secret of a rising market. Now again. As the great holding-company and investment-trust promotions were before, so the performance funds, hedge funds, growth funds, offshore funds, real estate funds and the gossamer creations of the computer age were now. By making it difficult for bad or weak companies to borrow money, the tight-money policy may well have hastened the end. Conservatives are notable for inflicting such suffering on themselves or their kind. But sooner or later the end would in any case have come.

However, the effect of monetary policy on price increases and unemployment, by now predictable, was to allow the worsening of both. Unemployment, which averaged 3.5 percent of the labor force in 1969, rose to 4.9 percent in 1970 and to 5.9 percent the following year. And wholesale prices, which were 106.5 in 1969 (1967 $= 100$), went up to 110.4 in 1970, and 113.9 in 1971.[6] Unemployment, as before, was not the alterna-

---

[5] *Economic Report of the President, 1974,* p. 328.

[6] *Economic Report of the President, 1974,* pp. 279, 305. Although there was increase in all categories, it was strong in durable consumers' goods and particularly in finished producers' goods. In both those parts of the economy the market power of corporations and unions is strong.

tive to inflation. There could, as before, be both. Monetary policy could suppress activity and increase unemployment, and especially in those industries—housing,
and the construction industry generally, being the leading examples—which depend on borrowed money. The
market power of corporations and unions meanwhile
could keep prices going up as before. The modern
capitalist economy could suffer inflation. And it could
suffer recession. And it could, up to a painful level of
unemployment, have both at the same time. However,
the economists whom Mr. Nixon had brought to Washington were not men of shallow faith. Concessions
might be made to the reality but this could be only out
of short-run political necessity.

Such concessions were made. Political courage is a
much admired force for public good. The benign impact of political cowardice deserves more praise than it
commonly receives. By the summer of 1971, a presidential election was only a year and a few months
away. All polls showed that the public reaction to the
new combination of inflation and unemployment was,
not surprisingly, adverse. The major candidates for
the Democratic nomination showed evidence in the
polls of swamping Mr. Nixon. Economists can urge
suffering for a principle. And they can urge the public
to exercise patience while processes, presumed to be ultimately benign, work themselves out. Unfortunately
patience cannot be legislated or achieved by Executive
Order. And pleas for its voluntary exercise have their
primary impact on those making them.

Strong overtures were made to higher economic
principle and to patience. On July 28, 1971, Paul W.
McCracken, the scholarly head of the Council of
Economic Advisers, affirmed stoutly the virtue and efficacy of the current reliance on monetary policy, the
unwisdom, even eccentricity, of any direct interference

with prices or wages. He conceded that a contemporary observer, the present author, who had urged that the market power of corporations and unions would defeat monetary policy unless unemployment was very severe, "has the merit of being logical within the limits of his peculiar view of the economic system." But he strongly rejected such peculiarity, dismissed the economics of a freeze of prices as "illusory" and warned solemnly that "General wage and price control would be a serious threat to individual freedom."[7] That corporations and unions already exercise such control and thus, presumably, endanger freedom was not stressed.

In his stand for principle, Dr. McCracken had the initial support of his President. At a press conference in early August, Mr. Nixon, recurring again to the same observer, said he was "unalterably opposed" to the "Galbraith scheme which is supported by many of our Democratic Senators," the scheme being modest direct intervention on wages and prices. The President noted that such policies were favored only by "extremists of the left," adding generously, "I don't say this in a condemning way, it is only an observation."[8] A few days later, on August 15, the extremist specter suddenly ceased to stalk; principle collapsed in face of overriding political need. All wages and prices, farm prices and a few others excepted, were frozen.

Simultaneously with the freeze, the budget was liberalized and tax reductions were requested, these being enacted at the end of the year. And monetary policy was relaxed. The ancient faith was not, however, jettisoned. The action against market power was temporary. The controls were "designed to create conditions in which a more expansive budget policy would be safer and more effective." All would then be well. The controls, by then, would have broken the inflationary thrust; they were "emergency expedients, required in

---

[7]The Washington *Post*, July 28, 1971.
[8]The *New York Times*, August 5, 1971.

a particular historical context but expected to fade away, leaving no permanent change in the system except the eradication of inflationary expectations."[9]

It is hard not to dwell on the foregoing statement. The combination of wishful thought and sheer recklessness is impressive. The problem addressed by the controls—that created by the market power of corporations and unions—is not new but old. No one suggested that corporations and unions would soon disappear. But the *problem* would disappear. The consequences of such irresponsibility are not small. Some people lose income in consequence; some lose their jobs; international and domestic economic affairs are disoriented; there is social tension and frustration; the reputation of capitalism suffers; so does that of economists. Least damaged, perhaps, are the scholars who make such statements, offer such hopes.

The controls were not seriously administered—more accurately, they were largely unadministered. In contrast with the World War II and Korean war experiences, no serious organization was established for administration. Those responsible, by their own subsequent candid admission, remained strongly opposed to the principle.[10] Firms had difficulty in getting answers as to what was required of them. Such interpretation as was available was frequently provided by members or former members of the industry affected —a form of self-dealing against which the World War II and Korean war price administrations had established the most careful safeguards. No enforcement

---

[9] *Economic Report of the President, 1972*, p. 24

[10] A point often made in conversation by Herbert Stein, who was soon to succeed McCracken as Chairman of the Council of Economic Advisers. C. Jackson Grayson, Jr., the administrator principally in charge, emerged from his service to mount an energetic attack on the policy. See his "Controls Are Not the Answer," *Challenge* (November/December 1974), p. 9.

arm was established; instead officers whose experience
and career prospects were in tax collection were borrowed from the Internal Revenue Service.

Nonetheless, in something between moderate and remarkable measure, the action achieved its purposes.
The increase in unemployment was arrested; in 1972,
as again in 1973, there were small decreases. Wholesale prices during the freeze in the latter months of
1971 were stable. Phase II, which followed the freeze,
limited the controls, broadly speaking, to union contracts and the prices of the large corporations, that is to
say to the areas of market power. It reflected not at all
badly the logic of control. Through all of 1972, under
this regime, industrial prices rose by 3.6 percent. Consumer products (other than foods, which were not controlled) rose over the year by 2.2 percent.[11] Writing
of the experience in January 1973, the Administration
economists said, not without satisfaction and not without reason, that, since August 1971, there had been
"a dramatic deceleration of the rate of inflation."[12] They
noted that the action had dealt with causes, not symptoms. The controls were "not merely a suppression of
price increases that would burst out if controls were
removed."[13]

None of this meant that the old faith was dead. Confidence was simultaneously expressed that the United
States did not face any problem of inflation "beyond the
capacity of prudent fiscal and monetary policy to control."[14] So the controls would now be jettisoned. On
January 8, 1973, Secretary of the Treasury George P.
Shultz, now the chief economic policy-maker of the
Administration, met with newspapermen to affirm
his continued opposition to the policy. He noted that
controls had worked well in a slack economy but ex-

[11]*Economic Report of the President, 1974*, p. 309.
[12]*Economic Report of the President, 1973*, p. 30.
[13]*Economic Report of the President, 1973*, p. 68.
[14]*Economic Report of the President, 1973*, p. 54.

pressed the conviction that they would work less well now that full employment was being approached and they were more needed. The election had also been won. Steps were taken to dismantle the controls.

The dismantling proceeded erratically and with some backtracking through 1973. On the whole, fiscal and monetary policy were, in fact, reasonably prudent. Revenues gained in relation to expenditures; a Federal deficit in the national income accounts of $15.9 billion in 1972 became a surplus of $600 million in 1973.[15] Money was kept tight and expensive; by the end of 1973, the rediscount rate was an unprecedented 7.5 percent. The lending rate of the large commercial banks—the prime rate—was above 9 percent.[16] A "prudent fiscal and monetary policy" thus received a remarkably fair trial. During 1973, the cost of living increased by nearly 9 percent, nearly three times as much as during 1972. Wholesale prices in 1973 went up 18 percent. Thus for the prescience of Secretary Shultz and his colleagues. A persuasive claim of success for their promise of what prudent fiscal and monetary policy would accomplish will require ingenuity and some literary skill.

In the autumn of 1973 came the Yom Kippur war, the oil embargo and a very large increase in petroleum prices. These were widely blamed by the Administration economists, among others, for the inflation. Around three-fourths of the price increases of

---

[15]*Economic Report of the President, 1974*, p. 328.

[16]*Economic Report of the President, 1974*, p. 318. It is argued, rightly, that these rates are not excessive from the standpoint of the one who receives them. The purchasing power of the money he is lending is declining. After offsetting this loss, the lender receives little if anything net from his lending. The argument is, however, less persuasive when interest is viewed as a cost to the borrower. Here it must be related to the income or revenues of the borrower, e.g., the would-be home-owner, which will not ordinarily have increased in proportion to such wide increases in interest costs.

1973 occurred before the war and before the oil prices went up appreciably.

In 1974, the prudent policies continued. The preliminary estimate of the Federal deficit on national income accounts was $7.6 billion.[17] Monetary policy remained tight until early autumn when, in response to bitter complaint from the affected industries and criticism from economists, it was slightly relaxed. During 1974, the further reward of what was proclaimed to be prudence was an 18.9 percent increase in wholesale prices, an 11.0 percent increase in living costs.[18] At the end of the year farm prices were leveling off. So were prices of raw commodities and evidently also of services. These are the areas of slight market power. Where there was market power, the resistance to constraint was predictably more stalwart. In December 1974, the United States Steel Corporation announced a nearly 5 percent increase in the prices of a wide range of steel products and later retreated fractionally at the request of the President. Large increases were being sought in utility rates, including telephone rates. Prices of most manufactured products were still being marked up, although, as inventories accumulated, with diminishing enthusiasm.

The costs of this approach to price stability were far from slight. Monetary restraint, the principal reliance, had by then produced an unprecedented slump in the housing industry. Once again that devastating discrimination of monetary policy against those who must do business with borrowed money. Economic output as a whole had also declined modestly for the year, and references to a healthy rate of growth had now an antique sound. Unemployment at the end of 1974 was the highest in absolute numbers since the Great De-

---

[17] *Economic Report of the President, 1975*, p. 329.
[18] *Economic Report of the President, 1975*, pp. 304, 309.

pression and, at 7.1 percent of the labor force, at very nearly the highest rate since those distant days. In Detroit, it was noted, the collection of unemployment relief checks involved a two-and-a-half-hour wait in line. A considerable sprinkling of higher-salaried white-collar workers and minor executives was to be found in the queue. However, the commitment to principle remained strong. In December of 1974, Mr. Alan Greenspan, the Chairman of the Council of Economic Advisers (replacing Dr. McCracken and his successor, Mr. Herbert Stein), summarized his position before a gathering of Washington economists in two notably elegant sentences:

> Thus once the inflation genie has been let out of the bottle it is a very tricky policy problem to find the particular calibration and timing that would be appropriate to stem the acceleration in risk premiums created by falling incomes without prematurely aborting the decline in the inflation-generated risk premiums. This is clearly not an easy policy path to traverse but it is the path which we must follow.[19]

Inflation was still a thing that, once exorcised, would be gone forever. Capitalism functioned normally on an even keel. Once man had put it there, God, a good conservative gentleman too, would keep it stable. All that was needed was the will to suffer the requisite pain. Such, in 1974, was the state of economic thought. And again, also, it was on a collision course with political necessity. In the closing moments of the year, with the inflation genie still very much out of the bottle, the President's advisers gathered on a snowy landscape in Colorado to concede that the pain was too great. Perhaps it would be better to have less unemployment, more inflation.

---

[19]Alan Greenspan, "Economic Policy Problems for 1975," an unpublished speech before the National Economists Club, December 2, 1974.

An unhappy passage proving, however, the power of faith in economics as opposed to experience.

With the American failure came world failure. In all of the industrial countries from the late '60s on, prices were being pulled upward by demand, pressed upward by wage claims. The two forces were, on closer view, both parts of a larger whole. In the last century and in the earlier decades of this one, incomes in the industrial countries were deeply stratified. So, conveniently, was consumption. It was taken for granted that a white-collar worker would have a higher standard of living than a blue-collar worker, a professional family more than either. Managers were meant to have yet more; property owners most of all. At the bottom, and at best only partial participants in the common product, were the ethnic poor—the blacks in the United States, the Irish in England, the Algerians in France, the Italians in Switzerland.

Increasingly, in all countries, these accepted and prescriptive limits on income and consumption were under strain. Everywhere the less privileged were asserting more strongly their claims to some part of the consumption that previously had been thought the natural right only of the privileged. Nothing, in modern times, has sustained more learned discussion than the prospect for more leisure for the masses, the hope for a more nearly classless society. And nothing has caused more dismayed discussion than the economic consequences of the decline in the work ethic, the ever more vigorous assertion of the income demands of those, the blue-collar workers in particular, who had always been thought content to accept less.

The tendency for the claims of consumers to press ever more insouciantly on the capacity to supply them —and the associated and by no means unnatural reluctance of governments to limit these claims—was one cause of inflation in the industrial countries. The incapacity or ineptitude, both in principle and in practice, of the effort to control inflation in the United States was the other. There is a notable asymmetry in the relation of the United States to the rest of the trading world. The United States is sufficiently self-contained in its economic relations with other countries so it can go far, given the will and wisdom, to stabilize its own prices. But if prices in the United States are rising, there are few other countries that can avoid the resulting impact. They can have more inflation than the United States; they cannot easily have less.

In the nineteenth century Britain and a gold-based sterling were fixed points in international economic policy; other countries adjusted their action to this known. In the '50s and earlier '60s—the good years—the United States and the dollar played a similar role. American prices were stable; dollars were an eminently safe asset that anyone would wish to hold. When dollars were being lost by a country, something was wrong. So, on this signal, governments took steps—tighter fiscal policy, higher interest rates, in the case of some exceptionally tractable countries such as Holland, a curb on wage increases—to put things right. *In extremis* there could be a devaluation. It was by such adjustment to the United States and to the dollar, not by meetings of central bankers and finance ministers, that coordination between the domestic policies of the industrial countries in these years was effected. Such internal coordination, in turn, is the first requisite for international-currency stability. Only if internal prices are relatively stable or moving in harmony with each other can exchange rates be stable and hence predictable.

It was this harmony that instability in the United States and related inflation in the other industrial countries in the late 1960s brought to an end. A further and complicating factor was a fundamental difference in movements in costs and productivity between the industrial countries—a difference dramatized by the contrasting position of Germany and Japan on the one hand and the United States on the other. In these years Germany and Japan, their arms expenditures restricted by the victorious powers after World War II and their enthusiasm for warlike activity usefully diminished by defeat, were using their savings to build new and efficient industrial plants. This, in turn, was producing civilian goods at low cost. The United States, by contrast, had come through World War II with its prewar industrial plants intact and thus, by comparison, obsolescent. And a large share of its savings was going into weapons systems and later into its eccentric misadventure in Vietnam. So, apart from the pull of demand and the press of wage claims, the United States was suffering also in these years from the higher costs of relatively inefficient production. For so long as the dollar was maintained at a fixed rate of exchange with the mark and the yen, there was great advantage in buying in Germany and Japan, selling in the United States. It was said in the late '60s that the dollar was overvalued. So it was.

In consequence of the foregoing, foreign corporations, beginning in the late '50s, accumulated dollars from their flush sales in the United States. These were not absorbed by the much smaller purchases from the United States. In the hands of the recipient firms or deposited by them in European banks, the dollars became the newest mystery of the monetary *cognoscenti*—the Eurodollars. And when borrowed or loaned, they became the Eurodollar market—as always, when examined, a simple thing. Numerous of the dollars so assembled, not surprisingly, were turned into gold. So now in the decade of the '60s the great gold hoard of the United States, with history going back to 1914, began to melt away. Partly this was a penalty of power. From 1914 until after World War II, when men of means thought of sanctuary for their wealth in the event of war, they thought of the United States. Now the United States, a superpower, entangled in Vietnam and one arm of the balance of terror, no longer seemed safe. Better Switzerland, even better Germany. In the late '60s the outward flow of gold from the United States became a flood.

At intervals through the '60s finance ministers, treasury secretaries and central bankers met to consider what might be done about the increasing disarray in international monetary affairs. They were described as emerging grim-faced from these meetings. Reporters questioned them under the handicap usual in monetary matters of having to simulate knowledge of the questions to be asked. After appropriate thought the participants almost invariably declined comment. The tradition of Schacht and Montagu Norman was still strong. Not surprisingly, nothing was accomplished at these meetings, for those attending had no access to the underlying causes of difficulty—to the varying rates of inflation, the varying movements in costs which were ultimately responsible for the disequilibrium.

In the late '60s the United States ceased, in effect, to furnish gold to all comers and confined itself to providing it to other central banks in settlement of their claims. The other central banks, in turn, undertook to restrict their gold sales to their sister central banks. Private individuals wishing to possess gold had to bid for it from other private holders. Gold now had two prices: There was the old or official price for settlement between central banks and the new open-market price established by private traders. This, in the further invention of the *cognoscenti*, was the two-tier market. It was the beginning of the final step away from gold.

The end came in August 1971. As part of the larger

package of policy changes announced during that month, the United States ceased to supply gold to other central banks in accordance with the arrangement just described. Not many noticed what would once have been an heroic act. That was at least partly because heroic language was avoided. Men did not speak of the final abandonment of the gold standard. Instead it was said that the gold window had been closed. No one could get much excited about the closing of a window. No one much noticed that the gentle Bretton Woods system had by now succumbed. It was not intended to cope, nor could it, with the larger, divergent movements in prices and in currencies that now were commonplace.

Dollars, as noted, now existed in large accumulations. Better bargains could be obtained by changing these into marks, yen or other currencies and buying goods in Germany, Japan or other lands. Safety also suggested these currencies as the ones to hold. In consequence, the dollar was now a weak currency. Other countries did not necessarily rejoice. A situation in which they could sell easily to the United States and were not unduly pressed by American competition was not without comfort. There was advantage in allowing a currency to go down with the dollar. This could be readily arranged, at least for the short run, by having the central bank sell the local currency freely for dollars. The dollar would thus remain conveniently overvalued.

Negotiations now got under way to arrange the devaluation and restabilization of the dollar. These were held in the late autumn of 1971 in the buildings of the Smithsonian Institution in Washington. Eventually new exchange rates were agreed upon; these reflected varying rates of devaluation of the dollar from approximately 17 percent for the yen and 12 percent for the mark down to little or none for the Canadian dollar. The participating governments pledged themselves, through their central banks, to buy and sell currencies so as to hold exchange rates within a range of 2.25 percent of the agreed parities. Congress, in a symbolic act required by the International Monetary Fund, dutifully reduced the gold content of the dollar. The result was described with relative modesty by Richard Nixon as the greatest monetary reform in the history of mankind. Secretary of the Treasury John B. Connally, who received credit for the agreement, basked momentarily in the esteem which people who do not understand what is happening accord to those who presume to knowledge of money. For both the Smithsonian Agreements and Connally the esteem was short-lived. Both were soon casualties of the times.

Early in 1973, coincidentally with the abandonment of the Phase II controls, there was a massive movement out of dollars into other currencies. This was in expectation of further inflation in the United States, a further devaluation of the dollar. Both expectations were soundly justified by events. (There were similar speculative movements in other currencies.) To maintain the Smithsonian parities proved impossible. Currency instability now became the approved policy; this also achieved a benign cognomen. It was called a float. The economists of the Administration graced their surrender with a superlative manifestation of bureaucratic prose:

In the area of international economic relations, the year 1973 may be characterized as one of continuing adjustment to past disequilibria as well as to new developments that entered the picture during the year. Early in the year the governments of most major countries abandoned attempts to fix exchange rates at negotiated levels. While central banks continued to intervene to some extent, foreign exchange markets played the major role in determining the exchange rates that would clear the market. This process was marked at times by unusually large fluctuations of market exchange rates. Nevertheless, the market performed its intermediating function well . . .[20]

The reference to "past disequilibria" was meant to shift the blame to predecessors, a tactic somewhat impaired by the fact that the writers were also the predecessors. The reference to "unusually large fluctuations of market exchange rates" was a euphemism for serious disorder in international business. Of the fact of disorder no one was very much in doubt.

In nearly all business transactions—international even more than domestic—there is an element of futurity. Bargains are made now against later payment. Such bargaining becomes difficult if neither party knows what the payment will be worth. This is the case if the buyer does not know what he will have to pay for the currency in which he makes the later payment. Or if the seller does not know what he will receive in his own money for the currency in which he accepts the payment. Such is the case if exchange rates are unstable.[21] As a matter of urgency, the central banks had in fact to intervene in order to provide a modicum of certainty. A floating currency thus became an imperfectly stabilized one. Floating became, as it was called, dirty floating. In 1974, the International Monetary Fund initiated discussions designed to formulate rules for the conduct of dirty floating by central banks.

The consequences of dirty floating for international trade were not immediately adverse. Aided by exceptionally large transactions in grain and other food products, international trade continued to expand in

---

[20]*Economic Report of the President, 1974,* p. 182.
[21]Futures contracts—buying currency for future delivery at prices quoted today—can reduce the risk. It is a device that is available only at considerable cost to sizable traders and not in all currencies.

1973. Not many, although there were some,[22] could imagine that this disorderly improvisation reflected progress. The hopes of Keynes and White at Bretton Woods were for something better. They were right to hope.

Beginning in 1973, but with full effect in 1974, came the great petroleum price squeeze. In keeping with much else in this history this too was extensively misunderstood. In part it resulted from the discovery of hitherto unused bargaining power by the producing countries; in part it was the product of inflation. The effect of high prices that are derived from strong demands, we have seen, has always been to turn the terms of trade to the favor of producers of food and raw products. The tendency of such producers is to operate at or near capacity, sell for what the market will bring. Strong demand raises such prices in relation to those who are better able to regulate supply. In the case of the oil-producing countries the effect was a slight variant; strong demand in the consuming countries made it possible for producers to raise prices without immediately suffering an excess of unsold oil that would threaten the agreement that sustained the price. To sustain the OPEC prices during a period of noninflationary demand would have been far more difficult. Such commodity agreements do not have a marked

---

[22] See Ronald A. Krieger, "The Monetary Governors and the Ghost of Bretton Woods," *Challenge* (January/February 1975). In addition to perceptive comment on the world monetary situation, some in conflict with the present conclusions, Professor Krieger contributes a valuable verse on the reaction of the Governors of the International Monetary Fund, meeting in 1974, to the collapse of the Bretton Woods system:

Humpty Dumpty sat on a wall,
Humpty Dumpty had a great fall.
All the king's horses and all the king's men
Formed an ad hoc committee to consider the situation.

record of success. Without inflation this one too could fail.

Everywhere the higher oil price was considered highly inflationary; in the United States it served invaluably as an excuse for official inadequacy in the control of inflation. In fact, it was deflationary. Especially in the Arab countries but also in Iran and elsewhere, the revenues accruing from the higher prices were far greater than could immediately be spent for either consumers' or investment goods. So they accumulated in unspent balances. Thus they represented a withdrawal from current purchasing power not different in immediate effect from that of levying a large sales tax on petroleum or its products.[23] The effect, increasingly evident as 1974 passed, was the predictable effect of fiscal astringency. As demand faded, prices in competitive markets—those for food, commodities, services—began to weaken. Prices subject to corporate market power continued to rise. So did unemployment. The oil-producing countries had provided the industrial countries with a surrogate tax increase. Its effect, like any general fiscal or monetary action against inflation, was to increase unemployment well before acting to arrest inflation.

Not much in the history of money supports a linear view of history, one in which the knowledge and experience from one epoch provide the intelligence for improved management in the next. Of those who give guidance on these matters history says even less. Out of the 2500 years of experience and 200 years of ardent study have come monetary systems that are as unsatis-

---

[23]This effect of the oil-price increases was perceptively identified at one of President Ford's so-called Summit Conferences on Inflation in the autumn of 1974 by Professor Richard N. Cooper. Few, not including the present author, saw the force of his position.

factory as any in the peacetime past. In recent times conservatives have reacted adversely to inflation, though not with great enthusiasm to the measures for preventing it. Liberals have thought unemployment the greater affliction. In fact no economy can be successful which has either. Inflation causes discomfort and frustration for many. Unemployment causes acute suffering for a lesser number. There is no certain way of knowing which causes the most in the aggregate of pain. It was the prime lesson of the '30s that deflation and depression destroyed international order, caused each nation to try for its own salvation, indifferent to the damage that its efforts caused to neighbors. It has equally been the lesson of the late '60s and early '70s that inflation too destroys international order. Those who express or imply a preference between inflation and depression are making a fool's choice. Policy must always be against whichever one has.

But also it is now evident that only in the extremes of inflation or depression is there a choice. Otherwise, if only the accepted and orthodox remedies are applied, we get both. For this combination no one, liberal or conservative, speaks. And at this combination, after 2500 years, we have at last arrived. Few histories could have a less happy ending.

CHAPTER XXI

Afterword

COULD IT BE BETTER? The answer is yes.

Proof begins with the people who manage money. If anything is evident from this history, it is that the task attracts a very low level of talent, one that is protected in its highly imperfect profession by the mystery that is thought to enfold the subject of economics in general and of money in particular. Inadequacy is protected further, we have seen, by the fact that failure is almost never at cost to those responsible. More often it has been an interesting subject for discussion, something that has given an added dimension to personality.

Finally, in monetary matters as in diplomacy, a nicely conformist nature, a good tailor and the ability to articulate the currently fashionable financial cliché have usually been better for personal success than an excessively inquiring mind. Effective action and associated thought provoke fear and criticism. It is for these and not the result that the individual is likely to be remembered. So, in the management of money, as in economic management generally, failure is often a more rewarding personal strategy than success.

There is reluctance in our time to attribute great consequences to human inadequacy—to what, in a semantically less cautious era, was called stupidity. We wish to believe that deeper social forces control all human action. There is always something to be said for tolerance. But we had better be aware that inadequacy—

obtuseness combined with inertness—is a problem. Nor is it inevitable. In the past, economic policy has been successful. We must assume that it was successful not by happy accident but because informed and energetic people made it so.

It will be no easier in the future than in the past for the layman or the lay politician to distinguish between the adequate individual and the others. But there is no difficulty whatever in distinguishing between success and failure. Henceforth it should be the simple rule in all economic and monetary matters that anyone who has to explain failure has failed. We should be kind to those whose performance has been poor. But we must never be so gracious as to keep them in office.

None of this is to suggest that success will be easy. Among the lessons from this history two stand out. The first is that the problem of money has now become fully coordinate with that of the economy, even with that of the polity. The second is that economic performance which a hundred years ago would have been accepted as inevitable and fifty years ago as tolerable is no longer accepted. What was then misfortune is now failure.

Specifically, in the last century and before, money was important. Corporations had no general power to move prices. Unions effectively did not exist. The taxes and expenditures of national states were controlled by the exigencies of war and peacetime need, not by what was required for the right kind of economic performance. What was used as money and how much there was of it made a difference; the instinct of the men who followed Bryan (and of those who opposed him) was not wrong.

In modern times, we have seen, the national budget has become a decisive factor in economic performance. It extensively determines whether demand will expand, prices rise, unemployment increase and—in consequence of government borrowing and the resulting deposit creation—whether the supply of money will expand. And beyond the budget is the power of unions and corporations directly to affect prices and, more than incidentally, to negate the restrictive effect of monetary and budget policy. As we have sufficiently seen, it is well within the scope of union and corporate power and advantage to shove up costs and prices while demand in the economy is shrinking and unemployment rising. Thus the distinctly disenchanting tendency in the modern economy for recession to be combined with inflation.

Corporate and trade-union power raise the further question of the distribution of power as a whole in the modern state and of the sovereignty of modern governments. And implicit in the effort to exercise such power by the state is a decision as to how income will be distributed. Thus monetary policy has become but a minor part of the whole economic policy. And economic policy has become an aspect of politics—of the question of who exercises power, who controls the rewards.

Nor is this all. We have seen that currencies now accumulate in large agglomerations outside the country of issue—the Eurodollars and the Petrodollars being the recent cases in point. And the transnational bank and the transnational corporation which hold or own these accumulations can move them into other currencies and out again in a volume that is far beyond the remedial and stabilizing capacity of existing machinery for monetary stabilization. Thus the modern problem of monetary management has a much greater international dimension than ever before.

There is yet a further problem. As the recent examples of petroleum and food amply show, supply and demand in the modern economy are now brought into equilibrium only after large movements in prices and in income. These have an extensive, unstabilizing effect on domestic price levels and international exchange rates. So stable prices and stable international exchanges also require action to prevent disruptive movements in the prices of individual products of major importance. This task too transcends national boundaries, goes beyond the reach of national authority.

Finally, to repeat, what served as adequate performance in the past is acceptable no longer. After the Napoleonic Wars in Britain and the Civil War in the United States, steps were taken to restore monetary stability and re-establish specie payments. Farm prices fell sharply. There was some increase in unemployment. There was much complaint but it was not operative. Economic hardship was then far from unnatural. Low prices, low wages and loss of jobs were not precisely acts of God. But they were not yet acts of government. Now, needless to say, they are.

Nothing, or anyhow not much, lasts forever. But what is well established is likely to last for a time. So the forces that have shaped past policy (or which past policy has resisted), if they have been correctly identified in this history, will, one may assume, continue to operate for at least a while in the future. They are, in the fullest sense, historical imperatives. This means that they are not matters for ideological preference as commonly imagined. To see economic policy as a problem of choice between rival ideologies is the greatest error of our time. Only rarely, and usually on matters of secondary importance, do circumstances vouchsafe this luxury. Far more often, institutions and historical circumstance provide the same straitjacket for liberals and conservatives, socialists and men of avowedly medieval mind. What works for one works for all. What fails for one is abysmal for all.

If the near future is an extension of the near and more distant past, there are six imperatives that will shape or control monetary policy and the larger economic policy of which it is now a lesser part. These are:

(1) The perverse unusefulness of monetary policy and the frustrations and danger from relying on it. This is perhaps the clearest lesson of the recent past. The management of money is no longer a policy but an occupation. Though it rewards those so occupied, its record of achievement in this century has been patently disastrous. It worsened both the boom and the depression after World War I. It facilitated the great bull market of the 1920s. It failed as an instrument for expanding the economy during the Great Depression. When it was relegated to a minor role during World War II and the good years thereafter, economic performance was, by common consent, much better. Its revival as a major instrument of economic management in the late '60s and early '70s served to combine massive inflation with serious recession. And it operated with discriminatory and punishing effect against, not surprisingly, those industries that depend on borrowed money, of which housing is the leading case. To argue that it was a success may well be beyond even the considerable skills of its defenders. Only the enemies of capitalism will hope that, in the future, this small, perverse and unpredictable lever will be a major instrument in economic management.

The central bank remains important for useful tasks —the clearing of checks, the replacement of worn and dirty banknotes, as a loan source of last resort. These tasks it performs well. With other public agencies in the United States, it also supervises the subordinate commercial banks. This is a job which it can do well and needs to do better. In recent years the regulatory agencies, including the Federal Reserve, have relaxed somewhat their vigilance. At the same time numerous of the banks have been involved in another of the age-old spasms of optimism and feckless expansion. The result could be a new round of failures. It is to such matters that the Federal Reserve needs to give its attention.

These tasks apart, the reputation of central bankers will be the greater, the less responsibility they assume. Perhaps they can lean against the long wind—resist a little and increase rates when the demand for loans is persistently great, reverse themselves when the reverse situation holds. But, in the main, control must be—as it was in the United States during the war years and the good years following—over the forces which cause firms and persons to seek loans and not over whether they are given or not given the loans.

It should be noted, in fairness, that the ineffectiveness, if not the danger, of monetary policy is being recognized by men of candid mind within the System. The President of the Federal Reserve Bank of New York has noted that the quantity of money, the magnitude of primary concern to those who have placed their faith in monetary policy, cannot effectively be measured. He has noted also that its short-run movements cannot be controlled, and also that such movements are without significant economic effect.[1] Not much hope for monetary policy remains, especially when it is remembered that all action must be taken in the short run, that long-run change is the aggregation of short-run changes. Similarly a recent Governor of the Federal Reserve System has observed that ". . . good monetary policy depends upon admitting how much we do not know [about the management of

---

[1] Alfred Hayes, "Testing Time for Monetary Policy." An address before the New York State Bankers Association in New York City on January 20, 1975. One problem, among others, in measuring money supply, as noted by Mr. Hayes, involves savings deposits. These, increasingly, are interchangeable with, or indistinguishable from, deposits subject to check.

money.]"[2] There is a strong case against relying on an instrument or an innovation of widespread but unknown effects. The examples of atomic energy, supersonic transport and even Freon gas come to mind.

Still, what happens when there is reliance on monetary policy is not all that unknown. The record has been made; it is adverse.

(2) The balancing factor in economic management will have to be the national budget, and the decisive need here is to overcome its presently fatal inelasticity for dealing with excess demand. This imperative lacks both novelty and subtlety. If monetary policy is unavailable for regulating aggregate demand in the economy, only fiscal policy remains. This, we have seen, operates with greater certainty than monetary policy for expanding demand; it was for this reason that it replaced monetary policy in the economists' faith during the Great Depression. And it operates with greater predictability of effect and much greater fairness for limiting demand. There is no grievous political or other problem in reducing taxes or increasing public outlays to expand aggregate demand. The Congress of the United States is especially cooperative and prompt when tax reduction is called for. Similarly, a sizable group of liberal economists resort, homeopathically, to tax reduction as a remedy for all ailments—even, on occasion, inflation. However, no similar enthusiasm is evident when a tax increase is required. Expenditure reduction is equally difficult, except as it invokes the oral enthusiasm of conservatives. And it operates against the high probability, one strongly believed by the present author, that civilian public needs in the United States are less amply supplied than the private consumption at least of the more affluent. There is the further structural difficulty that there is often, as in

[2]Sherman J. Maisel, *Managing the Dollar* (New York: W. W. Norton & Co., 1973), p. 311.

the case of construction and weapons procurement, a long lag between the decision to reduce an expenditure and the actual curtailment of outlays with its consequent effect on demand.

The solution, one which anyone who is uneasy about the excesses of executive power must come to with reluctance, is to separate the budget of the national government from the fiscal policy.[3] Expenditures would be determined and taxes established as now. One would hope this would be with a full and civilized appreciation of the need for a proper balance between public expenditure and private expenditure, public consumption and private consumption. Revenues would be expected to cover outlays so established when the economy was operating at approximately full employment levels. The taxes so set would redistribute income as deemed socially and economically desirable between income groups. Then authority for increases or decreases in taxes—within specified limits—would be allowed to the Executive purely for reasons of fiscal, i.e., larger economic, policy. These changes would be so designed as not greatly to alter the incidence of taxation as between different income groups.

(3) Direct wage and price control where there is market power is inevitable. It should not be used where such power does not exist—in agriculture, small enterprise, where there are no unions. There regulation of aggregate demand must suffice. Controls reflect a policy which few wish to accept but which, wishes to the contrary, will not go away. As we have sufficiently seen, at or near full employment the market power of strong corporations and strong unions can create an inflationary dynamic of its own. And, we have seen, it

---

[3]See the outline of this proposal in James Tobin, *The New Economics One Decade Older* (Princeton: Princeton University Press, 1974), p. 76 et seq. Impairment of the legislative authority over taxation is not something to be taken lightly. What is lacking is an alternative.

has repeatedly done so. Though it is possible to arrest this inflationary thrust, it requires a greater recession and more unemployment than either compassion or the simple dictates of political survival will tolerate. As this goes to press, yet another effort to arrest inflation by use of monetary and fiscal policy is coming to an end. The resulting unemployment and recession are severe—far more painful than politicians of either party are willing to accept. And these consequences have appeared well in advance of the end of the inflation they were designed to cure. Inflation, at least for a period, is being combined with severe recession.

The only alternative to these unpleasant effects is for the government to intervene directly where there is market power—where there is the power by private action to increase prices and wages well before full employment and equally in face of falling demand. This removes from the private corporation a deeply cherished power. Similarly from the union. It confesses the error of much past and present economic instruction.[4] But again the straitjacket of circumstance. And so, in face of all the reluctance, the question of controls returns and returns again.[5]

(4) Monetary and economic management are inextricably a part of the larger problem of income distribution in the modern economy. This too will be-

---

[4]Specifically it is in conflict with the general microeconomic assumption of competition and the view that the monopoly or oligopoly is responsive to reduced demand and not appreciably influenced by related horizontal movements in wage costs. And, of course, it is in conflict with the generally optimistic macroeconomic conclusion that fiscal and monetary policy will provide not an ideal but at least a tolerable reconciliation between employment and output on the one hand and price stability on the other.

[5]It must be emphasized again that this policy is useful only for the areas of the economy where there is market power. Recalling the discussion of the World War II experience, it fixes only prices that are already fixed. It is not useful and is in fact damaging if applied to such competitive markets as those for agricultural products, services, small enterprise generally or retailing.

come increasingly evident. Nothing is so attractive to the individual of conservative instinct as the thought that economic policy is a purely technical matter. No questions of social class or social policy are involved. Given the right technique—the skilled fine-tuning of Mr. Nixon's craftsmen—the economy is put right; power and income and their enjoyment remain unaffected. Liberals also have not been immune to the thought that monetary and fiscal policy—including the control of prices and incomes—are socially neutral.

It is not so. A central feature of modern economic society, we have seen, is the rejection by subordinate social classes of the prescriptive limits on their income and consumption. With this rejection go claims on production that cannot be met; from these claims comes inflation. If wages and therewith the consumption of blue-collar workers must be restrained in the interest of preventing claims on the economy that are beyond its capacity, the claims of other income recipients will also come up for consideration. What is required for profits, other property income, executive salaries, professional income will also be under examination. Nor will it be an answer that the consumption of the rich, or anyhow of the very rich, is a small part of the total. The question of equity—of some approach to equal treatment for all—is not less important than the aggregate of income involved. So movement toward a more consciously egalitarian income distribution will become an indispensable aspect of successful economic policy. We have sufficiently seen that successful policy will require restraint on trade-union claims. But there can be no future for a policy that selects wage- and salary-earners for such restriction and, however conveniently, leaves other claimants untouched.

(5) Planning for the supply and conservation of use of important products and services will, increasingly, be an aspect of monetary and economic management. As noted, the movements in prices that are necessary

to bring supply and use of important products—fuels, food, housing—into equilibrium can now be very great—great enough to put damaging strains on wage and price stability. The obvious remedy is to anticipate such shortages and, through public action, expand supply or reduce use. That such action has already been forced on modern governments in peacetime— and in the United States on an avowedly conservative administration—is a guide to expectation. (The character of the action is not changed by referring to planners as czars.) Since the problems of both supply and use are transnational, there will have to be cooperation between national planning authorities for these tasks. And supranational organization becomes a prospect. Again, notably in the cases of energy and food, circumstances are forcing the pace and, as ever, on those who are ideologically reluctant.

(6) The problem of instability in international exchanges will recur; no more in the future than in the past will unpredictability seem a solution. International currency stabilization will, however, only be possible when national economies are stable—when the industrial countries have succeeded in combining reasonably high employment with tolerably stable prices. Until then all talk of international currency reform will be in a vacuum and can safely be ignored except by those whose employment depends on the discussion. It can be assumed that any future system will need lending capacity vastly in excess of the Bretton Woods system, even as it has been enlarged in recent times.[6] On the assumption that large blocs of mobile currencies will continue to accrue in the hands of banks, multinational corporations and (in lesser degree) free-lance

---

[6] Through provision of Special Drawing Rights and other steps, the Bretton Woods system has been much enlarged beyond the original design, although with no really significant departure from the original loan principle. The amounts available remain small in relation to potential international transfers of funds.

speculators, eventual reform will have also to include some regulation of international currency movements.

There is another prospect—one for which we can profoundly pray. It is that policy in the future will be based not on forecasts but on the current reality. The reason for this we have sufficiently seen; not only is economic forecasting highly imperfect, something that is conceded even by the forecasters except when offering a new forecast, but official forecasting has an ineluctable tendency to error. On all but the rarest occasions it is biased by what policy-makers hope to have happen or need to have happen. Or, in the manner of the Vietnam war expenditures, it cannot contradict larger official promise. The solution is not better forecasts but prompt and unapologetic accommodation to what exists and prompt and unapologetic change when that no longer exists. In the late summer of 1974, Gerald Ford, newly arrived in the Presidency, proclaimed inflation the major threat to the American economy. Less than half a year later, with unemployment rising rapidly, production falling and prices leveling off, he proclaimed a recession to be the major threat. Such reversal of emphasis is not a confession of error. We should applaud prompt reaction to the current circumstance. The new President's error was not in changing his mind. It was in supposing that inflation could only be cured by recession—that the market power of corporations and unions could only be curbed by unemployment and declining output. No economic policy can be very satisfactory that provides only a choice between inflation and depression. But of this error there has been sufficient discussion.

There is one final prospect, also deeply rooted in this history. Nothing, it is worth repeating once more, lasts forever. That is true of inflation. It is true of recession. Each stirs the attitudes, engenders the action which seeks to bring itself to an end—and eventually does. But we have seen that the action required, including the action needed to avoid the increasingly probable combination of inflation with recession, is demanding and complex. And it becomes ever more so. The increasingly demanding character is the main message of this afterword. If anything is certain from this history, it is that those who see themselves as the strongest defenders of the system, those who proclaim themselves the most stalwart friends of free enterprise, even capitalism, will be the most fearful of measures designed to conserve the system. They will be the most antagonistic to the action that will improve its performance, enhance its reputation, increase its capacity to survive. Those who pray for the end of capitalism should never welcome the activist and affirmative spirit of the New Deal, World War II and after, or the New Frontier. This spirit, however on occasion the victim of its own enthusiasm, optimism or obligation to appease its opposition, is open to the efforts that make the system work. When motivated by such spirit, the system has worked—in the United States to the satisfaction of, at a minimum, something exceeding a majority. Those who yearn for the end of capitalism should pray for government by men who believe that all positive action is inimical to what they call thoughtfully the fundamental principles of free enterprise.

Index

ABOUT THE AUTHOR

JOHN KENNETH GALBRAITH, for many years Paul M. Warburg Professor of Economics at Harvard, is a past President of the American Economic Association, a former Ambassador to India, the author of the noted triology, *The Affluent Society, The New Industrial State* and *Economics and the Public Purpose,* and a veteran of the modern money wars of the United States. In World War II, he was principally in charge of price control and thus at the very center of the economic and anti-inflationary strategy of that important time. He has been very close to the center ever since.

MONEY TALKS!
How to get it and How to keep it!

We Deliver!
And So Do These Bestsellers.

THE NAMES THAT SPELL GREAT LITERATURE

Choose from today's most renowned world authors—every one an important addition to your personal library.

Hermann Hesse

☐	BENEATH THE WHEEL	2509	• $1.50
☐	MAGISTER LUDI	2645	• $1.75
☐	DEMIAN	2944	• $1.75
☐	NARCISSUS AND GOLDMUND	6891	• $1.75
☐	ROSSHALDE	7370	• $1.50
☐	STEPPENWOLF	7979	• $1.50
☐	GERTRUDE	10060	• $1.95
☐	THE JOURNEY TO THE EAST	10136	• $1.75
☐	SIDDHARTHA	10266	• $1.75

Alexander Solzhenitsyn

☐	AUGUST 1914	2997	• $2.50
☐	ONE DAY IN THE LIFE OF IVAN DENISOVICH	2949	• $1.50
☐	THE LOVE-GIRL AND THE INNOCENT	6600	• $ .95
☐	STORIES AND PROSE POEMS	7409	• $1.50
☐	CANCER WARD	8271	• $1.75

Jerzy Kosinski

☐	BEING THERE	2265	• $1.50
☐	STEPS	2597	• $1.50
☐	THE DEVIL TREE	7865	• $1.50
☐	THE PAINTED BIRD	8257	• $1.75

Doris Lessing

☐	THE SUMMER BEFORE THE DARK	2640	• $1.95
☐	THE GOLDEN NOTEBOOK	7747	• $1.95
☐	THE FOUR-GATED CITY	7937	• $1.95

André Schwarz-Bart

☐	THE LAST OF THE JUST	7708	• $1.50
☐	A WOMAN NAMED SOLITUDE	7880	• $1.75

Buy them at your local bookstore or use this handy coupon for ordering:

Bantam Books, Inc., Dept. EDG, 414 East Golf Road, Des Plaines, Ill. 60016

Please send me the books I have checked above. I am enclosing $_____ (please add 35¢ to cover postage and handling). Send check or money order—no cash or C.O.D.'s please.

Mr/Mrs/Miss_____

Address_____

City_____ State/Zip_____

EDG—8/76

Please allow three weeks for delivery. This offer expires 8/77.

Bantam Book Catalog

It lists over a thousand money-saving best-sellers originally priced from $3.75 to $15.00 —bestsellers that are yours now for as little as 60¢ to $2.95!

The catalog gives you a great opportunity to build your own private library at huge savings!

So don't delay any longer—send us your name and address and 25¢ (to help defray postage and handling costs).